Reading Nelligan

Reading Nelligan

ÉMILE J. TALBOT

McGill-Queen's University Press
Montreal & Kingston · London · Ithaca

ISBN 0-7735-2318-9 (cloth)
ISBN 0-7735-2479-7 (paper)

Legal deposit second quarter 2002
Bibliothèque nationale du Québec

Printed in Canada on acid-free paper that is 100% ancient forest free (100% post-consumer recycled) and processed chlorine free.

This book has been published with the help of a grant from the Humanities and Social Sciences Federation of Canada, using funds provided by the Social Sciences and Humanities Research Council of Canada, as well as a grant from the International Council for Canadian Studies through its Publishing Fund.

McGill-Queen's University Press acknowledges the financial support of the Government of Canada through the Book Publishing Industry Development Program (BPIDP) for its publishing activities. It also acknowledges the support of the Canada Council for the Arts for its publishing program.

National Library of Canada Cataloguing in Publication Data

Talbot, Emile
Reading Nelligan
Includes bibliographical references and index.
ISBN 0-7735-2318-9 (bnd)
ISBN 0-7735-2479-7 (pbk)
1. Nelligan, Émile, 1879–1941 – Criticism and interpretation. I. Title.
PS8477.E4Z885 2002 C841'.4 C2001-902810-5
PQ3919.N4Z885 2001

This book was typeset by Dynagram Inc. in 10.5/13 Sabon.

Earlier versions of some of the material in this book appeared in the journals *Québec Studies* and *La Revue francophone de Louisiane*, and in the volume *Émile Nelligan. Cinquante ans après sa mort*, edited by Yolande Grisé, Réjean Robidoux, and Paul Wyczynski.

For Elizabeth, Marc, Paul

Contents

Bibliographical Note

All quotations from Nelligan refer to his *Poésies complètes 1896–1941*, edited with intelligence and erudition by Réjean Robidoux and Paul Wyczynski, and are indicated in the text by pagination only. When indicating lines of verse, I have followed the common practice of counting from the first line of verse rather than from the title, as do Robidoux and Wyczynski. When I refer to the editors' critical or historical notes, I use RW in addition to the pagination. When referring to the companion volume, *Poèmes et textes d'asile. 1900–1941*, edited by Jacques Michon, I use M plus pagination.

Reading Nelligan

Introduction

In 1930, the British lecturer Joseph McCabe was asked after a talk in Toronto what prospects he saw for Canadian literature. With proper British hauteur, he replied with a question of his own: "Does it exist?" The questioner, it appears, was disconcerted, but E.K. Brown, then only twenty-five but on his way to becoming a respected literary scholar, thought that he need not have been. Writing in *Queen's Quarterly*, Brown suggested that the questioner "might have silenced Mr. McCabe, who is an excellent judge of poetry, with a single verse of Canadian poetry, 'Ma pensée est couleur de lumières lointaines,' and, for good measure he might fearlessly have continued with its sequent, 'Du fond de quelque crypte aux vagues profondeurs.'" Brown, who would later write several books on Canadian poetry in addition to his studies of Wharton, Arnold, and Cather, was convinced that "to quote these verses, recalling as they do the enigmatic music and the autumnal sensibility of Verlaine, is perhaps the readiest way with any bland scoffer at Canadian literature. The brief lyric of which they are the opening verses, ... supplied, until very recent years, the most admirable aesthetic experience that Canadian poetry in either of our languages had to offer. Minor poetry it is, if you will, but it is minor poetry of genius" (724).

Brown's rejoinder makes clear that Émile Nelligan, whom Brown identified as the author of the lines he had just quoted, was by 1930 recognized by some in English Canada as one of the shining lights of Canadian poetry. Nelligan had been introduced to educated anglophone Canadians in 1924 by Archibald Mac Mechan in his book *Headwaters of Canadian Literature*, in which he had affirmed that what Nelligan had achieved in his poetry was "unique in the history of Canadian literature" (158). In 1943, his standing as a poet was confirmed by Louis Dudek's translation of three of Nelligan's better-known poems, "Soir d'hiver," "Clair de lune intellectuel," and "Sérénade triste," with the endorsement that "there is nothing like him among our English Canadian poets" (20).

In Quebec, Nelligan's reputation had begun earlier, with the publication in August and September of 1902 of an essay by Louis Dantin in which he proclaimed that French-Canadian letters, past or present, had not yet produced someone as gifted "au point de vue poétique" (1997, 68) as this young man. This seminal essay, slightly revised, provided the preface for Dantin's edition of Nelligan's poetry in 1904. Nelligan had the good fortune of being presented by one who was not only the best French-Canadian critic of his generation but who also had, in the words of Réjean Robidoux, an "identification empathique" (1997, 20) with his subject. Dantin, a broadly cultured man endowed with great literary sensitivity, was able to recognize the influence of continental French poetry on Nelligan's writing while at the same time delineating aspects of the Canadian poet's originality and genius. Nelligan's reputation in Quebec was further enhanced by recognition from abroad. In 1907, the French critic Charles ab der Halden devoted some forty pages of his *Nouvelles Études de littérature canadienne-française* to an intelligent appreciation of his verse. The evidence of Nelligan's influence on the better poets of the next generation in Quebec is substantial.[1] Yet, except for some work on the formal aspects of his poetry by Gérard Bessette beginning in the late 1940s, most critical writing on Nelligan between ab der Halden and the late 1960s focused on the relationship between the work and the man,[2] sometimes resulting in what Jacques Michon has called a "fausse conscience du texte" (1979, 25).

Alongside the literary reputation, then, there emerged as well what might be called the "myth of Nelligan," a set of images of the man that has become part of the collective Québécois imagination. The elements for legend-making were surely there – the adolescent who devoted himself to poetry for three years, became insane, and was then interned for forty-one years – and it can be argued, as Pascal Brissette has, that the myth originated with Dantin's essay.

Moreover, beginning in the 1930s when various litterati, teachers, and students undertook to visit him at Saint-Jean-de-Dieu, Nelligan gradually acquired "une image médiatique" in Quebec (Marquis 1995, 24) and even developed into, according to one critic, a "personnage fétiche" (Giroux 17) in the manner of Rimbaud in France and James Dean in the United States. He became, in Claude Beausoleil's words, "la première star de la littérature québécoise" (216). His photo as a nineteen-year-old, "une tête d'Apollon rêveur et tourmenté," as Dantin put it (1997, 68), has been so frequently reproduced since 1900 that it is probably the best-known image of a poet in the history of French Canada. In Réjean Ducharme's *Le Nez qui voque* (1967), the narrator reveals how he and his friends (at the age of seven!) were so taken with this photo that they tore it out of the library's copy of his poetry and took it home with them. The Nelligan legend has inspired some fifty literary texts, mostly poems, which pay homage to Nelligan,[3] as well as a number of musical compositions.[4] These texts exalt his genius, his madness, and even his martyrdom. Michel Tremblay and André Gagnon's opera *Nelligan* (1990), which features a young bohemian on the verge of madness who is completely devoted to poetry in the face of an uncomprehending anglophone father, and Aude Nantais and Jean-Joseph Tremblay's *Le portrait déchiré de Nelligan* (1992), a "fiction dramatique" in which the young Nelligan is depicted as both a moral and poetic rebel persecuted by a conservative society, are the most recent examples. Bernard Courteau's attempt to prove that Nelligan was not insane but rather played the role of a madman as a protection against his oppressors is yet another twist of the myth-building process. Pascal Brissette has shown that the myth has responded to literary, ideological, and even personal exigencies and acquired new meanings over the course of the century since Nelligan's initial internment.[5] The myth of Nelligan has served the needs of the collective imagination in Quebec and will continue to do so for some time to come. If opinions differ on the interpretation of this phenomenon, there is no debate over the fact of its existence.

Ironically, this poet who has acquired such significance in the Quebec psyche was the author of texts that for a long time were not judged to be particularly Québécois. Nelligan himself does not appear to have considered his work in national terms and refers directly to Canada in only one of his poems (out of 174). He hoped to have his volume of poetry published in France (something his contemporaries Albert Lozeau and Jean Charbonneau would succeed in doing a few years later), and he sneered at the possibility of it being published in Montreal (Dantin 1997, 72). His readings were mainly European – French and Belgian, mostly – and his poetry is replete with intertexts of the European poetic discourse of the time. There is no need to review here the European influences on Nelligan that have been studied with thoroughness and intelligence by Paul Wyczynski and others.[6] Every reader familiar with nineteenth-century French and Belgian verse will readily detect its resonance in Nelligan's poetry. Moreover, if his verse contains some instances of romanticization of rural life (a major theme in traditional French-Canadian poetry), the persons mentioned in them tend to have Germanic names and the atmosphere is vaguely Graeco-Latin. All the geographic allusions in his work, with one exception, refer to foreign places: Europe, the tropics, and the Orient. All the artistic references are European.

This is undoubtedly why so many critics for so long refused to see him as a Canadian poet. Already in 1902 Louis Dantin was regretting the absence of a "cachet canadien" (1997, 81) in Nelligan's work and openly wishing that he could have taken "plus près de lui ses sources habituelles d'inspiration" (81). Charles ab der Halden stressed five years later "combien peu canadien est ce poète canadien" (348) compared to Fréchette, Chapman, and Lemay, who clearly smell of "le terroir"; of Nelligan, he affirms, "Nul, moins que lui ne chante sa province." There is nothing whatsoever in Nelligan, claims ab der Halden, that might allow "la moindre induction sur l'origine de son auteur" (349), an assessment repeated by Archibald MacMechan some fifteen years later (157). In turn-of-the-century France, the perceived dominance of religious, historical, and nationalist themes in French-Canadian literature had elicited only disdain. In a stinging article in *Mercure de France* in 1906, the French critic de Marmade warned his readers that "[le] respect idolâtre du passé, [la] résolution tenace de le reproduire dans le présent, telle semble être la *marque de fabrique* des produits littéraires du Canada" (26; de Marmade's italics). De Marmade scolded Canadian writers for their "lieux-communs religieux et patriotiques" (29) and affirmed that "la plupart des littérateurs canadiens écrivent mal et ne songent point à écrire mieux" (29–30). But, ab der Halden argued, it is precisely this religious, historical, and nationalist inspiration that is absent in Nelligan.

This view of Nelligan as intellectually divorced from his homeland was endorsed by the institutional criticism in French Canada beginning with Camille Roy, considered until the 1950s a leading authority in literary matters in Quebec, who affirmed in 1907 that "La poésie de Nelligan ... tient ... nullement à nos traditions nationales et religieuses. En quoi elle diffère des autres poésies canadiennes" (29). This non-attachment to the *terroir* is precisely what interested the forward-looking poets who founded the literary magazine *Le Nigog* in 1918 and for whom Nelligan was a clear inspiration. Robert de Roquebrune, Marcel Dugas, and Paul Morin did nothing to dispel the "non-Canadianness" of Nelligan, which they saw as a virtue, not a vice. In the 1930s, Albert Dandurand would confirm that "l'œuvre de Nelligan n'est pas la peinture de nos mœurs" (195), and Gérard Tougas, whose history of French-Canadian literature was the standard reference work during the sixties and seventies, affirmed that "Nelligan dédaigna les sujets dits canadiens" (99).

While there can be no doubt that Nelligan shunned historical, political, and patriotic themes, his verse is not altogether lacking in allusions to the "terroir," as Edmund Wilson, the first American critic to recognize Nelligan's genius, clearly perceived. While acknowledging that "one almost loses sight of the milieu in which these brilliant pieces were created" (98), Wilson understood that Nelligan's verse was not devoid of a sense of place. He pointed out that "the chill sternness of that milieu lies behind these bright tapestries in the background; it is suggested by the recurrent rhyme *givre-vivre*, which reminds one of the recurrent problem of survival in that paralysing climate" (98). These remarks, though conveying prevailing stereotypes concerning Canadian winters, have the merit of reminding us of the importance of cold and snow in Nelligan's work. That "Soir d'hiver" is one of Nelligan's best-known poems supports Wilson's observation. Yet, as Jean Larose has reminded us, the poet of "Soir d'hiver" found it necessary to "se re-présenter depuis 'la nouvelle Norvège'" (87). And, is Nelligan's "Canadianness" to be limited to the fact that his "vitre est un jardin de givre"?

The answers to this question have been few, passing, and vague. Gérard Tougas, for example, acknowledged that "au fond, Nelligan est le plus Canadien des poètes" (99), but without explaining his assertion. It remained to Gérard Bessette to oppose categorically the devalorization of Nelligan's Canadianness, which by the 1960s was understood as his *québécité*: "Il est faux de prétendre que l'auteur de 'Châteaux en Espagne' n'exprime ni notre milieu ni notre société. Seulement, il le fait en profondeur, sans recourir aux oripeaux du terroir, sans s'attacher à décrire des traits évidents et superficiels de nos coutumes. Le drame de notre psychisme collectif, il l'a vécu dans son propre cœur, au plus intime et au plus douloureux de sa conscience" (62).

This assessment has been endorsed by Réjean Robidoux (1992, 66), but what does it mean to be a French-Canadian "en profondeur"? For Bessette, it meant that Nelligan, in his relationship with his anglophone father and his francophone mother, expressed Quebec's unresolved collective Oedipal complex. But can his "Canadianness," however it might be defined psychoanalytically, be understood within his writing? This issue, touching on intricate matters of literary hybridity and the autonomisation of New World literatures that cannot be explored in their full ramifications in this focused study, is crucial to reading Nelligan. While he is clearly not the only writer for whom this question arises,[7] we are left with the problem of identifying his "Canadianness" in the light of the francophone European discourse present in his verse. Indeed, this discourse is so recognizable in Nelligan that it threatens to create a semic field that is *too* familiar and thereby a barrier to reading this Canadian poet. Confronted with a familiar language, we might easily conclude that Nelligan is merely a derivative poet, interesting perhaps in the context of the literary history of Quebec, but not of much interest beyond. Yet we cannot, as some have argued, put aside all references to French poetry in reading Nelligan, for to pretend to read these poems in isolation, outside a literary environment familiar both to us as readers and to Nelligan as poet, is to introduce artificiality into the dynamics of reading.

How, then, are we to avoid the trap of sources and influences that could ultimately reduce Nelligan's poetry to a set of interrelations with other texts? Reading Nelligan, I suggest, involves a process which might be called *reading through*. It consists of recognizing Nelligan's absorption of a nineteenth-century French poetic discourse but reading *through* that discourse to arrive at the French-Canadian text which is Nelligan's. Reading through does not mean ignoring the web of French poetics that constitutes the fabric of Nelligan's text, but rather using that web as a means of discerning Nelligan's particularity. In so doing, we acknowledge an insight with a long history, famously formulated by Kristeva and expressed succinctly by Sollers (and frequently paraphrased): "Tout texte se situe à la jonction de plusieurs textes dont il est à la fois la relecture, l'accentuation, la condensation, le déplacement et la profondeur. D'une certaine manière, un texte vaut ce que vaut son action intégratrice et destructrice d'autres textes" (75). Nelligan's poetry is indeed a junction of numerous texts: Romantic, Parnassian, Symbolist, and Decadent. Recognition of these European intertexts emerges as a condition for its comprehension, and reading through means acknowledging Nelligan's text as replication of an existing discourse from the legitimizing culture. However, it also requires that we perceive in his poetry the presence of a non-belletristic discourse proper to his own culture, understanding that his poetry stands in relation not only to European models but also to a larger, contiguous nexus of discourses of his society with which it entertains a fabric of relations. It further means discerning the intratextual coherences by which it maintains its immanent integrity and hence its difference.[8] My intent in proposing this approach is not to arrive at a totalizing reading of this surprisingly complex poet, but rather to illuminate facets of his writing that can make reading him more meaningful.

Nelligan's integration and destruction of other discourses, as well as his engagement with his own French-Canadian culture, will become evident as this book progresses, but a brief discussion at this early juncture of an example of intertextuality, understood in the broad Sollersian sense quoted above, will help clarify the need to "read through." I refer to an instance of lexical and syntagmatic absorption that disengages lexeme and syntagm from their meaning in the text of origin, in this case, a Parnassian one.

Although Parnassianism was not a homogeneous movement, there has long been a critical consensus on some of the traits that constitute it. Its Hellenistic and oriental leanings, its interest in ancient myths, its love of the visual and the plastic, its valorization of form and craftsmanship, its cult of impersonality, its aversion to vagueness and sentimentality, its proclamation of the autonomy of the artistic product are well known. If poets usually associated with these tendencies, such as Leconte de Lisle, Ménard, Banville, Mendès, and Heredia, are among the least read today, this was not the case in the last decades of the nineteenth century in France. To the contrary, their reputation, at least among the cultivated public, was considerable. The 5,000 copies of the first edition of Heredia's *Trophées*, for example, sold out within hours. This fame spread to Canada and particularly to Montreal, where Heredia's volume was hailed by *L'Écho des jeunes* as "un pur joyau dont s'enorgueilliront les lettres françaises" (qtd by Pierssens and Benardi 48).

While there is evidence that Canadians studying in Paris or travelling to France (several thousand a year by 1896) occasionally brought back volumes of verse, much contemporary French literature was also available locally. At the end of the nineteenth century, Montreal booksellers did not, as is sometimes believed, sell only works of history, patriotism, spirituality, and paeans to the joys of agricultural life. Current French poetry was available in several Montreal bookstores, such as the Librairie Beauchemin. Moreover, both ephemeral literary reviews and broader cultural magazines, such as *Le Samedi* and *Le Monde illustré*, regularly published French verse, making it available to those who could not afford to purchase volumes of poetry from France. Among the poets appearing in these two magazines were the Parnassians Banville, Mendès, Prudhomme, and Leconte de Lisle.

This literature left its mark in late nineteenth-century Montreal, attracting in particular the young poets who formed the nucleus of the École littéraire de Montréal during its first years. Henry Desjardins was, according to one of his commentators, strongly influenced by Leconte de Lisle, and his poem "Ton soupir" is "de forme toute parnassienne" (Saint-Bernard-de-Clairvaux 53). Jean Charbonneau was apparently attracted to Sully Prudhomme and Leconte de Lisle (Wyczynski 1960, 17) and Joseph Melançon was said to be "parnassien de tendance" (Légaré 95). Arthur de Bussières, "tout épris de la mode parnassienne," wrote poems that were, according to Wyczynski, "pleins de couleurs parnassiennes" (1960, 29), and was considered by his friends to be a devotee of Heredia. In fact, Bussières' obituary in 1913 states that his poetry was "d'une ciselure impeccable et d'une grande recherche de vocabulaire, à la manière de M. José-Maria de Heredia" (Condemine 113). His only volume of poetry, *Les Bengalis*, published posthumously, is clearly derivative, with a Parnassian tint discernible in both the title of the collection and those of individual poems, such as "Le Rêve du Dyak," "L'Éveil du Brahma," and "Khidirma la turque." His "Kita-No-Tendji," which appeared in the collective volume *Les Soirées du Chateau de Ramezay* in 1900, begins by evoking the weightiness of matter so prized by the Parnassians:

> C'est un temple de pierre aux structures énormes,
> Dont les contours pesants estompent l'horizon;
> Granits, marbres en blocs, pylônes à foison
> Flanqués d'ombre. (*Les Soirées* 347)

Bussières' poetry is, moreover, saturated with the exotic geography and imagery prized by Heredia and Leconte de Lisle. Clearly, Parnassianism provided a set of paradigms for the poets of the École littéraire de Montréal who were eager to renew French-Canadian poetry on bases other than those then prevalent in French Canada.

Nelligan was a sporadic member of the École littéraire, and a critical tradition dating back to his lifetime concurs in seeing Parnassian traits in his poetry as well. His contemporary Louvigny de Montigny said of him that he habitually lifted "un mot bien sonnant ou un terme exotique à Leconte de Lisle et à Heredia" (317). Nelligan's mentor and first critic, Louis Dantin, affirmed that Nelligan "se crut obligé d'écrire, après Heredia, des 'sonnets impassibles' " (1997, 80) and that "le plus scrupuleux des parnassiens" would readily acknowledge Nelligan's poem "Éventail" (81). Dantin further specified that while Nelligan's poetry was often symbolist in conception, it was always Parnassian in expression (93), an assessment shared by ab der Halden (366). Paul Wyczynski sees Heredia as a possible source for "Clair de lune intellectuel" (1960, 164), "Ruines" (174), and "Potiche" (179). He posits traces of Leconte de Lisle in "Noël de vieil artiste" (1960, 144), "Châteaux en Espagne" (199), and "Fantaisie créole" (82), as well as other poems (111, 119, 199, 208). Moreover, in their critical edition of the *Poésies complètes* Robidoux and Wyczynski allude to numerous *rapprochements* between Nelligan and Parnassianism, pointing out, for example, that "Gretchen la pâle" is "d'une forme délibérément parnassienne" (RW 404), that "Châteaux en Espagne" is written "en style parnassien somptueux" (RW 406), that "Les Angéliques" is "d'allure parnassienne" (RW 423), that "Vieille romanesque" is "un exercise poétique d'apprenti parnassien" (RW 486), and that "Paysage fauve" is a "petite contribution parnassienne" (RW 506). There is no need to challenge these assessments founded on considerable erudition and sound judgment.

Yet these scholarly findings do not cohere with the experience of reading Nelligan. When we read Nelligan, what strikes us is not Parnassian impassibility but rather its opposite: Nelligan readily emerges as extremely personal, intimate, tender unto tears, often afraid, and obsessed by death. In his poetry the "vague à l'âme" which so offended the Parnassians in Lamartine and Musset is in the forefront. How is it possible, then, to think of him as a Parnassian?

A careful study of a single syntagm associated with this movement can assist us in assessing the meaning of Nelligan's Parnassianism. Any reader of the Quebec poet will note, for example, that he shares the Parnassian affinity for the metallic, especially gold, references to which appear more than fifty times in his poetry. An examination of one nominal syntagm that consists of a noun (here called the base noun) followed by the preposition *de*, followed by the noun *or* is instructive in this case.

This nominal syntagm is frequently used by Heredia, as the following list, taken from *Les Trophées* (1893; his only published volume), illustrates:

1. crins d'or ("Centaures et lapithes")
2. yeux d'or ("Sphinx")
3. cheveux d'or ("Persée et Andromède")
4. lit d'ivoire et d'or ("Regilla")
5. timon d'or ("Le Cocher")
6. Cyclades d'or ("Pour le vaisseau de Virgile")
7. oiseau d'or ("Le Cydnus")
8. points d'or ("Antoine et Cléopatre")
9. copeaux d'or ("Le Huchier de Nazareth")
10. Hercule d'or ("L'Épée")
11. arabesques d'or ("A Claudius Popelin")
12. gorgone d'or ("Émail")
13. gumène d'or ("Carolo Quinto Imperante")
14. Castille d'or ("L'Ancêtre")
15. palmier d'or ("A un fondateur de ville")
16. panache d'or ("Au même")
17. uraeus d'or ("La Vision de Khem, III")
18. antenne d'or ("La Samouraï")
19. pollen d'or ("Fleur séculaire")
20. frisson d'or ("Le Récif de corail")
21. crinière d'or ("Vendange")
22. mailles d'or ("La Sieste")

23. algues d'or ("Bretagne")
24. branches d'or ("Soleil couchant")
25. brume d'or ("Le Bain"; "Les Conquérants de l'or")
26. besant d'or ("Blason céleste")
27. genêt d'or ("Armor")
28. voix d'or ("Au tragédien E. Rossi")
29. orbes d'or ("Sur un marbre brisé")
30. sable d'or ("Le triomphe du Cid")
31. nécropole d'or ("Les Conquérants de l'or")
32. trou d'or ("Les Conquérants de l'or")
33. sables d'or ("Les Conquérants de l'or")
34. onces d'or ("Les Conquérants de l'or")
35. laves d'or ("Les Conquérants de l'or")
36. vases d'or ("Les Conquérants de l'or")
37. moutons d'or ("Les Conquérants de l'or")
38. bergers d'or ("Les Conquérants de l'or")
39. bâton d'or ("Les Conquérants de l'or")
40. chateau d'or ("Les Conquérants de l'or")

As the above list clearly shows, when using this syntagm, Heredia in most instances refers literally to gold, that is to the precious metal. This is the case in no. 4, where the bed evoked is made of gold, as are the plow of no. 5; the Hercules of no. 10 (in the context of the poem, a handle of a sword made of gold); the arabesques of no. 11; the *gumène* (an anchor cable) of no. 13; the antennae of no. 18 (part of a helmet made of gold); the chain links of no. 22; the bezant of no. 26; the necropolis of no. 31; the ounces of no. 34; the vases of no. 36; the sheep and the shepherds (presumed to exist in yet undiscovered cities of South America) of nos. 37 and 38; the staff of no. 39; and the castle of no. 40.

When the referent is not the metal, it is then usually the colour. Such is the hue of the hair in no. 1; the eyes of a sphinx, sculptured in yellowish stone in no. 2; the hair of no. 3; the wood chips of no. 9 (to evoke the golden colour of the wood); the Gorgon of no. 12; the algae of no. 23; the branches of no. 24 (here evoking the rays of the sun); the fog of no. 25 (golden in this case because of the effects of the sun); the broom tree of no. 27 (because of its yellow flowers); the orbits of no. 29 (in the context of this poem, circles formed by the sun); the sand of no. 30; the hole of no. 32 (since it is the golden circle produced by the sun); the sands of no. 33; and the lava of no. 35.

In the great majority of cases, then, Heredia uses the syntagm noun + *de* + *or* to refer to either the metal gold or the colour gold. On first reflection, we might think that Nelligan follows Heredia's example, for he uses the same syntagm (roughly the same number of times) as Heredia, as the following list illustrates:

1. nymphes d'or ("Rêve fantasque")
2. l'Eden d'or ("Clavier d'antan"; "Fantaisie créole")
3. voix d'or ("La Sorella dell'Amore")
4. voix au son d'or ("Ma Mère")
5. soleil d'or ("Devant deux portraits de ma mère")
6. lampion d'or ("Le Talisman")
7. baisers d'or ("Le Berceau de la Muse")
8. pays d'or ("Tristesse blanche")
9. larmes d'or ("Sérénade triste")
10. étoile d'or ("Bergère")
11. vol d'or ("Maints soirs nous errons dans le val")
12. râles d'or ("Rêve de Watteau")
13. voix d'eau d'or ("Vasque")
14. vasque d'eau d'or ("Vasque")
15. cœur d'or ("Le mai d'amour")
16. son d'or ("Gretchen la pâle")
17. soirs d'or ("Salons allemands")
18. sonnet d'or ("Sonnet d'or")
19. chant d'or ("Sonnet d'or")
20. bruits d'or ("Pour Ignace Paderewski")
21. manteau d'or ("Notre-Dame-des-Neiges")
22. ailes d'or ("Les Communiantes")
23. nimbe d'or ("Communion pascale")
24. tristesse d'or ("Chapelle ruinée")
25. eaux d'or ("Fantaisie créole")
26. soir d'or ("L'ultimo angelo del Corregio")
27. ciel d'or ("L'ultimo angelo del Corregio")
28. lumière d'or ("À Georges Rodenbach")
29. choses d'or ("Vieille Armoire")
30. lueur d'or ("Le Roi au souper")
31. bras d'or ("Le Tombeau de Chopin")
32. grèves d'or ("Le Lac")
33. astres d'or ("Le Lac")
34. points d'or ("Paysage fauve")

35. rêve d'or ("L'idiote aux cloches")
36. scombres d'or ("Frère Alfus")
37. tourbillon d'or ("Un poète")
38. lunes d'or ("Clair de lune intellectuel")
39. juins d'or ("Sous les faunes")
40. cheveux d'or ("La Vierge noire")
41. vaisseau d'or ("Le Vaisseau d'Or")

For a late nineteenth-century reader, this syntagm would have marked this text as Parnassian. Clearly, Nelligan is absorbing a lexeme, *or*, as well as its semes of brilliance and preciousness, and, indeed, an entire syntagm, but it is also evident that something quite different than pure absorption is occurring. Nelligan's Parnassianism appears mainly lexical, for he adopts the lapidary vocabulary of the Parnassians to arrive at aims distinctly contrary to theirs. Heredia's base noun almost always refers to material objects made of gold, or to the colour gold, and constitutes part of a Parnassian aesthetic that emphasizes concrete, tangible realities in order to stress the visual and give the impression of objectivity. In Nelligan, syntactic identity with the Parnassian syntagm does not preclude semantic deviation from it: hardly ever does the base noun refer to something material. His base nouns refer to or derive from an interior reality, the domain of sensibility. What is golden in his poetry are voices, songs, tears, hearts, sadness. If something exterior is so designated, it is vague and imprecise. On the paradigmatic axis, Nelligan replaces Heredia's base nouns with substantives drawn from another register. In Nelligan, the semic space of precious metals does not found a poetics of the tangible and the concrete as it does in Heredia. There is an *Eden d'or* in which gold evokes precious memories of a happier past. A voice is also golden, *la voix d'or*, for it is a voice dear to him. If we were to analyse all forty of Nelligan's uses of this syntagm, we would come to the conclusion that the base noun is always something treasured by Nelligan in a very intimate and personal way. These syntagms valorize cherished memories. Gold, far from connoting glitter and light, stresses the contrast between a tender and joyful past and a cruel and sad present. By attributing *d'or* to signifiers relating to his personal past, Nelligan creates a climate of nostalgia, contrasting his erstwhile life with the present one. The Parnassians also sought to recreate the past, but theirs was the historical past. Heredia, Leconte de Lisle, Ménard, and Banville all sought to resurrect former civilizations which they largely idealized. For them, the signifier *or* valorizes the civilizations of yesteryear, especially those of Latin America and the Mediterranean, that is, the cultures of the sun. For Nelligan, the only important past is his own personal past, that of his own pre-adolescence, of his personal golden age.

This comparison could be extended to other syntagms, other signifiers, but the conclusion would be the same. While the syntagms and signifiers are similar, the context of interpretation is not. Nelligan uses the language of the Parnassians to overturn Parnassian aesthetics, to express what they abhorred, that is, what is most intimate and private. He thereby also distinguished himself from the poetic tradition in French Canada, which had long suppressed the poetic subject's self-expression. A signifier and syntagm favoured by the Parnassians are inserted into a poetic discourse whose semic density derives not from brilliance but from darkness. In such a context, the presence of gold renders the poet's experience all the more painful. Parnassian discourse has been woven into a new pattern and invested with a new meaning.

Lexical and syntactic replication, then, does not preclude original signification. A careful reflection on the language, form, and thematics of Nelligan's poetry enables us to see how the elitist discourse of nineteenth-century French culture provided the instrumentality by which Nelligan created verse that reflects an original intersection of personal compulsions and communal values. Discerning how these matrices intersect makes it possible for us to identify in what way he remains a French-Canadian, *en profondeur.*

1 To Be a Poet

Unlike the culturally unified cities of Quebec and Toronto, Montreal in the 1890s was divided into two cultures, one French, comprising roughly sixty per cent of the population, and the other English, accounting for about forty per cent. French speakers had been in the majority in the city since the mid-1860s, but theirs was not the culturally dominant group. The English-speaking community, though far from homogeneous and including persons living in poverty, controlled not only the levers of banking, commerce, and industry (anglophones residing in Montreal's "Golden Square Mile" had cornered, it is believed, about seventy per cent of Canada's wealth), but those of culture as well. The community could boast of an established university in McGill, an excellent library in the Fraser Institute, and an active Art Association that eventually gave birth to the Montreal Museum of Fine Arts. The Mechanics' Institute provided adult education and lectures and made available a good library. Theatres such as the Royal, the Academy of Music, Queen's Theatre, and, after 1898, Her Majesty's, provided a full schedule of dramatic performances.[1]

French cultural life rested on less wealth and a smaller elite and developed within constraints imposed by the Catholic Church. The Institut Canadien, an autonomous institution that had provided public lectures and a library since the 1840s, was forced, under pressure from Bishop Bourget, to close in 1871, and its books were eventually transferred to the Fraser Institute after the city of Montreal refused to accept them as a basis for a municipal library. Since the city provided no public library until 1917, the French-speaking population was limited to such resources as the Cabinet de lecture paroissial, under the direction of the Sulpicians. The Montreal division of Laval University, inaugurated in 1878 after years of intra-Church bickering, lacked the scope and prestige of McGill. Although French theatrical luminaries such as Bernhardt, Coquelin, Duquesne, and Monnet-Sully did perform in Montreal, the francophone community had only ephemeral amateur theatre companies, none of which were regarded favourably by the Church. The opening of the Monument National in 1893 was an attempt to provide a quality setting where plays might be produced that would be acceptable to the clergy. The Cercle Ville-Marie, a literary association active during this period, remained under clerical control and was suspicious of contemporary culture. The visits of a few French intellectuals to Montreal (Bourget in 1893, Brunetière in 1897) provided only a modest intellectual stimulus. Although limited in range and influence, the cultural effervescence created by the small, quasi-bohemian circles that began to form in the early 1890s[2] would, however, prepare the way for the founding in 1895 of the École littéraire de Montréal by young French-speaking intellectuals with no connection to the Church who were concerned with the low level of the language and literature of the time. It would become, for a few years, the focus of independent intellectual life for francophones in the city.

To be a poet in Montreal in the 1890s, then, required a choice of language and culture. Such a choice would not seem to be difficult, since the poet would be assumed to write in his native language, but for Nelligan, the issue was complicated by the fact that his father was English-speaking and his mother French-speaking. In the retelling of the Nelligan story in Quebec, Émile's father is sometimes depicted as monolingual and anti-French, but this perspective is faulty. David Nelligan spoke French and agreed to giving his son a French first name and a French education. He did want English to be spoken in the house when he was present, but there is no evidence that he was motivated by anything more than the desire that his children would be able to speak English. His son learned to speak both languages and could recite English and American poetry from memory. Alfred DesRochers, himself a major Quebec poet, pointed out that anglophone families in Quebec at the turn of the century usually had the works of Shakespeare as well as the major British poets of the seventeenth and eighteenth centuries in their home libraries. DesRochers even suggested Thomas Gray's "The Bard" as a source for Nelligan's famous image of the golden ship (191, 195). While such an influence remains conjectural, Jacques Michon's edition of Nelligan's hospital notebooks reveals that his considerable interest in English poetry lasted to the end of his life.

There is no basis, however, for supposing that Nelligan might have considered writing in the language of the dominant culture in Montreal at the time and becoming an English-Canadian poet. His choice of French can be attributed to the fact that it was the language most familiar to him, the language most often spoken at home (his father, a postal inspector, was frequently absent), and the language of his schooling as well. As the language of his mother, an accomplished amateur pianist, French may also have been associated with music in his artistic consciousness. Although he retained a lifelong interest in Thomas Moore and Edgar Allen Poe, continental French poetry of the late nineteenth century, which was highly innovative formally and thematically, was closer to his sensibilities than the English poetry of his time, which was dominated by Tennyson and his followers. In English Canada, the Wordsworthian poetry of Lampman, focused on nature, or the Tennysonian stances of Charles G.D. Roberts, Nelligan's almost exact contemporary, would not likely have attracted him even had he known of them, which does not seem probable.[3]

What did it mean to be a French-Canadian poet in 1896? To what indigenous traditions could a young poet turn for inspiration? While French poetry had been written in Canada since the eighteenth century, this poetry had largely consisted of predictable types: circumstantial verse commenting on current events; patriotic and historical poetry; political poems espousing partisan agendas; moral and didactic verse transmitting traditional values; and humorous verse.[4] In the half-decade prior to Nelligan's writing, an opening to new forms could be observed in young, marginalized writers such as Victor Grenier and E.-Z. Massicotte, whose literary magazine, *L'Écho des jeunes* (1891–95), welcomed current literary developments in France. Their influence is difficult to assess since their review never had, according to Massicotte, more than two dozen readers (see Pierssens and Benardi). The prevailing literary ideal at the end of the century remained that set forth by abbé

Casgrain in 1866, namely that writing be the expression of shared values and a collective history. Of French-Canadian literature, whose primary genre was then poetry, Casgrain wrote that "elle sera le miroir fidèle de notre petit peuple dans les diverses phases de son existence, avec sa foi ardente, ses nobles aspirations, ses élans d'enthousiasme, ses traits d'héroïsme, sa généreuse passion de dévouement" (qtd by Hayne 60). Such "poetry," however, hardly ever rises above the level of metered and rhymed prose. Its facility and predictability were emphasized by Octave Crémazie in 1867 in a frequently quoted letter to abbé Casgrain: "Faites rimer un certain nombre de fois *gloire* avec *victoire*, *aïeux* avec *glorieux*, *France* avec *espérance*, entremêlez ces rîmes de quelques mots sonores comme *religion*, notre *patrie*, nos *lois*, le *sang de nos pères*, faites chauffer le tout à la flamme du patriotisme et servez chaud. Tout le monde dira que c'est magnifique" (2:93). Though he did treat of death and the passage of time, Crémazie, the most famous of the mid-century poets, remains largely a patriotic, circumstantial poet whose verse seems lacking in inspiration.

The few instances of intimate poetry, by Pamphile Lemay and Eudore Évanturel, can be considered discrete exceptions. Alfred Garneau, another anomaly, published little and his collected poetry only appeared posthumously, in 1906. Adolphe Poisson, in a volume published in 1894 and reissued in 1895, the year prior to Nelligan's first poems, did refer to his own verse as "ces lambeaux de mon cœur" (XII), but his collection, except for a single poem, is largely composed of narrative verse and encomia to the famous, and would appear to derive primarily from what he later calls "les nobles champs de la pensée" (4). Indeed, to reveal one's inner self in poetry was considered to be in bad taste. In his preface to Albert Ferland's *Femmes Rêvées* (1899), Louis Fréchette specifically praised Ferland for not disclosing "devant le public les recours intimes de son être" (II). Fréchette's admonition constitutes part of an effort to repress the expression of subjectivity in nineteenth-century French-Canadian culture. As an example of this process, Pierre Nepveu has shown how abbé Casgrain chose to represent Marie de l'Incarnation as a heroic, messianic figure, thereby erasing the deep interior life that is a key to understanding her (43–4). Fréchette's own *Légende d'un peuple*, it has been pointed out (Beaudoin 176*ff*; Nepveu 44), does not acknowledge that the heroes of his vast epic might have been capable of introspection.

In the late nineteenth century, this same Louis Fréchette stood out as the most prominent of poets. Although his advocacy of progressive ideas and his appropriation of Romantic discourse had marked him with controversy, this prolific poet was much acclaimed and even widely hailed as "le barde national," particularly after being honoured by the Académie Française and received by Victor Hugo in 1880. In a self-legitimating manoeuvre, the École littéraire de Montréal named him its "président d'honneur" in 1898. Indeed, Fréchette would fit the definition of what Vigny in his essay "Dernière Nuit de Travail" defined as "le grand écrivain," that is the poet who holds "un peuple dans sa main, et l'opinion qu'on a de lui le tient dans le respect de lui-même et l'oblige à surveiller sa vie" (1:764). Nelligan, however, had in mind to be a poet who would fulfill Vigny's definition of a true poet as "une autre sorte de nature, nature plus passionnée, plus pure et plus rare" (1:764), who is incapable of anything but poetry. The true poet, Vigny had argued, is possessed by his imagination, which he does not control. Such a man "a besoin de *ne rien faire*, pour faire quelque chose en son art" (1:765; Vigny's italics). While he cannot be asked to do anything quotidian or utilitarian, he must be given the means to live. The testimony of those who knew Nelligan confirms Jean Charbonneau's recollection that Nelligan was willing to "sacrifier tout intérêt matériel au culte du Beau" (1935, 117). "Émile," recalled Lucien Lemieux, whose family summered at Cacouna along with the Nelligans in 1898, "ne voulait pas entendre parler de travailler pour gagner sa vie. La poésie seule l'intéressait" (qtd in Lacourcière 32).

While Nelligan's mother seems to have taken some pride in her son's poetry, such an exalted view of the poet would put the young man in conflict with his proper, bourgeois family. This situation has been discussed in detail in Paul Wyczynski's massive biography of Nelligan and need not be repeated here. A poet, in Nelligan's understanding of the word, was destined to be a social outcast, for while the bohemian circles of the 1890s might have been expected to be sympathetic, Canadian society, French or English, had produced no previous model of the type. Poets *were* highly esteemed in late nineteenth-century Quebec, to the extent that public figures and government functionaries found it useful to publish verse. Even the first premier of Quebec, P.J.O. Chauveau, wrote poetry. But poetry was seen as a cultivated pastime, a way for the elite to transmit and disseminate patriotic and traditional values. It was the work of middle-aged men, those "messieurs rubiconds et ventrus," as Dantin called them (1997, 66), who had stable positions and for whom poetry was compatible with an occupation. They accepted Boileau's admonishment in *L'Art poétique* – still influential in Quebec more than two centuries after its publication – that poetry *not* be an "éternel emploi" since "Il faut savoir encore et converser et vivre" (186) and would have been baffled by the suggestion that the poet might not be like other men.[5] Jean Charbonneau, writing about the atmosphere of 1895, when he himself was beginning to write poetry, described it thus: "Un jeune homme que sa famille destinait à une profession quelconque et qui, clandestinement, 'faisait de la littérature,' avait besoin d'être mis sous observation comme s'il était atteint d'une maladie mentale. Beaucoup en était convaincus" (1935, 282–3). Within a socio-cultural context that rejected the autonomy of art, a young man's assertion that poetry might be an exclusive calling – a notion widely accepted in literary circles in France – was incomprehensible. None of Nelligan's fellow poets who constituted the École littéraire de Montréal proposed such a view of poetry. Most were lawyers and journalists and several of the younger members later became provincial or federal functionaries. But it was precisely Nelligan's claim that the poet was different from other humans, that the poet was other.

It bears noting, however, that Nelligan's claims are modest compared to those that Paul Bénichou has carefully delineated in the French Romantic tradition. The self-exaltation, the claim to divine inspiration, and the pretension to a calling to enlighten society so frequent in Romantic discourse are absent from Nelligan's. Unlike his friend and fellow-poet Guy Delahaye, Nelligan did not view poetry as a kind of mystical knowledge of the universe,[6] and he was far removed from the Rimbaldian notion that the poet might be an alchemist of the Absolute. He imagined Chopin accomplishing for music "ce que fit à Florence / Maint peintre italien pour l'âge rajeuni" (257), but there are no indications that he saw himself as leading a similar renaissance in poetry. Conscious of having been touched by genius – "Je sens voler en moi les oiseaux du génie" (304) – he saw his difference as deriving not from his being chosen by the gods but rather from a special combination of intellectual and moral traits. The most evident of these is the way he thinks, for the real poet thinks in ways that are not those of other mortals. Nelligan confronts this issue in his poem "Clair de lune intellectuel." The initial poem in all editions of Nelligan's poetry until the 1990s, "Clair de lune intellectuel" is an exemplary Nelliganian text and an excellent introduction to his poetic universe. It recalls Verlaine's "Clair de lune," the opening poem of *Fêtes galantes*, with which Nelligan was clearly familiar[7] and which serves as an intertext for this poem, but "Clair de lune intellectuel" differs sharply from the Verlainian text in both form and signification. Verlaine's title is embedded in Nelligan's but is qualified by the adjective "intellectuel," which Nelligan uses only one other time in his poetry, in "Mazurka." The unexpected qualification is important, for Nelligan's poem is meant to be a statement about the nature of his own thought.

Unlike Verlaine, who uses a three-quatrain strophic form, Nelligan makes his statement through a fixed form, the rondel. Nelligan had a propensity for fixed forms, particularly for the sonnet, which other poets of the École littéraire de Montréal favoured as well, but also for the rondel, of which there are sixteen other examples in his corpus.[8] The genre, which dates back to the Middle Ages and particularly to Charles d'Orléans, does not appear to have been practiced in Canada, but had been given new life in France in the second half of the nineteenth century by two poets with whose work Nelligan was quite familiar, Théodore de Banville and Maurice Rollinat. It consists of thirteen lines, with the first two lines repeated as lines 7 and 8 and the first line repeated as the last line. The entire poem must be based on two rhymes only, with a set rhyme scheme, *ABba*, *abAB*, *abbaA*, which Nelligan adheres to. Yet the rondel, which is ordinarily used for light verse, provides Nelligan with an incomparable structure for a serious representation of thought, or rather, a special kind of thought, as poetry.

The structure of the rondel permits the statement that defines his thought, "Ma pensée est couleur de ... ," which emerges as the poem's major enunciation (identified as ME and printed in bold characters in the reproduction of the text below), to both frame and divide the poem evenly.

ME **Ma pensée est couleur de** lumières lointaines,
Du fond de quelque crypte aux vagues profondeurs;
MB *Elle a l'éclat* parfois des subtiles verdeurs
D'un golfe où le soleil abaisse ses antennes.

En un jardin sonore, au soupir des fontaines,
MB *Elle a vécu* dans les soirs doux, dans les odeurs;
ME **Ma pensée est couleur de** lumières lointaines,
Du fond de quelque crypte aux vagues profondeurs.

MB *Elle court* à jamais les blanches prétentaines,
Au pays angélique où montent ses ardeurs;
Et, loin de la matière et des brutes laideurs,
MB *Elle rêve* l'essor aux célestes Athènes.
ME **Ma pensée est couleur de** lunes d'or lointaines. (294)

The major enunciation, then, constitutes not only the first and last lines (1 and 13) but the middle line (7) as well. It is more direct and perhaps more effective than Verlaine's initial verse, "Votre âme est un paysage choisi," since Verlaine's line does not make it clear whether the poet is addressing an interlocutor or himself. The first person possessive, "ma," on the other hand, is crucial to Nelligan's context, for "pensée" alone of all the signifiers in the poem is so modified. The poet's one possession, his prized possession, is his thought.

Nelligan's poem, then, is structured in the following manner: major enunciation plus five verses plus major enunciation plus five verses plus major enunciation. What may be called the modes of being of thought ("Elle a l'éclat ... Elle a vécu ... Elle court ... Elle rêve" [identified as MB above]) occur at precise and equally spaced intervals (lines 3, 6, 9, 12). A conscious effort to create a highly structured text is clearly in evidence. Indeed, this seems appropriate as a formal mirror of the mind's logical, structuring power. What is striking about this poem, however, is that its highly structured form is at variance with its content. What this text signifies is not that thought is order, structure, clarity, and logic, but rather that thought, or this poet's thought, is non-ordered, that its primary quality is indeterminacy.

The first clue appears in the oxymoronic title. "Clair de lune" – a number of nineteenth-century poems bear this exact title (Verlaine and Hugo come to mind in particular) – invites *rêverie* (Verlaine is specific about it: "Au calme clair de lune triste et beau / qui fait rêver"); it evokes the free flow of thoughts, the mixture of thought and sentiment; it calls up the "rêves nébuleux" of which Nelligan speaks in "Amour immaculé." Indeed, if we were to expect *clair de lune* to be modified at all, it would be by the epithet *sentimental* as in Gautier's "Clair de lune sentimental" in *Émaux et Camées*. Its modification by "intellectuel" signals that in this poem the imaginative and the intellectual shall be conjoined.

This conjunction is emphasized within the first three lines where we encounter signifiers containing semes of indeterminacy: "lointaines" (line 1), "quelque" (2), "vagues" (2), "parfois" (3), "subtiles" (3). The first line, with its alliterative [l]s that recall the alliterative [l]s of the title and thereby create a phonetic link with it, establishes the tone: "Ma pensée est couleur de lumières lointaines." If Rimbaud could find colour in vowels, Nelligan sees his thought *as* colour. The operative verb of the first sentence, as in the initial sentence of Verlaine's poem, is *to be*, the verb of equivalency; in other words, colour is not presented as a quality of thought but rather thought is identified with colour, though, significantly, no specific colour is mentioned. Synesthesic combinations, we know, are not unusual in Nelligan nor in French poetry of the period. The colour evoked is associated in turn with faraway lights. "[L]ointaines," it should be noted, has temporal as well as spatial connotations. French accepts "époque lointaine," for example, as referring to a distant time. In the second line, the flow of the alliterative [l]s is arrested by the alliterative velars and dentals as the image of light is unexpectedly and dissonantly associated with semes of depth. The indeterminacy is still present, however, for the crypt is unspecified ("quelque crypte"), and its depth undetermined ("aux vagues profondeurs"). As an underground burial vault in some churches, a crypt has associations with death, a theme of consistent importance in Nelligan's poetry; as a subterranean chapel, it has religious connotations as well. Such a chapel is frequently older than the church under which it is found, so the word contains temporal as well as spatial semes (as does "lointaines"). Nelligan may also be seeking to actualize the etymological seme of *crypte*, which derives from the Greek *kryptós*, meaning hidden or secret. "Profondeurs" would seem to corroborate this seme, since its specific meaning in the plural refers to a place deep down under the surface of the earth or water. It contains semes of intellectual profundity as well, but in the poem these depths are vague. The crypt could be read as the poet's own mind, deep and secret in its recesses, from whence his thoughts proceed. But what do we know about the poet's thought from this distich? Very little that is specific, to be sure, but that is precisely the point. His thought seems to have bipolar associations: light ("lumières") and darkness ("crypte"); distance / height (again "lumières") and depth (again "crypte"). But we are not dealing with binary oppositions here as much as with a blurring of any sharpness of distinctions; the signifiers "lointaines," "quelques," and "vagues" have assured that. These are unusual notions in a culture that believed the purpose of poetry to be the expression of ideas.

Line 3 provides the first of four statements that elaborate on the modes of being of the poet's thought: "Elle a l'éclat parfois des subtiles verdeurs / D'un golfe où le soleil abaisse ses antennes." "Éclat," whose semes are supported by the assonant repetition of [a] four times in the first hemistich, challenges us as an attribute of thought, because its connotations of sharpness seem at variance with the indeterminacy prominent in the major enunciation. That *éclat* also connotes the intensity of bright light, vividness, and freshness, and sometimes magnificence and brilliance would seem to complicate our problem, since the light of the first distich is distant. The remainder of the sentence, though, makes possible the integration of *éclat* into the ambience of indeterminacy. This second distich describes a sunset, specifically a sun setting over a body of water, not an unusual scene in nineteenth-century poetry (consider, for example, Verlaine's "Soleils couchant"). The comparison being made, then, is between attributes of the poet's thought and the visual effects of a setting sun. These effects are expressed by the collocation "subtiles verdeurs." When applied to fruits or wine, *verdeurs* as a noun signifies primarily immaturity, a seme that seems to be active here, connoting the youthfulness of the poet's thought. That *verdeur* also refers to youth in the expression *la verdeur de l'âge* would cohere with the attribute of line 9, "Elle court à jamais les blanches prétentaines," *courir la prétentaine* being normally characteristic of youth. The other meaning of *verdeur*, namely crudity, as in *la verdeur de ses propos*, does not seem to be active in this context. It is also possible that Nelligan is activating the etymological seme of *verdeur*, which derives from *verd* (*verdeur* meaning "green" is attested in the twelfth century). From this perspective, "subtiles verdeurs" could refer to the delicate green of the water, and "éclat" earlier in the verse would also be attenuated. *Subtiles* does have meanings of ingenuity or perspicacity (as in *esprit subtil*) or subtlety and shrewdness (as in *question subtile*). One has the impression, then, of a thought that is both youthful and ingenious. Nelligan is not defining thought as being sharp, but he is including sharpness as an occasional characteristic of it (note "parfois"). While anomalous within the semic field that is emerging in the first quatrain, the semes of sharpness, combined with semes of *rêverie*, light, darkness, distance, depth, and the past, contribute to the non-definition of poetic thought, to the assertion that poetic thought cannot be defined but only described as indeterminate.

If the first stanza translates thought into sight, the preferred sense of the Parnassians, the first distich of the second stanza associates it with hearing and smell: "En un jardin sonore, au soupir des fontaines, / Elle a vécu dans les soirs doux, dans les odeurs." The only one of the modes of being of thought to be expressed in the past, thereby maintaining a semic link with "lointaines" and "cryptes," it will be repeated as part of the refrain in verses 7 and 8. The sighing fountains remind us of the last stanza of Verlaine's "Clair de lune":

Au calme clair de lune triste et beau
Qui fait rêver les oiseaux dans les arbres
Et sangloter d'extase les jets d'eau,
Les grands jets d'eau sveltes parmi les marbres. (*Fêtes galantes* 33)

But while Verlaine's poem begins on a note of apparent gaiety and changes to deep melancholy, Nelligan's rondel maintains its positive tone. In this instance, his distich seems to have as its purpose to propose a contrasting attribute of his thought. Sharpness and brightness give way to *mollesse*, to a kind of lethargic serenity. Balmy nights, garden smells, water fountains: these provide the ambience for *rêverie*, strengthening the central message that the poet's thought is not exclusively rational, that it is indistinguishable from free-flowing, indiscriminate mental activity.

This leads to what may be identified as "Part II" of the poem, that is, verses 9–12, in which two sentences express attributes of the poet's thought, with this difference: the first two attributes ("Elle a l'éclat ... Elle a vécu ...") had expressed states, while the attributes of this section express activities ("Elle court ... Elle rêve ..."), the first taking place on a horizontal plane, the other on a vertical one. A wandering that is aimless ("Elle court à jamais les blanches prétentaines"), continuous ("à jamais"), and somehow fresh and pure ("blanches") evolves into a specific, focused activity, the dream of attaining the realm of idealized art – the "pays angélique," far from "la matière et [l]es brutes laideurs" to which the poet aspires. He dreams of celestial Athens, in the plural, cities of light, learning, and the arts, perhaps. *Athènes* might also recall Athena (or Athênê), the goddess of thought, the arts, the sciences, and industry, who gave her name to the city. But the primary signification seems to be a realm out of this world. Recalling that "crypte" contains semes of death, it is possible to suggest that the celestial Athens which are dreamed of also connote death, since that is the only way to escape "la matière et [l]es brutes laideurs." The line recalls Baudelaire's "Élevation" and that poet's desire to flee "ces miasmes morbides," but betrays as well a fundamental Nelliganian exigency to "planer au divin territoire" ("Châteaux en Espagne"). Nelligan's thought is otherworldly, and properly belongs in the idealized world of art. As Jacques Michon has pointed out, the real enemy in Nelligan's poetry is not death or even hell, but rather life itself (1983, 44). Yet, in contrast to other poems of Nelligan that I discuss later, in which the dream of celestial cities of the arts is subordinated to a strained effort to escape this world, this poem retains its hope and its serenity. I see no reason in the text for believing, as one critic has, that this poem "n'est en réalité que le bercement mélancolique de sa rêverie inquiète" (Wyczynski 1986, 426). "Clair de lune intellectuel" is one of the few of Nelligan's poems not to have any lines end in either a question mark or an exclamation point. The subdued rhetoric translates a calm confidence in the potentialities of poetic activity, a confidence that will be shaken in other poems.

The indeterminateness of poetic thought is further revealed in the very form that, as I have pointed out, is so tightly structured. The last line of the poem, "Ma pensée est couleur de lunes d'or lointaines," is a reprise of the major enunciation, but with a difference: "lumières lointaines" has been changed to "lunes d'or lointaines." This alteration is significant because it is part of a double departure from the chief nineteenth-century model of the rondel, namely Banville's *Rondels composés à la manière de Charles d'Orléans* (1875). In all twenty-four of Banville's rondels, the last line is an exact repetition of the first (Nelligan makes a change in line 13 in about half of his rondels), and in Banville the last line forms part of the third stanza, creating a five-line strophe (in all of

Nelligan's rondels, the thirteenth line stands alone). Rollinat, a less influential but more prolific writer of rondels (he wrote over 120 of them), never deviates from this model, his thirteenth line always being an exact replica of line 1 and always part of a five-line stanza. The return of the refrain is clearly considered essential by both Banville and Rollinat. Yet Nelligan, who always does more than merely imitate European sources, insists on altering this refrain both by making a semantic change in the final hemistich and by isolating the final line. These changes undoubtedly strengthen the effect of the poem, but in what way?

In the first place, the substitution of "lunes d'or" for "lumières" finally makes sense of the title – nowhere in the body of the text has moonlight yet been mentioned – thereby confirming the temporality of the poem, since sunset was evoked in lines 3 and 4. It also adds semes of verticality – an important dimension of Nelligan's literary imagination – strengthening these connotations already present in "célestes Athènes." More importantly, it marks an enrichment, the vague "lumières" now having become moons of gold. *Or*, as I noted in the introduction, is a highly positive marker in Nelligan, as it is most definitely in this poem. By letting his thought roam, by exploring distance and depth, the poet has enriched himself. The moon, which almost always has sombre associations in Nelligan's poetry (with the exception of the light, pastoral "Violon de villanelle"), emerges here as a positive symbol, quite unlike its role in Verlaine's poem. The nocturnal anguish so prominent in other Nelligan texts is absent.

One final aspect of the closing line needs to be noted: it is a truncated version of the distichs which constitute verses 1–2 and 7–8. In accordance with the rules of the rondel, the second line – the only phonetically and semantically dissonant line in this poem – disappears. There is no longer any question of depth; the crypt, evoked twice previously, has been eliminated. In a sense, this provides focus and tends to suggest that the dream of ascent negates the origins of depth. Yet, this clear focus is balanced by the fact that dropping the second half of the distich makes the poem not only a perfect rondel but an incomplete sonnet as well – the simple repetition of the missing line would have created the fourteen lines required for a sonnet. That Nelligan should have chosen a thirteen-line form, a form designed to be incomplete, for a poem defining his thought is significant, for by frustrating the reader's desire for the return, as in the past, of the whole distich, he once again reminds us of the indeterminacy of his thought.

In Nelligan's understanding, the poet's difference lies not only in the otherness of his thought processes but also in his moral superiority. The concept of the poet as morally superior has a long history. It had regained considerable prominence in the Romantic period, and remained an implicit assumption of a number of nineteenth-century poets. Yet few poets claim in their own verse to be pure. Such, however, is Nelligan's assertion, as his poem "Mon Âme" makes clear:

Mon âme a la candeur d'une chose étoilée,
D'une neige de février ...
Ah! retournons au seuil de l'Enfance en allée,
Viens-t'en prier ...

Ma chère, joins tes doigts et pleure et rêve et prie,
Comme tu faisais autrefois
Lorsqu'en ma chambre, aux soirs vers la Vierge fleurie
Montait ta voix.

Ah! la fatalité d'être une âme candide
En ce monde menteur, flétri, blasé, pervers,
D'avoir une âme ainsi qu'une neige aux hivers
Que jamais ne souilla la volupté sordide!

D'avoir l'âme pareille à de la mousseline
Que manie une sœur novice de couvent,
Ou comme un luth empli des musiques du vent
Qui chante et qui frémit le soir sur la colline!

D'avoir une âme douce et mystiquement tendre,
Et cependant, toujours, de tous les maux souffrir,
Dans le regret de vivre et l'effroi de mourir,
Et d'espérer, de croire ... et de toujours attendre! (295)

The poem's title reverberates throughout the text, as "âme" is repeated five times. The initial sentence, "Mon âme a la candeur d'une chose étoilée, / D'une neige de février" (lines 1–2), establishes the purity ("neige de février") and the innocence ("candeur") of the poet's soul. "[C]andeur," whose etymological seme (<Latin *candor* = white) strengthens this declaration of purity, reappears in its adjectival form, "candide" (9), in the third stanza, again referring to his soul, as does "neige" (11), to which his soul is likened. The simile in the fourth stanza that compares his soul to muslin, here probably white muslin, is part of the same semic sphere, as is the novice nun, who would have been robed in white, who handles it.

The poet's purity, however, is in conflict with the world in which he finds himself, for this world is "menteur, flétri, blasé, pervers" (line 10). While such a depreciation of earthly existence would not have been at odds with religious thinking in late nineteenth-century Quebec, the Baudelairean harshness of this series, its unexpectedness, and its centrality (it constitutes the tenth line of a twenty-line poem) bring into sharp focus what appears to be a primary reason for the poet's nostalgia for the more innocent time of his childhood. Lines 3 to 8 constitute a direct address to an unnamed female person who is dear to him ("Ma chère"),[9] whom he summons to return with him "au seuil de l'Enfance en allée" (3). The capitalization of "Enfance" signals its importance, and its qualification by "en allée" reminds us that it is no more, that the poetic voice is therefore that of an adult. Informed by the poet in lines 1 and 2 that his soul is as pure as snow, the reader easily concludes that the poet, though no longer a child, has retained his childhood innocence. The woman is summoned to join him for prayer (line 4). The second stanza describes, however, not their common prayer but hers, mingled with tears and reverie, and implies through the polysyndetic construction ("et pleure et rêve et prie") that tears, daydreams, and prayer are part of a single process. This might indicate that the woman has also come into contact with "ce monde menteur, flétri, blasé, pervers" (10). It would appear that she habitually joined him in his room ("en ma chambre") for evening prayers. These were directed, it will be noted, to the Virgin, rather than to God, Christ, or some other saint. This Virgin, presumably represented by a statue in the boy's room, is said to be "fleurie." In its ordinary usage, this word means festooned with flowers, and it is quite possible that a statue of the Virgin inside a private home in Quebec in the 1890s would have been garnished with flowers, particularly in May, the traditional "month of Mary." In this instance, "fleuri" also likely carries the meaning that it has in the expression *teint fleuri*, in which the complexion is said to be fresh and sparkling, thereby recalling both "candeur" (freshness) and "chose étoilée" (sparkling).

These prayers to the Virgin are a signal that this poet's anguish derives from something more complex than the Romantic opposition between the poet and society. Semes of purity are traditionally attributed to the Virgin with whom the poet, who is also pure, is thereby associated. The Virgin is pure because she was untainted by original sin (the doctrine of the Immaculate Conception) and gave birth without ever being defiled by sexual relations (the doctrine of the Virgin birth). The triumph of purity over sexuality that the Virgin represents is not without significance to the reading of this poem. The strong presence of religious semes in "Mon Âme," which contains a series of signifiers with clear religious connotations ("prier," line 4; "prie," 5; "Vierge," 7; "sœur novice," 14; "couvent," 14; "mystiquement," 17; "espérer," 20; "croire," 20), does not require elaboration. Moreover, in at least two instances, semes of purity overlap with religious semes ("Vierge" and "sœur novice"). The religion of reference in this and other poems is, of course, nineteenth-century French-Canadian Catholicism, a historical and geographical version of Christianity which called forth much idealism and selflessness but which at the same time envisaged sexuality as something sordid.

In this poem, purity is associated with semes of coldness, with a frigidity that could be related to sexual reticence: "neige" (twice), "février," "hivers." The poet himself makes the link directly in the third stanza when he specifies that his soul is like "une neige aux hivers / Que jamais ne souilla la volupté sordide" (lines 10–11). That "volupté," i.e., pleasure of the senses, should be qualified by the adjective "sordide" identifies it as part of the quasi-Jansenist religious discourse common in nineteenth-century Quebec, a subject to which I shall return in subsequent chapters. The poet is proclaiming his faithfulness to the ideal of sexual purity in contrast to the "pervers" world about him.

The first two lines of the fourth stanza, "D'avoir l'âme pareille à de la mousseline / Que manie une sœur novice de couvent" (lines 13–14), suggest the poet's wish to subordinate the claims of sexuality to those of purity. In this simile, his soul is likened to a fine, delicate, and unblemished cotton that is being handled by a young nun. The poet imagines being touched in the deepest part of his being by a young woman, but desire remains safe, for the woman has committed herself to a chaste life. This overwhelming of sexual semes by religious ones is apparent as well in the two opening stanzas in which the poet invites a woman to join him in his room at night. Any erotic intimations that might emerge from the association of a bedroom, nighttime, and a female companion, are held in check by the strong religious semes: the bedroom is the site of bedtime prayers, the woman is his companion in prayer, and the prayers are addressed to the Virgin, the guarantor that the erotic semes will not be actualized.

The poet, who lays claim to purity, identifies himself specifically as a poet only in lines 15–16 where he compares his soul to "un luth empli des musiques du vent / Qui chante et qui frémit le soir sur la colline." The introduction of the lute, the traditional symbol of lyric poetry, is somewhat clumsy, for this stringed instrument is strangely filled ("empli") with the music of the wind. This image, which Lamartine had used in "Le Poète mourant,"[10] may suggest that the poet captures the sounds of the cosmos, but Nelligan does not elsewhere in his work show any indication that he subscribed to Hugo's celebrated description of the poet as an "écho sonore" of the universe. The simile would appear to be little more than an awkward effort to identify himself as a poet. Yet, the lute's music is that of the wind which not only sings ("chante") but also trembles ("frémit"). Does the poet fear his own gift? Does he tremble at his plight in this sinful world? Or does the eerie music of the wind over the hill remind him of his mortality (*cf* line 19, "l'effroi de mourir")? No direct answer is given in the text, but the poet's plight as he conceives it is cause for his discomfort.

After the two initial heterometric stanzas, the third stanza (the first of three in alexandrines) begins with the interjection "Ah!" This hackneyed device, already used in line 3, signals the poet's frustration at the inevitability of his conflict. The assonant [a] in "Ah! la fatalité ..." [alafata] reinforces this sense of being in a trap not of his own making, of having a soul that cannot adapt to this sinful life (while strengthening the link with the incipit where the same assonance occurs: "Mon âme a la candeur ..." [amala]). The expression "la fatalité" governs not only the infinitive immediately following it, "d'être une âme candide," but also the anaphoric infinitives of line 11, "D'avoir une âme ainsi qu'une neige," line 13, "D'avoir l'âme pareille à de la mousseline," and line 17, "D'avoir une âme douce et mystiquement tendre." He does not have options;

he cannot choose another, different soul (in line 9, he *is* his soul). His is "douce et mystiquement tendre" and hence subject to continual suffering. The entire first hemistich of the eighteenth verse consists solely of two conjunctions and one adverb ("Et cependant toujours"). This has the effect of emphasizing duration while at the same time deferring "de tous les maux souffrir" to the second hemistich and thereby stressing the condition. The poet is caught between his sorrow at living and his fear of dying. He is destined to hope and to believe. It is not certain what governs the infinitives "d'espérer, de croire," but the most likely possibility is "la fatalité" of line 9. Hope and faith are two of the theological virtues (the third, love, is absent), but the religious connotations remain muted in this instance, for there are no objects to these infinitives. To hope and believe in what? The three suspension points after "croire" sow doubt as to the existence of such an object. Hence, he is always waiting: "et de toujours attendre."

What is he waiting for? Like Beckett's Vladimir and Estragon, for some kind of salvation, to be sure, but one that remains unnamed. In Nelligan's culture, salvation came from and through Christ whose absence here is telling. Indeed, the failure to identify the person or event awaited may be the key to the poem: the poet's distress derives from his not knowing what or whom he is waiting for. In contrast to "Clair de lune intellectuel," where the poem ends with the enrichment of his thought/imagination, this poem stresses the poet's anguish.

Strikingly similar concerns are to be found in "Rêve d'artiste":

Parfois j'ai le désir d'une sœur bonne et tendre,
D'une sœur angélique au sourire discret;
Sœur qui m'enseignera doucement le secret
De prier comme il faut, d'espérer et d'attendre.

J'ai ce désir très pur d'une sœur éternelle,
D'une sœur d'amitié dans le règne de l'Art,
Qui me saura veillant à ma lampe très tard
Et qui me couvrira des cieux de sa prunelle;

Qui me prendra les mains quelquefois dans les siennes
Et me chuchotera d'immaculés conseils,
Avec le charme ailé des voix musiciennes;

Et pour qui je ferai, si j'aborde à la gloire,
Fleurir tout un jardin de lys et de soleils
Dans l'azur d'un poème offert à sa mémoire. (157)

This text might first appear as one more rendition of the old topos – particularly in vogue in the Renaissance – of the poet who seeks inspiration from a lady and promises to render her immortal through a poem. "Rêve d'artiste," which Nelligan recited at a poetry reading sponsored by the École littéraire de Montréal in 1899, reveals itself, however, to be considerably more complex. Its publication in *La Patrie* in that same year carried a dedication to Robertine Barry (identified as "Mlle R.B."), a friend of his mother and something of a muse for the young poet. Several critics have therefore assumed her to be the "sœur" alluded to in the poem. While there may be some legitimacy to this attribution, the woman here evoked is clearly not the historical Robertine Barry. In one way, she resembles the woman in "Mon Âme," for she, too, is called upon to help the poet pray. Yet, the woman in "Mon Âme" is clearly a human person who is alive and known to him while the one dreamed of in this poem is represented as otherworldly. The adjective "angélique" applied to her in line 2 is not purely metaphorical, for in line 5 she is also referred to as "éternelle," and in line 8, the poet specifies that it is from her position in the heavens ("des cieux") that she will offer her help and protection. There is reason to suggest that she is (or has become) an angel (her wings are even evoked in the expression "charme ailé" [11]). Since the sonnet ends with the promise to write a poem in her memory, it could be suggested that she has already passed on to another world. That the poet wishes her to have a "sourire discret" is an indication that he is thinking of a woman who will not openly manifest her sexuality. The woman of his dreams is not one he wishes to seduce in the manner of Renaissance sonneteers. Rather, she is to be his intellectual helpmate, his adjuvant in the realm of the imagination and art, hence the purity of his desire ("ce désir très pur" [5]), and the insistence on referring to her as his sister.

Although in nineteenth-century French poetry "sister" sometimes designates a lover (as, for example, in Baudelaire's "L'Invitation au voyage"), the prominence of the appellation in this poem brings the signifier closer to connotations of sisterliness. The word occurs three times in the first three lines, each time moving closer to the beginning of the verse, and is repeated twice again in the first two lines of the second stanza. In the version that Nelligan published in *La Patrie* and then in *Les Soirées du Chateau de Ramezay*, he uses "amie" instead of "sœur" in line 5 (a wording he retains in his hospital transcriptions of 1934, 1935, and 1939), a clear indication that he wished to stress this *ange-femme*'s role as a friend. Moreover, an expression in the first tercet shows that the relations between the poet and his angelic muse are purely fraternal. The potential eroticism as she holds his hands – fulfilling the request made to Gretchen in "Frisson d'hiver" – and whispers in his ears is dissipated by the fact that she whispers "immaculés conseils," advice that is pure and sinless. In fact, in the poem as Nelligan published it in *La Patrie* in 1899, as it appeared in *Les Soirées du Chateau de Ramezay*, and as Nelligan himself transcribed it years later, this line reads "maint fraternel conseil" (see RW 409). The change to "immaculés conseils" – a revision that Réjean Robidoux has called a "trouvaille" (1997, 20) – seems to have been the work of Nelligan's first editor, Louis Dantin, but Nelligan clearly wanted "fraternel" which coheres with the importance he had given to *sister* earlier in the poem. Nelligan is not invoking a carnal or even a sensual relationship with this angelic woman whose goodness and tenderness was affirmed in the first line.

The reason is clear: the woman is above all an artist's dream – such is the significance of the title – who is to help him in the realm of art, which Nelligan consistently associates with the Ideal. This poet, who takes art seriously, identifies himself as an artist in the title and capitalizes the word "Art" in line 5 to indicate the value he attaches to it, a procedure he replicates in "À une femme détestée" and "La Romance du vin." Yet, the first stanza makes no reference to art, and the reader might therefore be tempted to read it in the manner of the first two stanzas of "Mon Âme" where the woman was also asked to assist him in prayer. It is specifically his desire here that she teach him "doucement le secret / De prier comme il faut, d'espérer et d'attendre" (lines 3–4). He thereby confesses his lack of aptitude for these activities, whose performance he assumes to require strategies he does not possess. The second hemistich of line 4, "d'espérer et d'attendre," further recalls the last line of "Mon Âme": "Et d'espérer, de croire … et de toujours attendre." Again, the object of hope and waiting is unidentified.

The first quatrain, however, appears to be a kind of prologue for the rest of the poem. It ends with a period, while the second quatrain and the tercets, which specifically address the question of art, constitute a single, complex sentence. It becomes clear in the second stanza that the woman is to do more than teach him to pray, hope, and wait, for she is to be his sister "dans le règne de l'Art" (line 6). There is, however, a relationship between the desire for an angelic woman who would teach him prayer and resignation and one who will console him in the realm of art. The second quatrain, which introduces the matter of art, begins by repeating, with a slight alteration, the introductory phrase of the first quatrain, thereby cementing the link between the two stanzas. The poet now hopes for a woman who will be faithful ("sœur éternelle") and loving ("sœur d'amitié"), specifically in aesthetic matters. She will assist him and protect him as he works late into the night (7) – Nelligan was not immune to Romantic clichés – and counsel him with the musical voice of angels.

Retrieving the Renaissance strategy of seduction in the final stanza, the poet offers in return to write something in her honour and memory. If he becomes famous ("si j'aborde à la gloire" [line 12]), then he will see to it that a poetic garden of lilies and sunflowers (common metaphors for poetry in nineteenth-century verse) bloom in her memory. The metaphors seem mixed here, but we detect exaltation on the part of the poet as he closes his sonnet with allusions to brilliant colours: white ("lys"), yellow/red ("soleils"), and blue ("azur"), the only such combination of colours in all of Nelligan's poetry. The last line of the poem as it appeared in *La Patrie* read "Dans l'azur des beaux vers d'un livre à sa mémoire" (the line in *Les Soirées du Chateau de Ramezay* is close to this). The changes, which again appear to be the work of Louis Dantin, do not alter the meaning of the line. The poet affirms that he will be grateful, but the manner in which he will express his gratitude confirms that his only talent, his only gift, is poetry.

Still, the poet's discourse is marked by a certain tentativeness. The poem's initial word, "parfois," suggests infrequency as well as repetitiveness. The poet hopes that the angel-muse might "sometimes" take his hands (dare he not hope for more?), while the poem to her memory will be composed only if he becomes famous. Such tentativeness and the deference and diffidence that accompany it seem to have been to no avail. An unnamed woman who may very well be the one alluded to in "Rêve d'artiste" reappears in "À une femme détestée" as a woman of flesh and blood who has incited the poet's anger:

Car dans ces jours de haine et ces temps de combats
Je fus de ces souffrants que leur langueur isole
Sans qu'ils aient pu trouver la Femme qui console
Et vous remplit le cœur rien qu'à parler tout bas.
Georges Rodenbach

Combien je vous déteste et combien je vous fuis:
Vous êtes pourtant belle et très noble d'allure,
Les Séraphins ont fait votre ample chevelure
Et vos regards couleur du charme brun des nuits.

Depuis que vous m'avez froissé, jamais depuis,
N'ai-je pu tempérer cette intime brûlure:
Vous m'avez fait souffrir, volage créature,
Pendant qu'en moi grondait le volcan des ennuis.

Moi, sans amour jamais qu'un amour d'Art, madame,
Et vous, indifférente, et qui n'avez pas d'âme,
Vieillissons tous les deux pour ne jamais nous voir.

Je ne dois pas courber mon front devant vos charmes;
Seulement, seulement, expliquez-moi ce soir,
Cette tristesse au cœur qui me cause des larmes. (158)

In a link with the angelization of the previous poem, this woman's abundant hair and seductive brown eyes are seen as the work of seraphim, but she is clearly a living woman whose sin seems to be that she has rejected the poet. The critical speculation has been that the woman is again Robertine Barry, since the poem was in her possession when Nelligan was interned and since it was she who, nine years later, first published it in *Le Journal de Françoise*, a magazine she edited. Critics have speculated that Nelligan had a crush on her and was rejected when he made it known. The unusual harshness of

Nelligan's tone, Bessette maintains (53), argues for such a hypothesis. The connection with Barry is possible and even plausible, but less important than the fact that the poet here proclaims that his sole love is for Art, an assertion repeated in "Le Berceau de la Muse" where he insists that his muse is his sole mistress (115). Even if this affirmation is the protest of a rejected lover, it nevertheless proclaims the centrality of Art in the poet's life.

This woman is, to be sure, attractive, even seductive. She is beautiful, noble in stature, has distinctly ample hair (an erogenous zone in nineteenth-century French poetry, as readers of Baudelaire know), and beguiling eyes ("charme" has the classical French meaning here of "seductive enchantment"). The description of her charms, however, follows "pourtant." In spite of these physical attractions, he both flees and detests her. The second quatrain specifies that she has offended him, even caused him suffering. The "intime brûlure" might indicate a rejection of his love, and the volcano to which he compares himself might well contain the lava of passion. But the point of the poem, it seems to me, is that in the first tercet the poet himself explicitly rejects this reading.

He protests that love, for him, is purely aesthetic: "Moi, sans amour jamais qu'un amour d'Art, madame" (line 9). Would that this woman had been like the noble Viennese lady in "Les Balsamines" who tearfully recalls

> Ce pauvre guitariste aux yeux où se reflète
> Le pur amour de l'art, qui près de sa tablette,
> Venait causer, humant des fleurs dans un bocal. (218)

The Viennese woman understood that the artist who sought her out acted through love of art alone. That Nelligan wished to project such an image of himself is clear. Jean Charbonneau, writing in 1916, recalled that Nelligan had told him, "Ma philosophie, mais elle réside toute entière dans mon amour de l'Art" (90). This remark to Charbonneau and the first line in this poem's sestet might be considered a reply to Louis Fréchette, who in his preface to *Mes Loisirs* had proclaimed that he wrote poetry "par pur délassement, par amour de l'art" (8). Nelligan, perhaps recalling Verlaine's lines, "Le Poète, l'amour du Beau, voilà sa foi / L'Azur son étendard, et l'Idéal, sa loi!" (1977, 43), wishes to emphasize the exclusivity of his love of art, one that for him is hardly a "délassement." The concept of the poet as the servant and lover of Art dates back to the Jeunes-France in the early 1830s, but was not part of the French-Canadian poetic tradition.

In any case, it would appear that the woman has misunderstood him. It is in this context that the epigraph, taken from the prologue of Rodenbach's *La Jeunesse blanche*, has some pertinence. Rodenbach's poem is also addressed to a woman. She is good, understanding, forgiving, and obviously older. After four stanzas of detailing her attributes, he begins to tell her of "Tout le bonheur obscur de mon heureuse enfance" (1:6). The stanza Nelligan has chosen seems to reflect what Rodenbach is experiencing at the time of his writing: "nos jours de haine et nos temps de combat" (6). The Belgian poet's problem is related to his inability to find "la Femme qui console / Et vous remplit le cœur" (6). Yet, Rodenbach's poetic voice has no sensual or amorous yearnings. The woman to whom he speaks was like a mother to him ("[vous] ... que j'aime à jamais comme on aime une aïeule" [5]), and there is no reason to believe that he is now seeking a romantic relationship. Nelligan's choice of this poem coheres with his intention to clarify that the relationship he envisaged was purely artistic.

The direct address, with its repetition of "vous" six times and "vos/votre" three times within the space of a sonnet, creates an atmosphere of indictment. *She* was the aggressor; *he* is the one fleeing. She has been unable to recognize the anguish that is boiling within him, ready to erupt ("en moi grondait le volcan des ennuis" [line 8]). Her indifference and lack of sensitivity are such that he never wishes to see her again. Yet, the poem's closure reflects the poet's incomprehension of what is going on inside him. The repetition of "seulement" in the next to the last line, causing the adverb to occupy the entire first hemistich as it acquires the conjunctive force of "yet," stresses that he does not understand his sadness. He is forced to ask the very woman who has spurned him to help him discern its meaning. This may indicate that the love of Art is insufficient to assuage his pain and perhaps that love and art are not for him as separate as he would want to believe.

That link is prominent in "La Romance du vin," the poem that closes both Dantin's and Lacourcière's editions,[11] and which may be read as the poet's answer to those who have spurned him. It provides an appropriate closure to Nelligan's poetry since it was intended as his reply to his detractors, since his public reading of it on 26 March 1899 was a personal triumph (suggesting that the sentiments he expressed were not his alone), and since, less than three months after this reading, he was interned for the rest of his life. Moreover, it is a text whose genesis is well known: Nelligan was incited to this response by criticism of his poetry by E. de Marchy, a Frenchman temporarily in Montreal.[12] Given the mildness of that criticism, I am inclined to concur with Jean Larose that Nelligan's strong reaction must derive at least in part from the fact that it came from a representative of the culture in which he had so heavily invested (see Larose 30). While much has been written about this incident, the poem it provoked has not itself received serious attention, having been overshadowed by its biographical and sociological dimensions.

I propose to enter into the text by its median verses, namely lines 18 and 19: "De se savoir poète et objet du mépris / De se savoir un cœur et de n'être compris" (300). These syntactically parallel anaphoric verses – the only usage of anaphora in this poem – appear at the very centre of "La Romance du vin": seventeen verses precede them; seventeen follow (for purposes of analysis, I shall refer to the seventeen preceding verses as the first part and the seventeen which follow as the second part). These median lines express certainties. This poet, so frequently unsure of himself, proclaims his certitude that he is the object of disdain and incomprehension. The line that precedes these two emphasizes the poet's scorn with an alliteration of [r]s: "C'est le règne du rire amer et de la rage" (line 17). The verse that follows (20) states that only the elements of nature (moonlight, storms) are capable of understanding him. Nelligan is clearly appropriating that discourse of Romanticism which posits an inevitable and irreparable opposition between the poet and society.[13] From this perspective, "poetry and society" must be rewritten as "poetry *or* society," for the choice of one prevents commerce with the other and leaves the poet destined to incomprehension and suffering. In another text, "Les Corbeaux," the horrific vision of the "grands corbeaux venus de montagnes célèbres" (273) who devour his flesh and finally his soul can be interpreted as referring to those in positions of authority who have descended from their lofty perches to destroy him. The "hommes aux fronts moroses" in line 23 of this poem are surely those, including his father, suggests Bessette (72), who are opposed to his poetry.

The poet's aspirations are clear and signaled even at the graphemic level: the only two words that carry a capital letter in this text are "Art" and "Idéal." In "Vive le vin et l'Art!" (line 13), wine, in lower case, finds itself diminished next to art, which is capitalized. But what is this art that he seeks?

> J'ai le rêve de faire aussi des vers célèbres,
> Des vers qui gémiront les musiques funèbres
> Des vents d'automne au loin passant dans le brouillard. (14–16)

He seeks fame for his poetry, yet he disdains the crowd that could give him that fame.[14] Ironically, this very poem was a crowd-pleaser: it lead to a boisterous ovation followed by the poet being carried atop the shoulders of his friends through the streets of Montreal to his home. Michel Biron has suggested that this reaction was possible because Nelligan's poem was in harmony with the liberal ideology of the time, which preached personal initiative and success (see Biron's "Nelligan: la fête urbaine"). Yet, while Nelligan does portray himself as acting individually, the thrust of his poem leads in a direction opposite to that of liberalism. He wished to be recognized as a poet – "autrefois, j'ai songé à la gloire," he told Thomas Lamarche in the thirties (XLIII) – but his understanding of success is qualitatively different from that preached by economic liberals. Indeed, his poem could be read as a reply to the liberalism expressed by the main speaker that evening, Wilfred Larose, in his lecture "Le succès dans la vie," a text that appears highly incongruous in the company of the poetry recited at that soirée, as Annette Hayward has pointed out (165–7). The famous verses he dreams of writing will produce only "musiques funèbres / Des vents d'automne au loin passant dans le brouillard." The Lamartinian attenuation – the winds are afar, the fog clouds vision – contributes to an atmosphere of dreamy sadness. Moreover, in line 16 an opposition emerges between the desired season and that of the poem, which is spring. On a beautiful evening in May, the poet wishes, in true Romantic fashion, for a windy, foggy autumn day.

The opposition between the poetic self and society is further highlighted by a semic axis which reflects what he perceives to be his community's attitude towards him. We note semes of ill-will ("méchanceté," line 12), disdain ("mépris," 18; "qui dédaignez," 24), incomprehension ("de n'être compris," 19), and laughter ("vous qui riez," 21). Nelligan, we may assume, is not reacting solely to de Marchy's criticism of his "Le Perroquet" but to all those who have mocked his art, beginning with his teacher, Jesuit Father Lalande, who once seized one of his poems and ridiculed it in front of the class. Those hostile to him, he seems to suggest, are reacting in this manner because of their own incapacity. We detect in this poem a series of signifiers that carry semes of song: "chœur" (line 2), "prélude" (4), "mélopées" (6), "chante" (9), "hymne" (26), and "chanté" (33), but the sources of this music are never directly human. Rather, birds, organs, crystal, and bells are its causes. Society, "la foule méchante" (12), is perhaps also that which "méchante," that is, which sings badly, is incapable of song, is incapable of poetry.

Nelligan expressed elsewhere his conviction that the world around him was filled with "des méchancetés dures, sordides, crues" ("Le Crêpe" 250) and deplored "L'affluence des sots aux atmosphères viles" ("Soirs d'octobre" 297). In this poem, the saddened poet attempts in the face of the hostile crowd to stimulate his own euphoria.[15] "Je suis gai!", repeated several times in the first part (twice in line 9 and twice in 13), is illocutory: it seeks to do as well as to say, or rather, it wants to achieve the doing by the saying. By dint of repeating "je suis gai," the poet, with the assistance of alcohol, believes he can become joyful. The movement is similar to that in another of Nelligan's poems, "Je veux m'éluder," which opens in the following manner:

> Je veux m'éluder dans les rires
> Dans les tourbes de gaîté brusque
> Oui, je voudrais me tromper jusque
> En des ouragans de délires. (306)

The desire for self-deception is expressed in this instance with extraordinary lucidity: "je voudrais me tromper." The second part of "La Romance du vin" returns to this litany of self-deception in the two clotural stanzas where the false declarations of joy take on additional force. The repetition of "Je suis gai! Je suis gai!" in line 29, followed by its amplified reiteration in the following line ("Je suis follement gai") and its repetition in an intensive mode in the two last lines ("Je suis si gai, si gai ... / Oh! si gai ..."), do not point to a successful result. The reader recognizes that the speech which sought to summon the emotion has not succeeded. The affirmations at the end are ironic and even bitter, similar to those of the opening lines of "Banquet macabre":

> À la santé du rire! Et j'élève ma coupe,
> Et je bois follement comme un rapin joyeux.
> Ô le rire! Ha! ha! ha! qui met la flamme aux yeux. (308)

The words "Ha! ha! ha!" represent not authentic laughter but rather its imitation. In "La Romance du vin," his gaiety is proclaimed in the fear of sobbing, as the poem's concluding line makes clear: "Oh! si gai, que j'ai peur d'éclater en sanglots!"[16] In "Banquet macabre" he also has recourse to wine "Pour étouffer ... la rage des sanglots" (308). Feigned good humour cannot create joy, and the poet's dysphoria persists.

Reading the poem in this way concurs with the traditional interpretation of "La Romance du vin" as expressing the well-known nineteenth-century theme of the poet's bitterness and sadness in the face of a hostile society.[17] This poem, as well as several others, contributes to the image of Nelligan as one who "se donne tout entier à la poésie et ... conçoit et exécute son œuvre envers et contre tous" (Ferron 1970, 46). But this may very well be but a partial reading. Must we limit Nelligan's plight solely to his experience as a poet in the modern world?

We need to return to the two median lines and discern that the certitude they express has two objects. The first, which I have discussed above, is the knowledge of being a poet and the object of disdain expressed in line 18. But line 19 does not merely repeat the preceding verse. To be sure, "se savoir un cœur" could be read as a gloss on "se savoir poète," as an expression of the poet's belief that the heart is central to being a poet. Yet it is also possible to read "se savoir un cœur" as carrying a different signification.

The word "heart," taken in its literal or figurative sense, finds itself situated, except in physiological treatises, most often on the axis of love. This axis, more evident in the second part of the poem, is already apparent in the first, particularly in the third line where the poet speaks of "espoirs naguères à mon cœur." The comparison of "espoirs naguères" to "oiseaux en chœur," a simile whose newness was noted by Jeanne Paul-Crouzet (123) tightens the link to the semes of love. The poet, moreover, directs the attention of the reader to "naguères" by rendering it in the plural and thereby turning an adverb into an adjective. The poet's hopes are those of the past, those that no longer exist. With the sole exception of the hope expressed by the monks in "Le Cloître noir," this sentiment is never realized in Nelligan's poetry. For him, "Tous les espoirs gisent gelés" ("Soir d'hiver") and he is therefore disillusioned. But disillusioned of what? Another Nelligan text can help us here. "Le Lac," one of his lesser known but no less important poems, a poem of reminiscence, love, and death, ends with the following affirmation:

> Ainsi la vie humaine est un grand lac qui dort
> Plein sous le masque froid des ondes déployées,
> De blonds rêves déçus, d'illusions noyées,
> Où l'Espoir vainement mire ses astres d'or. (263)

The hope referred to here, spelled with an initial capital letter – the graphemic level is always important in Nelligan – this hope which is disillusioned, is the hope of love: the preceding stanzas have informed us of the death of the lovers.

More than twenty years ago, Gérard Bessette affirmed that "le drame et la névrose de Nelligan sont liés à des préoccupations amoureuses" (47). Every attentive reader of Nelligan will have noted the tension in his poetry between purity and sexuality: the ideal of chastity is confronted by guilt of the flesh. The "âme candide" which resists "la volupté sordide" in "Mon Âme," which I discussed earlier, is just one example. I shall treat the topos of sensuality in Nelligan's verse in greater detail in the following chapter, but it may be useful to note that semes of guilt are not prominent in "La Romance du vin," as they are in a number of others dealing with love. The season of this poem, namely the month of May, could, however, provide tension between the flesh and the spirit. While in another poem, "Le mai d'amour," the poet appeals to the "Jeunes filles de bel humour" that they may give him "le mai d'amour" (149), the month of May could be an ambiguous time for this Catholic adolescent. May is springtime, the season of love, but is also, especially in Quebec during Nelligan's lifetime, the month of Mary, and therefore the month of purity, and even virginity. In Nelligan's poems of nostalgia, spring is associated with the innocence of childhood. The "mai d'amour" of which he dreams in the poem of this title is never realized. All the sentimental experiences

Nelligan evokes end in failure, and the May that he does find, that of "La Romance du vin," is not "le mai d'amour" that he might have wished. This is perhaps why he prefers autumn (line 15), the season of melancholy poetry, to spring.

The word "cœur" is also found in the second stanza in the following distich: "Et les rayons, ainsi que de pourpres épées, / Percent le cœur du jour qui se meurt parfumé" (7–8; 300). The preceding lines had described the sounds of a distant organ suddenly bursting into a "froide mélopée," suggesting a distinctly dysphoric atmosphere. In this distich, whose first line, as Paul-Crouzet has noted, could have been written by Heredia (137), the heart is inserted into a very dense metaphoric texture, but the signified is clear: it refers to a setting sun. When the essential part of the day, its heart, is attacked, the day dies, the victim of the same sun that sustained its life. These two lines contain other semes that in addition to the semantic range of "cœur" can also be linked to the axis of love: those of suffering ("percent") and death ("se meurent"). These are potential semes, not actualized at first reading, but subject to actualization during a rereading. Before undertaking this rereading, however, I need to comment further on the second part of the poem.

After the affirmations of knowledge in verses 18 and 19, the axis of love reveals itself anew and more clearly in distichs 21–2 and 31–2. In lines 21–2, the poet defies the women who have not wanted him: "Femmes! je bois à vous qui riez du chemin / Où l'Idéal m'appelle en ouvrant ses bras roses" (301). It would appear that the poet is angry at women for not having understood his poetic vocation, but these verses contain an image that goes beyond this simple affirmation. Since the Ideal is calling him "en ouvrant ses bras roses,"[18] the poet perceives the ideal as a woman – an association Baudelaire would not have rejected – and, more particularly, as a welcoming woman. Art, then, plays the role of a woman, replaces the woman, and reveals itself to be the substitute of love. The symbolic order replaces the passional order: text replaces sex. Or, as Nelligan himself says with sadness in "À une femme détestée," "Moi, sans amour jamais qu'un amour d'Art" (158). Yet, text cannot successfully replace sex, as my first reading has demonstrated. The two lines following those in which he drinks to the women who have mocked him remind us of this: "Je bois à vous surtout, hommes aux fronts moroses / Qui dédaignez ma vie et repoussez ma main!" (23–4; 301). "Surtout" seems to indicate that his anger at the men who have shown disdain for his vocation as a poet is greater than for the women who have spurned his love.

The poet who marches "à tatons dans [s]a jeunesse noire" (line 28) is a youth groping to find his way, both in the ways of art and in those of love. It is he who has revealed in another poem that his soul was "le donjon des mortels péchés noirs" ("Confession nocturne" 281), that his sadness derives from his being very unsure of himself in matters of the flesh. The penultimate stanza affirms anew, in an amplified mode, the joy of the poet, one that the reader knows to be false:

> Je suis gai! je suis gai! Vive le soir de mai!
> Je suis follement gai, sans pourtant être ivre! ...
> Serait-ce que je suis enfin heureux de vivre;
> Enfin mon cœur est-il guéri d'avoir aimé? (29–32; 301)

The last line of the stanza, the only interrogative sentence in the poem, expresses the poet's ultimate hope, which he does not expect to be realized, for a healing of the pains of love. His hostility towards society in certain poems, beyond its obvious source in his vocation as a poet, is also related to his problems of disillusioned love. "Le Regrèt des joujoux," an anodyne poem at first reading, weeps the loss of a childhood friend:

> Or, depuis je me sens muré contre le monde,
> Tel un prince du Nord que son Kremlin défend,
> Et, navré du regret dont je suis étouffant,
> L'Amour comme à sept ans ne verse plus son onde. (107)

The young girl of this poem, Lucile, "belle et gracieuse et blonde," is no longer, and has not been replaced. It is the loss of love, the lack of love, that saddens him, Love with its initial letter capitalized, which no longer pours over him its consoling waters, that causes him to retreat behind imagined Kremlin walls. "[C]omme un monstre cadavre," he announces in another poem, "Mon cœur vaisseau s'amarre au havre" ("Je veux m'éluder" 306). This poet is not sad solely because of the incomprehension of his role as poet, but also, and perhaps especially, because of his incomprehended love.

Beyond the revolt of the poet against society's failure to understand him, "La Romance du vin" therefore also reveals a "drame intime." A rereading of the first part, after reading the second part and after a reflection on the question the poet poses to himself, "Ainsi mon cœur est-il guéri d'avoir aimé?", permits us to actualize the semes of love that at first remained at the potential level. Like the day in line 8, this poet has been struck in what is most essential – the heart, the faculty of love. He also dies "parfumé," this farewell song constituting his final fragrance. This poem reminds us, as do numerous others by Nelligan, that poetry and love are not only indissociable for him, but that poetry exists because love is not possible.

Its theme of love notwithstanding, "La Romance du vin" does confirm Nelligan's acceptance of the Romantic belief that the poet was destined to be misunderstood. The issue is more sharply addressed in "Un Poète," which was directly inspired, it would appear, by Arthur Guiterman's poem "A Dreamer" (RW 528). This poem, which Nelligan cut out of the *London Sun* and pasted in his scrapbook (RW 528), is constructed around the repetition of a phrase, "He is a dreamer," reiterated thirteen times in the course of a thirty-two-line poem, with an admonition at the end of each of the four stanzas: "let him be" (stanza 1), "let him dream" (stanza 2), "let him be" (stanza 3), and "let him pass" (stanza 4). The notion that the poet is a dreamer who should be left alone is central to Nelligan's text:

> Laissez-le vivre ainsi sans lui faire de mal!
> Laissez-le s'en aller; c'est un rêveur qui passe;
> C'est une âme angélique ouverte sur l'espace,
> Qui porte en elle un ciel de printemps auroral.
>
> C'est une poésie aussi triste que pure
> Qui s'élève de lui dans un tourbillon d'or.
> L'étoile la comprend, l'étoile qui s'endort
> Dans sa blancheur céleste au frisson de guipure.
>
> Il ne veut rien savoir; il aime sans amour.
> Ne le regardez pas! que nul ne s'en occupe!

Dites-même qu'il est de son propre sort dupe!
Riez de lui! … . Qu'importe! il faut mourir un jour …

Alors, dans le pays où le bon Dieu demeure,
On vous fera connaître, avec reproche amer,
Ce qu'il fut de candeur sous ce front simple et fier,
Et de tristesse dans ce grand œil gris qui pleure! (293)

This poem, recalling the opening "Qu'il passe en paix, au sein du monde qui l'ignore" of Hugo's "Le Poète" (1968, 145), demonstrates what we know from other Nelligan texts, namely that his conception of poetry differs considerably from the one expressed by Guiterman. For, the existential anxiety which is the condition of Nelligan's text is completely lacking in the former's poem:

He reads the writing in the grass;
His seeing soul in rapture goes
Beyond the beauty of the rose. (lines 2–4)
… .
His days are calm, majestic, free; (7)
… .
… all the day
Blest visions find him on his way, (10)
… .
… and doth long
To glad the world with a happy song. (27–8; RW 528)

Nelligan may have borrowed the idea of the poet as a dreamer passing by, but he accepts none of the serendipity that Guiterman associates with this calling. If he sees the poet as pure, as an angelic soul (line 3) marked by candour (15) – note the homology with "Mon Âme" – we need to keep in mind the crucial importance of line 5 and recognize its implication that a "pure" poet assumes a "sad" poet. Kierkegaard, answering his own question, "What is a poet?", had replied that he was "an unhappy being whose heart is torn by secret sufferings, but whose lips are so strangely formed that when the sighs and cries escape them, they sound like beautiful music" (1987, 1:19). In speaking of poetry as the escape of the poet's personal anguish, Kierkegaard is subscribing to the Romantic myth of poetry as an uncontrollable impulse. Lamartine had claimed that poetry is the lava of the imagination, something that flows out of the poet and over which he has no control. This exalted concept of poetry persists in "Un Poète," for poetry "s'élève de lui dans un tourbillon d'or" (line 6).[19] This suggests that poetry arises from him naturally, without conscious effort. The image of the golden whirlwind valorizes the activity. The poet is not concerned with the everyday world, especially the world of history and politics that had so interested previous versifiers in Quebec. The first hemistich of line 9, "Il ne veut rien savoir," might well indicate his refusal of the ideological battles of his time. Although the call is to let him be, the poet's deep sadness, reiterated in the last line of the poem, stems not only from society's persecution but also from the existential condition of the poet himself. Vigny provided the axiom: "Le poète est toujours malheureux parce que rien ne remplace pour lui ce qu'il voit en rêvant" (2:887).

It is further implied that the vocation of the poet can be understood only by the spiritual world: by stars, by the hosts of the heavens, and by God himself. Given the importance that the poet places on the purity of his soul in "Mon Âme," it is not surprising that "Un Poète," an apology for the vocation of poetry, would place poetic activity under the sign of purity. The poet, like the one represented in "Mon Âme," is "une âme angélique ... / Qui porte en elle un ciel de printemps auroral." His poetry is "pure" and understood by the star "dans sa blancheur céleste aux frissons de guipure." After his death,

> ... dans le pays où le bon Dieu demeure,
> On vous fera connaître, avec reproche amer,
> Ce qu'il fut de candeur sous ce front simple et fier. (13–15)

There is irony in the poet's insistence that he be left alone, for he concludes by reminding those who shun him now that God will hold them accountable for their negligence, but the important point seems to be that poetry has become the domain of purity, the privileged place of angelic souls where sensual temptations do not penetrate. This text, whose date is unknown, complements Nelligan's famous clotural poem. What renders "La Romance du vin" tragic, what makes it so effective for bringing closure to editions of Nelligan's poetry, is the affirmation on his part that society has rejected his effort to substitute textual expression for the love he cannot seem to attain. He has nothing left to do but lose himself, not in the poetics of purity, but in the purity of poetry.

Beyond rejection by family and society, a total abandonment to poetry carries the further risk of jeopardizing one's sanity. Nelligan's statement to Dantin, "Je mourrai fou. Comme Baudelaire" (Dantin 1997, 66) may represent an "obscure sentiment d'orgueil," as Paul-Crouzet has suggested (127) and as Dantin himself intimated when he wrote that Nelligan looked upon his impending madness with "coquetterie et fierté" (66). A discussion of Nelligan's psychopathology is not the object of this book, which focuses on *reading* Nelligan, an activity that does not require knowledge of his subsequent illness, although some aspects of this complex issue will be revisited in subsequent chapters. While Nelligan, unlike Nerval, left no narrative detailing his mental derangement, he clearly saw madness as a possible outcome of his single-mindedness. It was a consequence, however, that he was willing to accept, although there is no evidence that he espoused a systematic program of "dérèglement de tous les sens" in the Rimbaldian sense. Jacques Michon properly formulated Nelligan's perspective when he proposed that for him poetry and madness had become "complices, unis par un rapport obscur et constitutif" (1983, 31). The madman and the poet, both shunned and ridiculed, seem to have merged in his mind. Nelligan, Dantin affirmed, would not have rejected the proposition that madness and poetry constituted a single lunacy (1997, 67).

The word *fou* occurs about a dozen times in Nelligan's poetry, sometimes referring to others, such as Angel Valdor, the woman of "L'Idiote aux cloches," and the priest of "Le Puits hanté," but at other times directly to the poet who declares himself to be "malade et fou" (180). While his madness is often associated with sadness and despair, that dysphoria is frequently the result of having been rejected. In "Prélude triste," he concludes with this tercet:

Je surgirai mal mort dans un vertige fou
Pour murmurer tout bas des musiques aux Anges
Afin de retourner et mourir dans mon trou. (241)

This poem's importance lies not so much in its being a "synthèse prémonitoire" of his tragic destiny (RW 491) as in its linking of madness to rejection:

> Je m'en vais sans personne et j'erre dans les soirs
> Et des jours, on m'a dit: Va. Je vais sans réplique.
>
> J'ai la douceur, j'ai la tristesse et je suis seul. (241)

While it may be his love that has been rejected, the poet is careful to maintain his identity as a poet, as one who murmurs "tout bas des musiques aux Anges" (241). His startling statement "Je veux être fou" (306) in "Je veux m'éluder" clearly lays claim to madness in the face of the monstrous vampires who are sucking his heart and those whose ferocious laughter derides his "vierge Intelligence" (306).

The willingness to accept madness as the price of commitment highlights the importance of faithfulness to one's calling as an artist. The theme of artistic fidelity unto death appears a number of times in Nelligan's poetry. In "Noël de vieil artiste," a poem of which Nelligan was sufficiently fond that he could still write it from memory in his fifties, the artist in question "est mort en plein combat, / Les yeux rivés à sa sculpture" (224). A similar image appears in "Sculpteur sur marbre" where he speaks of "le sublime sculpteur / Mort au pieds de la Mort, son dernier grand chef-d'œuvre" (222). The theme is most developed in one of Nelligan's longer poems, "L'Ultimo Angelo del Corregio," where he depicts the last moments of a dying Corregio who, despite his impoverished condition, remains "le cœur ferme et sans regret" (227) and resolute in his will to paint: "Il veut peindre" (227). What he chooses to paint is the portrait of his newborn son. The pathos – if such an effect was desired – is unsuccessful, but the point here seems to be a need to acknowledge that on his deathbed, Corregio's "génie coule à flot profond" (228) and that, to the end, "Le cœur d'idéal fut plein" (228). Like a religious vocation which once chosen could never be renounced (in Nelligan's culture, at least), the artist is called to maintain his vows against family and society, in defiance of his mental health, until death.

What, then, can he expect as a poet and for his poetry? We get an indication of the answer in a number of *tombeaux* that Nelligan wrote, following the model of a genre that reappeared in the last three decades of the nineteenth century as a variation on the numerous types of poems on death, beginning with the Greek threnody, that haunt the Western poetic tradition. The name *tombeau* was given in the sixteenth century to collections of poetry containing pieces honouring a famous deceased person, such as, for example, *Le Tombeau de Marguerite de Valois, royne de Navarre* (1551).[20] Its meaning was later extended to include not only a collection of poems but also a single poem in honour of a deceased person. Towards the end of the nineteenth century, both meanings were current. The better-known examples of the genre in the collection mode were *Le Tombeau de Théophile Gautier* (1873) and *Le Tombeau de Baudelaire* (1896). Mallarmé contributed to both of these collections, as well as to *Edgar Allan Poe: A Memorial Volume*, which dates from 1877, but which is conceived differently from the French volumes. Mallarmé wrote other *tombeaux*, on Verlaine and Wagner particularly.

It is not unexpected that Nelligan, who was keenly aware of what was happening poetically in France and who probably knew Mallarmé's *tombeaux* (see Wyczynski 1987, 306–7; M 454), would himself write such verse. Three of his poems are specifically titled "*tombeaux*": "Le Tombeau de Charles Baudelaire," "Le Tombeau de Chopin," and "Le Tombeau de la Négresse." Moreover, his hospital notebooks contain a distich which would seem to be the beginning of a *tombeau* for Verlaine. Two other poems, though they do not carry the word *tombeau* in their titles, are, in fact, *tombeaux* since they are testimonials to deceased persons. These are "Charles Baudelaire" and "À Georges Rodenbach." All these poems are sonnets, a form Nelligan was fond of and which was often used in this kind of poetry (more than forty per cent of the collection *Le Tombeau de Théophile Gautier* are sonnets). Nelligan's *tombeaux* poems, I suggest, are not without pertinence to his understanding of the ultimate destiny of poets and their poetry.

First, however, I need to note that Nelligan's *tombeaux* are not all of the same mould. "À Georges Rodenbach," for example, differs from other *tombeaux* by the fact that only the first stanza deals with Rodenbach. The second quatrain and the tercets are contextual stanzas that evoke the Flemish milieu. "Le Tombeau de Charles Baudelaire," of which there are two versions of the tercets, is the only one of these five poems to present itself as a dream, the sole poem in Nelligan's corpus to begin with the words "je rêve." We readily recognize an activity dear to Nelligan, but we discern as well that by coming back to the verb *rêver* in the next to last line of the second tercet, Nelligan is thereby framing the poem within a dream. "Gnôme," "elfe," and "farfadet" further assist in creating an atmosphere of the "merveilleux." This poem is also unique among Nelligan's *tombeaux* in presenting itself consciously as a *tombeau*, the only one to refer precisely to the monument placed over the remains of a deceased person, the only one, then, to operate in the double semantic field that always remains one of the possibilities of the genre. Nelligan dreams of an appropriate gravestone for Baudelaire, "un tombeau épouvantable et lunaire / Situé par les cieux ..." (258). "Le Tombeau de la Négresse" is, for its part, exceptional in paying homage to an anonymous person, although her identity is known from other sources.[21] Despite these divergences, which need to be acknowledged, a sufficient concordance exists among these poems for us to draw from them certain characteristics of Nelligan's *tombeau* poetry as a whole.

Nelligan follows the expectations of the genre, which require that the poem allude to the life or the work of the person commemorated. In "Charles Baudelaire," signifiers recall Baudelaire's work: in calling him an "enchanteur du pays du soleil," Nelligan evokes those Baudelairean poems that focus on tropical regions, the "pays parfumé que le soleil caresse" that opens "A une dame créole" (86). Baudelaire's wings are, moreover, vast, much like those of his own poet-albatross. His poetry is a "poison," a probable allusion to his poem "Le Poison" if not to the poison that we find in "Le Balcon" and "Le Flacon," but the designation may also be a barb aimed at the conservative critical establishment of the time which liberally referred to Baudelaire's poetry in this manner.[22] The flowers whose rebirth Nelligan predicts in the second tercet recall that Baudelaire saw his poems as flowers. In "Le Tombeau de Charles Baudelaire," Nelligan returns to the idea that Baudelaire is the "Cygne ... du pays du soleil" (258) or, in another version, the "chantre ... des pays du soleil" (503). The unexpected appearance of a rag-picker in the poem reminds the reader as well of Baudelaire's *chiffonnier.*

"Le Tombeau de Chopin" is even more allusive, with references to Chopin's personal life ("les faux baisers de la Floriani")[23], his health ("ô pale consomptif"; "ton maigre profil"), his native land ("le sol des palatins";[24] "de la Pologne"), and his adopted country ("bras d'or de la Gaule"). Nelligan's distich "Sur le tombeau de Paul," which would have been part of a *tombeau* for Verlaine, is likewise full of Verlainian allusions: "Verlaine, clair de lune odorant les jardins, / Sanglots fous des jets d'eau pleurant à la nuit vaine" (M 214). We immediately recognize both the thematics and the vocabulary of "Clair de lune," the initial poem of *Fêtes galantes*.

The most striking allusiveness, however, occurs in "À Georges Rodenbach," where Nelligan engages in an intertextual feast in which virtually every word is an allusion to Rodenbach's work. "Blanc, blanc, tout blanc," the opening words of the poem, are certainly meant to recall Rodenbach's collection of verse, *La Jeunesse blanche* (1886), where in the first poem the words "blanc," "blanche," and "blancheur" appear five times (in 1930, when Nelligan transcribed a slightly different version of this *tombeau*, he gave it the same title as Rodenbach's book: *La Jeunesse blanche*).[25] The "brouillards gris" and the allusion to the north recall the poem "Les Gris des ciels du Nord." The "mortes cités" alluded to are certainly a reference to Rodenbach's novel *Bruges-la-morte*, especially since Bruges is apostrophized in the following verses. The *béguines* addressed in the final tercet evoke their presence in the Rodenbachian corpus, specifically in his short story collection, *Musée de béguines*, and in his poems "Béguinage flamand" and "Cloches du dimanche." As well, the bells, the "glas" which "volent, corbeaux d'airain dans l'air sans hâles," conjure the tintinnabulesque atmosphere which saturates Rodenbach's poetry (see, as an example, "La Ville du Passé"). In subscribing to a strategy of strong allusiveness, Nelligan is indicating his solidarity with a certain manner of conceiving art which was not that of his own culture. His desire to align himself artistically with Baudelaire, Chopin, Rodenbach, and Verlaine becomes clear when we look at the manner in which he addresses them.

Catulle Mendès, in a letter to Coppée soliciting his collaboration for the collection that would become *Le Tombeau de Théophile Gautier*, specified that he would need to address himself to an image of Gautier and added, "la forme '*tu*' est recommandée" (qtd by Davies 14). While maintaining an attitude of respect towards his subjects, Nelligan spontaneously addresses Chopin, Baudelaire, and Rodenbach directly, using the familiar *tu*. The first word of "Charles Baudelaire," probably the first of the five *tombeaux* to be written, is "Maître" (the appellation is repeated in the first tercet),[26] an epithet frequently used in the French *tombeaux*. Nelligan identifies himself as a pupil, but one who permits himself an intimate tone with his master. Not only does he address himself directly to Baudelaire in a familiar way ("Tu nous charmes"; "tu n'es plus mais tu vas vivre encore"), he furnishes us with a sequence of possessive adjectives in the second person singular ("ton Vers"; "ta grace nouvelle"; "ta lyre"; "ta pure et vaste aile"; "ton vers de vermeil"; "ta trace"; "ton siècle"; "ton déclin"). Eleven *tu*s, *ton*s, and *ta*s in fourteen lines can be considered a considerable emphasis on familiarity. "Le Tombeau de Chopin" follows the same procedure ("ta souffrance"; "ton maigre profil"; "ton art"; "ta marche du tombeau"; "ton soleil mélancolique"). Nelligan thus creates an intimacy between himself and great artists, willingly placing himself within an artistic elite.

Inherent as well in the genre is a tendency to euphemism. The question of death frequently arises in Nelligan's poetry: aging and the flight of time are obsessions and death is an internalized presence. "J'ai grandi," he claimed, "dans le goût du tombeau" ("Le Cercueil" 252). About twenty of his poems deal with death. The noun *mort*, the adjective *mort/morte*, the verb *mourir*, as well as their synonyms, have a strong presence (they appear more than sixty times) in his poetry which, in this instance, shows its affinities with French decadent verse. What is astonishing, however, is the absence of these very words in his *tombeaux*. In these poems, with one exception, neither the word *mort* nor any of its synonyms appears in the text. The word for death finds itself erased, occulted. A good example of this recourse to euphemism is in "Le Tombeau de Chopin," where the word *dors* begins both the first and the last stanza, thus framing the poem not in death but in dreams.[27] Of the African woman in "Le Tombeau de la Négresse," Nelligan expresses the wish that she sleep "en paix dans les mois verts" (256). The only use of the substantive *mort* in these five poems is in "Charles Baudelaire," but *mort*, occurring in the first line of the second quatrain, does not refer to Baudelaire: "Les Classiques sont morts; le voici le réveil" (97). It is not death that we need to associate with Baudelaire, but rather a reawakening. He is the "Grand Régénérateur," as the following line makes clear. The *tombeaux* published in France, I would note, also tend to avoid the word "death." In the two major collections, *Le Tombeau de Théophile Gautier* and *Le Tombeau de Charles Baudelaire*, in the large majority of cases, death is spoken of without recourse to the signifier which most clearly and commonly identifies it.[28] The word appears in Mallarmé's "Le Tombeau d'Edgar Poe" and "Le Tombeau de Verlaine," but refers neither to the death of Poe nor to that of Verlaine.

Another characteristic is the secular representation of immortality. Religion, religiosity, and piety are often evoked in Nelligan's poetry where numerous saints, angels, archangels, nuns, monks, chapels, church windows, altars, angeluses, rosaries, and crucifixes abound. But there are no allusions to any of these in the *tombeaux,* where we find only one religious reference, an appeal to the *béguines* at the end of "À Georges Rodenbach." Nelligan's fellow Montrealer, Albert Lozeau, may have seen Baudelaire as a "chrétien sous des dehors pervers" (192), but Nelligan eschews any such considerations. The existence of God, the salvation of Christ, the immortality of the soul are never evoked in his funereal verse. To be sure, one line of "Le Tombeau de la Négresse," "Au limon moite et brut où nous la retournâmes," could recall the familiar theme of the Ash Wednesday liturgy that seeks to remind the faithful of the ashes from whence they come and to which they must return. But it is not envisaged that the Negress might return to anything but the earth. If, as seems likely, Nelligan was inspired by the story "Martha la négresse," which appeared in Dantin's magazine, it is all the more remarkable that he adopted none of the religious themes of that story, in particular the strong faith of the young black woman and the miraculous non-corruption of her body when she was exhumed twenty-five years later.

When the possibility of survival beyond this earth is evoked in these poems, it reveals itself to be a perpetuance without religious connotations. Baudelaire's permanence, for example, derives from his impact on poetry:

> Verlaine, Mallarmé sur ta trace ont suivi.
> O Maître, tu n'es plus mais tu vas vivre encore,
> Tu vivras dans un jour pleinement assouvi.
>
> Du Passé, maintenant, ton siècle ouvre un chemin
> Où renaîtront les fleurs, perles de ton déclin.
> Voilà la Nuit finie à l'éveil de l'Aurore. (97)

The flowers, "Les fleurs, perles de ton déclin," – a direct allusion to the *Fleurs du mal* – will be reborn. The semantic structure of this poem rests on recurring semes of regeneration first signified by the collocation "Grand Régénérateur" in line 6. Chopin is also a regenerator. The phrase "Quand tu nous vins, Chopin ...," by its verb and its tense, takes note of an important event, somewhat akin to Boileau's often quoted "Enfin, Malherbe vint." The remainder of the stanza stresses the musical rebirth occasioned by Chopin's work. The survival evoked in "Le Tombeau de la Négresse" is "un grand lys noir entre des roses blanches" which will perhaps burst forth "dans les buissons latents." In "À Georges Rodenbach," it is striking that the swan, namely Rodenbach, takes flight not towards heaven but towards a terrestrial paradise, Eden. Mallarmé, writing "Ne crois pas qu'au magique espoir du corridor / J'offre ma coupe" in "Toast funèbre" (65), clearly rejects the possibility of a spiritual afterlife. In fact, none of the poems in the collection *Le Tombeau de Charles Baudelaire* assumes an immortality other than that of the work, and fewer than ten per cent of the poems constituting *Le Tombeau de Théophile Gautier* make any references to an afterlife.

In reading these five poems, the reader is indeed struck by the total absence of the religious melancholy that Nelligan had appreciated in Millevoye's elegies and which permeates his earliest surviving text, "C'était l'automne ... ." Indeed, the rarity of melancholy of any kind in these poems is astonishing for a poet such as Nelligan. While he speaks elsewhere of his deep sadness ("Le Regret des joujoux," "La Cloche dans la brume"), his sombre and desperate state ("Amour immaculé"), his uncontrolled tears ("Devant mon berceau," "Le Jardin d'antan," "Banquet macabre," "Marches funèbres"), and his ennui ("Devant le feu," "Rêves enclos"), none of these sentiments appear in Nelligan's *tombeaux*. When melancholy does appear, it is attributed to a third party. In "Le Tombeau de la Négresse," the "tristes soupirs" of the second quatrain are those of the birds, and the subject of the verb *pleurer* in the first tercet is a bengalee. Nelligan seems to have adopted the attitude that Mallarmé expresses so sharply in a verse of "Toast funèbre": "J'ai méprisé l'horreur lucide d'une larme" (65).

Nelligan also appropriates another characteristic of the genre, namely the tendency to speak in the first person plural and to frame a collective discourse. Mallarmé, it will be recalled, does not speak in his own name either but in the name of a group of which he is a part: "O de notre bonheur, toi, le fatal emblème ..." ("Toast funèbre" 65). Nelligan's poetry as a whole provides numerous examples of the personal pronoun *je* and the possessive adjectives *ma* and *mon*. But there are few such examples in the *tombeaux*, the notable exception being "Le Tombeau de Charles Baudelaire." Moreover, the collectivity for which Nelligan speaks is not his national community. When in "Le Tombeau de la Négresse" we read "Au dernier ciels pâlis de mars, nous la menâmes ..." (265), we immediately perceive the "nous" to refer to persons living in the tropics. The communities of "Charles Baudelaire" ("Tu nous charmes," "Notre langue frémit sous ta lyre si belle," "Nous buvons ce poison doux qui nous ensorcelle") and of "Le Tombeau de Chopin" ("Quand tu nous vins, Chopin ...") are not French-Canadians of Nelligan's time but the elite of artists and lovers of the arts. In his *tombeaux*, Nelligan distances himself both from his own corpus, which focused on an outpouring of the self, and from traditional French-Canadian poetry, which saw itself as the voice of the nation.

A reading of Nelligan's *tombeaux* poems reveals, then, that his own production in this sub-genre is remarkably close to European practice. The *tombeau* of the late nineteenth century had abandoned the nostalgia, melancholy, and religiosity that characterized the elegiac tradition and the "graveyard" poetry much in favour at the end of the eighteenth century in order to create a new funereal poetry that would be more sober, more detached, more secular. The goal was to insist on the survival of the work, not on the poet's continued existence in an afterlife in which these poets no longer believed. A writer's immortality derives from his words. In Nelligan's understanding, Baudelaire's *tombeau* is "bâti colloquialement" (258), that is, verbally, with words. This is strongly affirmed in a poem he published in 1898, "Sur un portrait de Dante," which ends with a proclamation of Dante's *literary* immortality:

> Et tu vivras, ô Dante, autant que Dieu lui-même,
> Car les cieux ont appris aussi bien que l'Enfer
> A balbutier les chants de ton divin Poème. (230)

In a second version, the lasting nature of Dante's fame is strengthened further: "Et tu vivras aussi longtemps que Dieu lui-même" (231). Nelligan's conclusion thereby constitutes an important deviation from Auguste Barbier's "Dante," which served as a source for Nelligan's information on Dante (RW 482), but which makes no reference to such an immortality. While Nelligan shies away from the more extreme Romantic claims to the equality of poets and gods, in this instance he comes close to attributing to great poets an eternal continuation such as that of the gods. Having discerned the non-rational nature of his poetic thought and the purity of his quest, having experienced the incomprehension and disdain of family and society, Nelligan remained committed to what he saw as a calling, even unto insanity. In his *tombeaux* poems, he distances himself from his own national community in order to place himself alongside an artistic elite that has responded to such a calling, an elite to which he feels he belongs and in the name of which he speaks, a stance he confirms in "Musiques funèbres": "Que m'importe l'amour, la plèbe et ses tocsins? / Car il me faut à moi des annales d'artiste" (287). The *tombeaux* poems allow him to envisage the possibility that this stressful and dangerous adventure was not for nothing, that in addition to the survival of his soul or perhaps even in place of the survival of his soul, there could be the survival of his work.

2 Spirituality and Sensuality

It is clear from the discussion in the previous chapter that Nelligan's desire to be a poet cannot be disengaged from the tension between his spiritual yearnings and his sensual temptations. Poems such as "Mon Âme," "Rêve d'artiste," and "À une femme détestée," in which the ideals of poetry are intertwined with religious themes and yearnings for sexual purity, or a poem such as "La Romance du vin," where poetry itself might be seen as a substitute for the love that is refused to the poet, are indications that the calling of the poet is not immune from either spiritual ideals or sensual cravings. Nelligan's spirituality derives from his culture in which most aspects of life were under the tutelage of the Catholic Church. While the Church harboured serious internal dissensions regarding its electoral involvement and was the occasional target of anti-clerical pamphlets, its spiritual and moral discourse remained uniform during this period and its broad societal impact undiminished. Not only parish activities but also social and cultural events, public welfare (assistance to the poor, orphanages, hospitals), and schooling were either under direct Church control or strongly influenced by the Church. Nelligan's family practiced the faith regularly, engaged in common evening prayer (Wyczynski 1987, 80), a devotion alluded to in his poetry ("Prière du soir"), and attended weekly mass (while a student at the Collège de Montréal, Nelligan was required to attend mass daily). His mother, whose family included several priests, seems to have been particularly devout. Nelligan's schooling was largely in the hands of religious orders up through the last school he attended, the Collège Sainte-Marie, which was managed by the Jesuits.

That a sixteen-year-old boy steeped in such a culture would write verse in which religion plays a role is not surprising. Early critics such as ab der Halden and Camille Roy who attempted to distinguish Nelligan from other French-Canadian poets by insisting that he avoided religious themes were able to do so only by overlooking a number of poems. Even the edition of his poetry published by Dantin, the only one available to critics prior to the 1950s, includes at least twenty poems containing references to chapels, stained glass windows, saints, Virgins, the crucified Christ, and prayers. While Nelligan's poetry occasionally makes use of imagery derived from Graeco-Roman mythology, it relies heavily on the traditional themes and images of Roman Catholicism. "Notre-Dame-des-Neiges," for example, features a virgin surrounded by the typical symbols of Christian iconography: a golden cape, flowers, angels, celestial music, a regal throne. Subjugating Satan, she protects Montreal, or Ville-Marie, hence *her* city. The poet calls upon her to expel "l'étranger" (188) – a sentiment that makes this the only "nationalist" poem that Nelligan is known to have written – and to give strength to the city's citizens. In "Petit Vitrail," the figure of Christ has a blond beard and tender eyes and is accompanied by a choir of cherubim. Present as well in Nelligan is the gamut of traditional religious thematics (including, in "Les Déicides," a reflection of the anti-Semitism of the period).

If, in poems such as "Petit Coin de cure," Nelligan was willing to poke fun at the clergy, other texts express a strong religious fervour, which may or may not reflect Nelligan's own piety (that Dantin was able to write and publish religious verse at a time when he no longer believed leads to caution in this regard). Among Nelligan's poems steeped in belief are "Les Petits Oiseaux," in which the poet, claiming inspiration from the medieval Dutch mystic Ruysbroeck, is led to pious thoughts upon observing hummingbirds, and two poems which celebrate a central sacrament of Catholicism, namely "Les Communiantes," with its mystical imaginings, and "Communion pascale," with its deep faith in the eucharistic mystery. While these poems do not represent the "religiosité factice" that ab der Halden detected in those few texts that he was willing to acknowledge as religious (349), they do constitute undistinguished religious verse of a type not uncommon in the period and are not particularly revealing of any specificities of Nelligan's faith.

MUSIC AND SPIRITUALITY

Other poems, however, reveal the particular role played by music in Nelligan's spirituality. Nelligan himself signaled the relationship in the title he envisaged for his future collection of poetry, *Le Récital des anges*. The importance of music in his life and work is, moreover, well attested (see, on this subject, Wyczynski 1971). His mother was an accomplished pianist, and he himself, though he does not seem to have played a musical instrument, was a great lover of music, and could hum, his friends reported, pieces from Bach and Mozart (Wyczynski 1971, 22). Paderewski's concert in Montreal in April 1896 seems to have been one of the high points of his life. "Pour Ignace Paderewski," probably written some time after that concert, contains a number of references to the otherworldly characteristics of music in such expressions as "astrales musiques," "rythmes séraphiques," and "prestige divin" (179). Another poem of the same period, "Mélodie de Rubinstein," refers to the Russian composer's music as "l'écho d'un sacré concert" (96). "Mazurka," for its part, suggests that Chopin's rhythms are borrowed from archangels. In "Prière du soir," in which he recalls with great fondness his own mother playing the piano in the evening, Nelligan associates her music with that of the angels and hence with spirituality:

> Et pendant que de Liszt les sonates étranges
> Lentement achevaient de s'endormir en nous,
> La famille faisait la prière à genoux
> Sous le lointain écho du clavecin des anges. (186)

The musical compositions referred to in these poems are not religious. Unlike sacred vocal music in which melody and harmony reinforce a verbal religious image, the spirituality of these pieces derives neither from the intent of the composer nor their use but from the sounds themselves, an insight with which twentieth-century theoreticians of the relationship between art and the holy, such as Gerardus van der Leeuw, would concur. For Nelligan, music, as an earthly correspondence of angelic sounds, is inherently spiritual. In the case of "Prière du soir," the family's prayerfulness is heightened by the acoustic memory of the pieces just heard.

Three poems, sometimes referred to as the Saint Cecilia Cycle, offer strong evidence for the link between music and spirituality in Nelligan's thought. Saint Cecilia, a third-century Christian virgin and martyr who, since the Renaissance, has been represented iconographically with a viola or a small organ, is recognized as the patron saint of musicians. In late nineteenth-century Montreal, her feast day on 22 November was marked with festivities, some of which Nelligan may have attended. In any case, Nelligan seems to have had a particular affection for Cecilia, referring to her twice as "la Sainte adorée" in "Le Récital des anges." This poem, which may have been written as early as 1897, provides a good example of the role of music in Nelligan's spirituality:

Plein de spleen nostalgique et de rêves étranges,
Un soir je m'en allai chez la Sainte adorée,
Où se donnait, dans la salle de l'empyrée,
Pour la fête du ciel, le récital des anges.

Et nul ne s'opposant à cette libre entrée,
Je vins, le corps vêtu d'une tunique à franges,
Le soir où je m'en fus chez la Sainte adorée,
Plein de spleen nostalgique et de rêves étranges.

Des dames défilaient sous des clartés oranges;
Les célestes laquais portaient haute livrée,
Et ma demande étant par Cécile agréée,
J'écoutai le concert qu'aux divines phalanges,

Elle donnait, là-haut, dans des rythmes étranges ... (206)

The poet's dysphoria is a given and the cause of his nostalgic spleen and strange dreams is not revealed. It may be pertinent to note that while Verlaine's "rêve étrange" in "Mon Rêve familier" is for an unknown woman of flesh and blood who would console him, Nelligan's "rêves étranges" lead him to a woman who, as a saint in the heavens, is outside the sphere of sexuality. The poem is an imaginative narrative in which the poet relates an incident – his attendance at a concert of angels in heaven led by Saint Cecilia – that assuaged his anxiety. The heaven evoked is not, however, a particularly Christian one. The woman to whom he is attracted is a Christian saint, but heaven is referred to as the empyreum, a designation associated with Pythagorean cosmology and Greek mythology. With its parading ladies and lackeys in full livery and with no hint of the presence of God or Jesus, this appears more as a *soirée mondaine* than the celestial resting place of the elect. The important point, perhaps, is that he presented himself uninvited (though properly attired, "vêtu d'une tunique à franges" – there is a Biblical resonance in this detail) and that his entry was approved by Saint Cecilia, one of only two welcoming figures in Nelligan's poetry (the other is his mother). She combines femininity, purity, and all the qualities associated with music. The combination is salvific, as the two other poems of the cycle confirm.

The unusual rhythms of the music she conducts echo the strangeness of his dreams, and, in "L'Organiste du Paradis," his melancholy. In the latter poem, Cecilia conducts the orchestra of archangels, a post to which she has been appointed by the Virgin. The quatrains that present this situation begin with the line "La belle sainte au fond des cieux," but the remainder of the poem is addressed to "*Ma* belle Sainte," to whom he expresses his wish:

Loin du monde diabolique
Puissé-je, un soir mystérieux,
Ouïr dans les divins milieux
Ton clavecin mélancolique,
Ma belle Sainte au fond des cieux. (207)

Cecilia has become *his* saint, now endowed with a capital letter, to distinguish her from other saints. Since she is twice referred to as being in the furthermost part of the heavens, we may wonder about her accessibility, but Nelligan seems more interested in her being distant from the "monde diabolique" that constitutes earthly existence.

For heavenly music provides an escape from a diabolic world impregnated with sin, a perspective strongly corroborated in the poignant "Rêve d'une nuit d'hôpital" which Nelligan appears to have written shortly after his mental crisis in 1899 while he was hospitalized at Notre-Dame, a neurological clinic, prior to being sent to an asylum.[1] He now imagines Saint Cecilia, haloed and dressed in white, in the company of God, Mary, and Joseph. Then,

> Soudain au flamboiement mystique des grands lustres,
> Éclata l'harmonie étrange, au rythme bref,
> Que la harpe brodait de sons en relief. . .
> Musiques de la terre, ah! taisez vos voix rustres!. . .
>
> Je ne veux plus pécher, je ne veux plus jouir,
> Car la sainte m'a dit que pour encore l'ouïr,
> Il me fallait vaquer à mon salut sur terre.
>
> Et je veux retourner au prochain récital
> Qu'elle me doit donner au pays planétaire,
> Quand les anges m'auront sorti de l'hôpital. (208)

The music is still strange, as it was in "Le Récital des anges," but it surpasses all its earthly varieties. The first tercet, however, links further hearing of this music to the moral life. Hence his resolution: "Je ne veux plus pécher, je ne veux plus jouir," a verse that might be read as an admission that his illness has its roots in the immoral life he has been leading. If, as it seems logical to conclude, the sins and the *jouissance* refer to sins of the flesh, then music is represented as a higher pleasure. So great is his desire to hear this music again that he will renounce his sensuality to assure it. "Hôpital" may be read literally, referring to the clinic where Nelligan happened to be, or metaphorically as the sick world in which we live, from which he expects the angels to rescue him. For Nelligan, heaven is music, and heavenly music is salvation.

A SOMBRE SPIRITUALITY

Music as salvation is, however, only a minor part of Nelligan's religious discourse, much of which betrays a clear propensity for the sombre side of religion. Even a light poem about Jesus's childhood, "Diptyque," ends with an evocation of the death and suffering that will befall him. One of the two poems that focus on the crucified Christ, "La Réponse du crucifix," evokes Christ's mercy, but in the final tercet of "Christ en croix" the poet recalls an evening when, having sighted a crumbling cross, he heard within himself "des marteaux convulsifs / Renfoncer les clous noirs des intimes Calvaires" (189). The Christ depicted in the opening quatrain of this poem is not, in any case, the Christ of compassion and forgiveness depicted in "La Réponse du crucifix," but rather the Christ of judgment, more Pantocrator than Saviour. The "monastic" poems, especially "Les Moines," "La Mort du moine," "Les Carmélites," and, to a certain extent, "La Bénédictine," emphasize not the joy of monks and nuns but rather their sorrow. In "Les Moines," the monks, their heads bowed, walk in dark labyrinths on "la splendeur funéraire des dalles" (200). These cloistered men, whom he calls "silencieux spectres de Jésus-Christ" (200), live as if they were already dead. The monks of "La Mort du moine" are sad and the nuns of "Les Carmélites" walk "parmi le deuil du cloître" (202). Even the nun in "La Bénédictine," a poem that does have a joyful ending, frequently feels "ennui" (203).

Nelligan's attraction for the melancholy, macabre dimensions of nineteenth-century Catholicism is already much in evidence in his earliest surviving piece of writing, an assignment required of him at the Collège Sainte-Marie in 1896 entitled "C'était l'automne ... et les feuilles tombaient toujours." Since the Jesuits encouraged imitation, it is quite possible that a model was suggested or even imposed. Similarities with the language of Chénier, Lamartine, and especially Millevoye have been noted by various critics (see, especially Wyczynski 1960, 47–8; 1969, 775; RW 348) The piece, which contains some inaccuracies (such as the angelus ringing at eleven o'clock at night), is more than an exercise, however, for its themes reverberate throughout Nelligan's poetry.

This short prose text describes the last moments of a dying boy who, in his final suffering, consoles his mother with the thought that they will meet again in the next life. The opening sentence is calculated to evoke a maximum of pathos: "L'Angélus sonnait, et l'enfant sur sa couche de douleur souffrait d'atroces maux; il avait à peine quinze ans, et les froids autans contribuaient beaucoup à empirer son mal" (85). The charged vocabulary ("couche de douleur," "atroces maux"); the solicitation of pity through the evocation of the subject's youth ("à peine quinze ans"); and the use of nature as an adjuvant of his suffering reveal a mastery of the rhetoric of sentiment in this sixteen-year-old writer. The abundance of clichés notwithstanding (virtually every noun in the text is modified by an adjective drawn from the repertoire of sentimental discourse), the writer creates an atmosphere in which fading, dissolving, and disappearance dominate, reflecting the boy's own fading away into death: the sounds of the church bell are weak (although we are told that the church is nearby); the vista is unclear; daylight is waning; the horizon is darkening; the blue mountains seem dark. The threefold evocation of the falling leaves, the third of which closes the text, contributes further to the congruence between the death of the boy and the condition of the nature that surrounds him. Yet the scene is intended to be religious, even containing a Christological reference, as the boy's mother is compared to Mary who, at the foot of the cross, accepted the suffering of her son.

Three lexical clusters dominate the discourse of this text. One of these brings together a considerable number of lexical items that relate to religion: *Angélus*, *céleste supplication*, *crucifix* (twice), *prière*, *Dieu* (twice), *cloche de la petite église*, *Marie*, *calvaire*, *croix*. Nelligan deviates here from his alleged models, Millevoye's "La Chute de feuilles" and Chénier's "Le Jeune Malade," neither of which have strong religious references. Another cluster contains words related to melancholy, suffering, and death: *douleur* (thrice), *souffrait*, *atroces maux*, *mal*, *lamentait*, *attristait*, *yeux éteints*, *tristement*, *glas funèbre* (thrice), *s'assombrissaient*, *sombre*, *tristesse*, *gémissements*, *malade* (thrice), *mourant*, *souffre*, *sacrifice*, *tristes* (twice), *lugubres*, *pleurer*, *mortuaire*, *cadavre*, *meurt*. A third grouping of signifiers relates to nature: *autans*, *nuit froide*, *campagne*, *ombragée*, *peupliers*, *montagnes*, *oiseaux*, *bocages*, *fauvettes*, *feuilles* (thrice), *brise d'automne*, *ramure*, *grand chêne*, *fleur*, *champs*, *nature*, *bois*, *arbres*, *vallée*. A confluence of these three clusters is not unusual in late eighteenth- and early nineteenth-century poetry in which the contemplation of nature produces melancholy which in turn invites reflection on mortality and the afterlife. Nelligan's imitative discourse might be dismissed were it not that its thematics (faith, death, the afterlife), its imagery (bells, the angelus, the caring mother, falling leaves, the autumn breeze) and its primary literary convention (atmospheric conditions as a reflection of the moral and psychological conditions expressed) are replicated throughout his work.

If a few poems such as "Communion pascale" reveal a simple and unproblematic faith, Nelligan's religiosity is most often marked by the melancholy of his first text. In most of his poems, the gloom is personal, for it is the poet himself who is sorrowful and weeps openly. But this melancholy is also represented as being inherent to all living things. All of nature is sad, including the flora and the fauna: "Les sylphes vont pleurant comme une âme en détresse / Et les cœurs des arbres ont des plaintes de morts" ("Nuit d'été" 91). Terrestrial existence itself appears disconsolate: "Ici-bas tout geint, casse ou pleure" ("La Chanson de l'ouvrière" 92). Nelligan is here adopting a religious thematics dating from the Fathers of the Church, which was appropriated by the popular spirituality of French Canada in order to stress that this life is hard, miserable, and necessarily sorrowful. We live in a "valley of tears," as a well-known prayer of the time put it. Consolation lay in the fact that this life is not the only life, that another lies beyond that is infinitely better, if we merit it. "L'essentiel, c'est le ciel," the saying went.

While "Petit Vitrail" features the image of a smiling, tender-eyed Jesus, three poems dealing with chapels situate themselves within European pre-Romanticism and emphasize the gloomy dimensions of religious belief. By its very title, "La Chapelle de la morte" brings together religion and death. The scene is worthy of the graveyard school, as the poet presents himself alone, moving about tentatively ("à pas discrets") in an ancient closed chapel (we observe again Nelligan's predilection for closed-in spaces) where he hears the sounds of his feet reverberate on the flooring stones. An unspecified golden age is evoked, as the stones on the floor express "les regrets / De toute une ère parfumée" (209). The image of an "ère parfumée" is a striking one, replete with intimations of a scented Eden, while playing with the homophone "air parfumé."

The second stanza recalls a woman, "ô bien-aimée," who has died. The topos of the deceased lover is common enough in lyric poetry that it is quite unnecessary to posit, as do Robidoux and Wyczynski, that the woman alluded to here is the same as the one in "Amour immaculé," namely Saint Cecilia (RW 461). Indeed, the supposition is unlikely, since the word "morte" is not used to refer to saints in Catholic piety. Nor is it likely, as Lemieux suggests (48), that the reference is to an actual woman whom Nelligan had loved. Nelligan is more probably drawing from a store of themes and images from the poetry he knew. In line 7, beginning the second half of the poem, he creates an extended metaphor by which his surroundings take on the traits of the deceased lover. The chapel becomes the soul, the altar the body, the nave the shroud, and the windows the eyes in a hallucinatory recreation of the dead woman. The metaphors are mixed and unconvincing, but eros, thanatos, and hieros are conjoined in a linkage that is a constant of Nelligan's poetry.

"Chapelle dans les bois" creates another pre-Romantic scene as the poet recalls a time when he and another child found themselves alone at night in a deserted sylvan chapel. The opening stanza accentuates the contrast between the children, presumed to be small, and the altars, specified as large. In fact, the "deux enfants blêmes / Devant les grands autels à franges" (210) could be expected to be intimidated or at least in awe, as they gaze up to the altars. Then, an additional contrast emerges between the pale and sad children (the first line, "Nous étions là deux enfants blêmes," is glossed by line 9, "Nous étions là deux enfants tristes," in which the qualifying adjective alone is changed), and Mary and the angels who are laughing amidst the chrysanthemums. The latter is an unusual iconography, for art history records no instance of Mary laughing. Nelligan creates it, as well as the contrast in size between the children and the altars, to stress the distance between the children and the sacred and thereby to emphasize the difficulty in their finding succour in this chapel. The second stanza, which draws from nineteenth-century Gothic imagery, seems to reinforce the total otherness of the sacred as it describes the ray of moonlight skirting the rigid icon of a "grand Saint livide" (line 8). The images of the first two stanzas, then, seem to intimidate rather than comfort.

Nevertheless, comfort is what the children do find in this chapel. By the third stanza, the sacred space has begun to effect a change in them. Repeating the first line of the poem while changing the designation of the children from "pâles" to "tristes," Nelligan describes them as absorbing the peace of the sanctuary, although, it needs to be noted, the spiritual is still associated with death: "sous la veilleuse mortuaire" (line 11). By the following stanza, their voices are in ecstasy, rising to the heavens like prayers. Yet, here too a note of melancholy persists, for their prayers are compared to "un angélus des dimanches, / Dans le lointain, qui prie et pleure ..." (15–16). Nelligan seems rarely able or willing to represent unlimited peace or joy. For him, the coupling of "prie et pleure" seems necessary, its terms inseparable. This poem is about the peace of religion, but that peace exists only within the context of a "valley of tears."

Even such a mitigated serenity seems but a dream, an illusion, however, as another "chapel poem" clearly demonstrates. "Chapelle ruinée," an unsuccessful poem constituting some of Nelligan's weakest verse, again relies on the commonplaces of European pre-Romanticism: on a windy, rainy, autumn day, the poet returns to a ruined park where a crumbling chapel is situated. His opening statement that this is a repeated act ("Et je retourne encor" 211) can be read as another indication of this poet's penchant for decaying things. But there is an ambiguity in the function of the adverb *encor*, since in this line, "Et je retourne encor frileux, au jet des bruines," "encor" could also be read as modifying "frileux," thereby emphasizing a continuous existential condition: the absence of warmth in the poet's life. What is clear is that the haunting space and the unpleasant climatic conditions mirror the state of his soul: "Et je sens se briser mon cœur dans ma poitrine" (line 8). This poem allows for no solace. The statue of Christ in the adjoining park is referred to as "ce grand Jésus debout," an intimidating image that recalls "le grand Saint livide" of "Chapelle dans les bois," and suggests the unreachability of God. The chapel is there, but it is physically in ruins, perhaps signifying religion's incapacity to help the poet. The bells, with their dark timbres, are those of "âges morts" and can only strengthen the "mornes désespoirs" that he harbours. It is also possible to suggest that when the poet says in the penultimate line, "Je pleure ces débris de petite chapelle," he is also weeping for himself. The soul as a chapel, church, or temple was a common metaphor in Catholic popular spirituality, which often referred to the soul as the "temple of the Holy Spirit."

A fourth poem, in which the word "chapel" does not appear, reveals clear thematic links with the three poems just discussed. In "La Cloche dans la brume," the poet addresses his soul, asking it to listen to the sounds coming from afar:

> Écoutez, écoutez, ô ma pauvre âme! Il pleure
> Tout au loin dans la brume! Une cloche! Des sons
> Gémissent sous le noir des nocturnes frissons,
> Pendant qu'une tristesse immense nous effleure. (214)

The scene – moaning bells heard through the fog – is hackneyed pre-Romanticism, to be sure, though with a Verlainian touch. Once again, the immense sadness experienced by the poet and his soul appears to be consonant with his surroundings. The indefinite, impersonal subject in the collocation "il pleure" (literally, it weeps) signals a situation out of the poetic persona's control.

Yet, in the second quatrain and the sestet, the poet abandons the shared emotion. "Nous" does not reappear and the poet stresses "vous," repeated six times in the second and third stanzas in what develops into an accusation levied against his soul: "Vous qui ne priez plus" seems to explain the malice of his soul, which he calls "pauvresse" (line 6), echoing "ma pauvre âme" of line 1. Then, in line 7, in what begins the second half of the poem, the soul's distress is compared to the ancient bell – we presume it to be a church bell – that dreams of the angeluses it used to announce, "Comme elle vous geignez, funèbre et monotone, / Comme elle vous teintez dans les brouillards d'automne" (214). Just as the church is nostalgic for the faithful who once frequented it, so the poet's soul regrets "l'exil des Espérances" (line 14). No longer praying, having lost Hope and thereby, we imagine, Faith as well, the soul's distress has nothing to console it. This seems to corroborate the reading of the line "Je pleure ces débris de petite chapelle" in "Chapelle ruinée" as also referring to his own soul. It is not without interest that the religious poems of Nelligan's mentor, Dantin, have been read as expressions of Dantin's struggles with his faith during this same period (see Blais 1993, 68–9).

GUILT AND FORGIVENESS

A weakening of faith does not, however, necessarily result in a diminution of guilt, a condition that seems to have seriously afflicted this adolescent. Lilian Feder has reminded us that "inappropriate, pathological guilt" constituted one of the more common mental disturbances in Western societies "so long as the authority of state, church, and patriarchal family was assumed" (5). There is no doubt that such conditions obtained in late nineteenth-century Quebec. Moreover, pastoral practice remained under the strong influence of what I would call the founding discourse of Quebec spirituality. The history of that spirituality still remains to be written, but I suggest that it is indebted to the so-called "French school," a counter-Reformation religious movement whose leader was Cardinal Pierre de Bérulle. One of Bérulle's most fervent disciples was Jean-Jacques Olier, the founder of the Sulpicians, who wanted to be a missionary in Canada and who authorized a Sulpician mission there before his death. Olier's religious status was given a boost in the young colony of New France when Jeanne Mance, the co-foundress of Montreal, was miraculously healed after visiting his tomb in France. For almost two centuries, Olier's Sulpicians were the dominant religious force in Montreal (an elementary school named after Olier, which Nelligan attended for three years, exists to this day). The importance of the French school in the austere mysticism of some of the early religious figures of New France has been noted by scholars (Lemire 1991, 86). Marie de l'Incarnation, who would become an icon of Quebec religious history, combined the spirituality of the school with Ignatian, Salesian, and Teresian strains. Her choice of a religious name, Marie de l'Incarnation, acknowledges the importance that Bérulle and his school placed on the mystery of the Incarnation. The seventeenth-century founders of the Séminaire de Quebec drew upon Bérullian spirituality, particularly on his emphasis on the priest as *alter Christus*, but more generally in the promotion of an ascetic daily routine and on the need for personal abnegation (see Baillargeon 108). The Sulpicians, through their Grand Séminaire, would themselves eventually train all parish priests in the diocese of Montreal.

The French school was a creative endeavour to bring theology and spiritual practice closer together. Its teaching was based on the recognition of the grandeur, the majesty, and the mystery of God, but also on the lowliness of the creature, on the necessity, even, of the *anéantissement* of the creature in the face of such an august God. This gave rise to a spirituality capable of authentic mysticism, but also one that gravitated around interdiction, abnegation, guilt, and deep pessimism about this world. These perspectives are clearly evident in Marie de l'Incarnation, whose sense of her own nothingness, unworthiness, and guilt have been underscored by Pierre Nepveu in his fine commentary on this authentic mystic (31–41 passim). This spirituality was promulgated in Quebec throughout the eighteenth and nineteenth centuries through the writings of Bérulle, St Jean Eudes, St Louis-Marie Grignon de Montfort, Olier, and acolytes of lesser stature, such as Étienne-Marcel Faillon, a French Sulpician who in the nineteenth century zealously preached Olierian spirituality in the province.[2] Bérulle's and Olier's Christocentrism was often subordinated to their insistence on human depravity, and what had been a mystical renaissance provided the discourse for a culpabilization of the faithful. Bérulle and Olier, as well as the leader of the first Sulpicians in Canada, Father Queylus, were accused of Jansenism (falsely, it would appear, but one can understand why the accusation might have been taken seriously). The Liguorism promulgated by the Oblates in Canada in the nineteenth century might have been expected to temper this severe moralism, but the Liguorism then being preached had become more rigorous, especially in sexual matters, than that preached by Liguori himself. The teaching of the Jesuits, also a force in the province, did not differ essentially in its moral and spiritual demands. The Christian pedagogy prevalent in Quebec emphasized God's harsh judgment, implying that more would be damned than would be saved. Not surprisingly, the fear of God's justice was stressed over confidence in his mercy. The "pastorale de la peur" that Jean Delumeau has chronicled in France in the seventeenth and eighteenth centuries (365–627) found its mirror reflection in nineteenth-century French Canada. If Nelligan's sombre view of religion owes something to the discourse of pre-Romanticism, as I've noted above, it is also derivative of the religious discourse of his culture. The culpabilization of that discourse did not spare Nelligan.

Inappropriate guilt is certainly much in evidence in "Premier Remords," a poem that Nelligan read at a meeting of the École littéraire de Montréal in 1899, six months prior to his internment, in which he dramatizes his mother, her lips on a crucifix, weeping because of her son's truancy. The scene, as he tells it, was his first encounter with remorse. Exaggerating the fault implies a greater need for forgiveness, and in much of Nelligan's poetry, spirituality is associated with a need to assuage his sense of guilt. This is already clear in one of his first poems, "Nocturne":

à Denys Lanctôt

C'est l'heure solennelle et calme du silence,
L'Angélus a sonné notre prière à Dieu;
Le cœur croyant sommeille en un repos immense,
Noyé dans les parfums languissants du Saint-Lieu.

C'est l'heure du pardon et de la pénitence,
C'est bien l'heure où l'on fait notre plus vaste aveu,
Où nos yeux ruisselants, pleurs de reconnaissance,
Retrouvent à la fin l'ardeur du premier feu.

O Soir si consolant pour mon cœur ravagé,
Soir de miséricorde au pécheur affligé
Qui demande à son Dieu la manne bienfaisante,

Pénètre de ton ombre une âme à la tourmente,
Recueillement subit du passé dans ton sein,
Pour qu'elle puisse avoir paix et joie au Matin. (94)

While clearly not of the greatest originality or quality, "Nocturne" is instructive for understanding Nelligan's spirituality as well as its trajectory. This early poem testifies to a deeply felt recognition of the consolations of religion by a person of authentic faith. There is no reason to believe that "cœur croyant," whose two components are linked phonetically by initial velars and adjoining [r]s, does not represent the belief of the poetic voice. These sentiments, however, are absent from later poems, as I've already noted. The title links religious feeling with melancholy, a constant association in his poetry, for "nocturne" refers both to a tender and melancholy piece of music and to a part of the religious office of matins, the prayers said before dawn. Prayer, of course, is what this poem is about, although the prayers in question are said at night. The angelus is recited morning, noon, and night, but "soir," repeated twice in the tercets, determines which prayers are referred to.

The first stanza exudes serenity and peace, as the first line, a flowing alexandrine replete with alliterative [l]s, presents the hour of prayer as solemn, calm, and silent. The semes of community ("notre prière"), the poetry of the bells, the heart at rest and bathed in sweet smells, complete the picture. It is important that the comforts of religion be established, for they will be needed to console a disturbed heart. Indeed, the second quatrain and the two tercets depict a poetic voice in search of inner peace, recognizing that now is the hour of forgiveness and penance, the time to confess one's greatest sins ("notre plus vaste aveu"). There has been sin, for line 7 speaks of eyes streaming with tears, but the moment of evening prayer is a time for regaining a past purity, for savouring anew "l'ardeur du premier feu" (line 8). The tercets confirm the extent to which the poet is troubled. Such expressions as "cœur ravagé" (line 9), "pécheur affligé" (10), and "âme à la tourmente" indicate the sense of guilt that permeates his relations with the deity. In evening prayer he seeks consolation (line 9), mercy (10), comfort (11), and finally peace and joy (14).

No peace or joy is envisaged in "Confession nocturne," however:

Prêtre, je suis hanté, c'est la nuit dans la ville,
Mon âme est le donjon des mortels péchés noirs,
Il pleut une tristesse horrible aux promenoirs
Et personne ne vient de la plèbe servile.

Tout est calme et tout dort. La solitaire Ville
S'aggrave de l'horreur vaste des vieux manoirs.
Prêtre, je suis hanté, c'est la nuit dans la ville;
Mon âme est le donjon des mortels péchés noirs.

En le parc hivernal sous la bise incivile,
Lucifer rôde et va raillant mes désespoirs
Très fous! ... Le suicide aiguise ses coupoirs!
Pour se pendre, il fait bon sous cet arbre tranquille ...
....
Prêtre, priez pour moi, c'est la nuit dans la ville! ... (281)

The rondel, with its repetition of line 1 as line 8 and again (in Nelligan's practice, usually with a variation) as the last line of the poem and the repetition of the second line as line 7, is a most appropriate form to translate an obsession: "je suis hanté" (lines 1, 7, 13). In "Le Salon," a relatively early poem, the poet described himself without explanation as "hanté par le remords" (182), and it is surely such a state that haunts him now. That is his confession to the reader. But the "confession nocturne" of the title also carries sacramental semes, since he is making it to a priest. Yet the form of address, "Prêtre," used three times anaphorically, is not the normal designation used in addressing a priest directly and certainly not during a confession. Indeed, the form has a hostile tinge to it and sets up a distance between the person speaking and the cleric he addresses (there is no evidence to suggest that the priest is Dantin, as Lemieux affirms [239]). The Church's confessional formula, "Bénissez-moi mon père," intended to create a filial, respectful relationship, is absent from this poem. Missing as well is the expression of repentance expected of the sinner in such situations.

The poet's guilt is deep, for the offenses – unnamed – are serious: "des mortels péchés noirs." The imagery used – the soul as a dungeon of dark sins – is the reverse of the imagery of metanoia, which is most often expressed as a movement from darkness to light. In Catholic moral theology, a mortal sin is one of such gravity that death while in that state leads to eternal damnation. The seriousness of the sins and the obsessive guilt are mirrored in the poet's surroundings, creating a concordance between exterior setting and internal conditions: the night is cold and it is raining with an unpleasant wind, all reminders of the dark storm within the poet himself. The city is deserted, perhaps because his sin has cut him off from the rest of men, but probably also because solitude and isolation represent the most common situation of the poet. From one of his first poems, "Silvio Corelli pleure," in which a wandering violinist regrets that he has no friends on earth, to later poems such as "Prélude triste," in which he proclaims "j'ai la tristesse et je suis seul" (241), this poet declares his sense of abandonment. No human support is forthcoming: "Et personne ne vient de la plèbe servile" (line 4). He is imprisoned within his own sin: "Mon âme est le donjon des mortels péchés noirs" (lines 2, 8). The rain, mentioned immediately after the dungeon, is sure to evoke Baudelaire's "Spleen LXXVIII," in which the rain is represented as forming the bars that imprison the poet. That the city is calm does not prevent Lucifer, the prince of devils, from roaming about and mocking the poet's despair. His only issue seems to be the suicide that he contemplates in lines 11–12. The full line of suspension points following line 12, which could be read as a continuation of the three suspension points at the end of the preceding line, indicate a pause during which suicide could be contemplated as a serious possibility. Hence, the anguish of the last line, which Nelligan alters to substitute "priez pour moi" for "je suis hanté." His announcement in "Rondel à ma pipe" that since "le ciel me prend en grippe" (213), he is prepared to smoke his pipe peacefully with Satan in hell, appears, in the light of this poem, to be a piece of bravado. Baudelaire's suggestion that sin might be a legitimate means of transcending convention has no echoes in Nelligan's poetry.

If in "La Cloche dans la brume" the poet reproaches himself for having abandoned prayer, in "Mon Sabot de Noël," it is Jesus who seems to have forsaken the poet. This poem, which is intended to celebrate the feast of Christmas (a time that should be doubly joyous for Nelligan, whose birthday was Christmas Eve), contrasts sharply with the Christmas poetry published at the time, in which the tone was invariably joyful or prayerful (as an example, see "Chant de Noël" by Nelligan's friend, Arthur de Bussières [see *Franges d'Autel* 89]). The poem initially rejoices for young children awaiting the arrival of Jesus at Christmas:

Soyez heureux, ô chérubins!
Chefs de Corrège ou de Rubens. . .

Et dormez bien parmi vos langes,
Où vous ferez mourir les anges.

Dormez, jusqu'aux gais carillons
Sonnant l'heure des réveillons. (225)

These opening verses fall easily within the tradition of pious Yuletide poetry. Contrary to the expectations of the genre, however, Nelligan's poem transforms itself in the second part into a series of despairing distichs, for the poet realizes that "Jésus ne descend plus pour nous" (line 19), the "nous" in this verse referring to the "fils errants de la Bohème," that is "les meurt-de-faim et les artistes" who represent the poet and his friends. His "rêve d'une nuit d'hôpital" that he might be welcomed into heaven by Saint Cecilia is negated by the refusal of Jesus. The poet's "sabot de Noël" will remain empty. The poem reveals a subject impregnated with the religious teaching of his time, which is for him a source of anguish rather than comfort. Jesus no longer descends for Nelligan and has no solace to offer the likes of him. His situation is not unlike that of his mentor, Louis Dantin, who in "Noël intime" describes the joy of those who witnessed the birth of Jesus in Bethlehem only to confess his own exclusion from the euphoria and, one is led to believe, from salvation as well (1932, 152–4). What distinguished Nelligan from other French-Canadian poets of the nineteenth century is not, as has sometimes been suggested, the absence of a religious thematics, but rather the fact that this poet, conscious that he is lacking in the practice of faith (as I've noted in "La Cloche dans la brume"), finds little consolation in these themes.

Did Nelligan experience a crisis of faith? Some critics have posited such a crisis prior to the fall and winter of 1898–99 (see, for example, Lemieux 187–9), and it is not implausible that at some point one did indeed occur, although any chronology based on the poetry, most of which is undated, is open to caution. When the poet in "Christ en croix" sees that the large, daunting crucifix before which he used to bow in adoration is now but a piece of crumbled plaster, we may conclude that the image reflects his own crumbling (or crumbled) faith. Nelligan's religious itinerary appears to have been an inconclusive process of uncertainty, representing an erosion, rather than a loss, of faith. No bold anti-religious verse of the type that Baudelaire produced in the "Révolte" section of *Les Fleurs du Mal* has come down to us (although some poems were apparently lost or destroyed). The erosion is clearly related to his sensual yearnings. "Petit Coin de cure," seen by Robidoux and Wyczynski as a "joyeuseté irrévérencieuse" (463), acknowledges that even a priest can experience sensuality. This young curate falls asleep "par l'exotique odeur des boudoirs de Sultane" (212), a line that was more explicit in the version published in *Les Débats* in 1900, in which it read "Songeant aux gros péchés de quelque courtisane" (464). Nelligan's longest poem, "Frère Alfus," features a learned monk who goes so far as to experience doubt:

> Parfois, il se disait, marchant dans les hauts saules,
> L'index contre le tempe et le missel au bras,
> Dieu peut être est chimère ainsi que vains nos rôles.
>
> À quoi nous servirait ainsi jusqu'au trépas
> De cambrer nos désirs sous les cilices chastes
> Et vivre en pleine mort pour un Ciel qui n'est pas? (283)

The tension between sensuality and spirituality in this young poet surfaces once again in the second of these stanzas. If it is true, as Robidoux and Wyczynski maintain, that Alfus's questioning is at the metaphysical and theological level (522), what seems to afflict him most is that belief requires him to stifle his desires with hair shirts and live as if he were dead sensually. His doubt seems to be motivated by a desire to unleash his passion. Cognitive factors appear to mask volitional ones. If the monk's doubts are resolved after a vision and a sleep of one hundred years, it is not altogether clear the poet has found the same certitude. His own final words, "pour nous, selon le gré du ciel, qu'il soit ainsi!" are more a prayer that he be given the certitude of faith than an affirmation that he has achieved it. We know that Nelligan's mentor, Dantin, did not achieve it. The text provides no evidence for Lemieux's assertion (187–8) that it represents a religious conversion on Nelligan's part. The allusions to suicide – the only unforgivable sin, according to Catholic theology – in "Confession nocturne" and in "Soirs hypocondriaques" ("Je cherche à me suicider," line 11) call for circumspection regarding a conversion. Alfus's questioning of the worth of sexual self-repression in the face of the possibility that God does not exist invites a more careful consideration of Nelligan's expression of sensuality.

LIGHT AMOROUS VERSE

While love was not a common theme in nineteenth-century French-Canadian poetry, some discreet poems of affection were penned by Chapman, Fréchette (see his lightly sensual "Louise" and "Le Premier Baiser"), Charles Lévesque, Eudore Évanturel, and Alfred Garneau, not to mention the occasional anonymous and pseudonymous amorous ditties that appeared in newspapers, especially after 1860. Love is clearly one of Nelligan's important themes, and one he almost always treats seriously, for his poetry contains fewer than a half dozen examples of light verse dealing with love. "Le Mai d'amour," a pleasant piece meant to be sung on a folk melody, is one example. Recalling that the time for love will not last, this is the closest Nelligan came to writing *carpe diem* poetry. Although the poet focuses his attention on the sole young woman at a May gala who has "un cœur triste" (150), the poem's tone is joyous. So is the tone of "Violon de villanelle" which celebrates the joy of young men and women happily dancing to music on a moonlit night. In a slightly different vein is the only Nelligan text that combines love and the renewal of nature. "Sonnet d'or," whose title is positively marked, contains more positive signifiers and syntagms than any other Nelligan wrote. From "soir triomphal" in the first line to "Avril de gloire" in the penultimate line, this sonnet brims with the euphoria of nascent spring. The air, the songs of the birds, are intoxicating. Within this atmosphere, the poet asks his loved one to come outside with him to savour the sounds and sights of spring, all of which are to be preferred to the Mozart and Handel she is playing inside. This text provides the unique instance in his poetry in which nature is elevated over art.

Another poem that also deals with love in an unapprehensive manner, "Placet pour des cheveux," was first published in 1902, after Nelligan's internment:

Reine, acquiescez-vous qu'une boucle déferle
Des lames des cheveux aux lames du ciseau,
Pour que j'y puisse humer un peu de chant d'oiseau,
Un peu de soir d'amour né de vos yeux de perle?

Au bosquet de mon cœur, en des trilles de merle,
Votre âme a fait chanter sa flûte de roseau.
Reine, acquiescez-vous qu'une boucle déferle
Des lames des cheveux aux lames du ciseau?

Fleur soyeuse aux parfums de rose, lis ou berle,
Je vous la remettrai, secrète comme un sceau,
Fût-ce en Éden, au jour que nous prendrons vaisseau
Sur la mer idéale où l'ouragan se ferle.

Reine, acquiescez-vous qu'une boucle déferle? (151)

The title and first line of this rondel place it within a courtly tradition. A "placet" is a written request for a favour that carries with it the feel of the good manners of times gone by. The first word of the poem directly addresses the woman as "Reine," a title with connotations of an earlier, courtlier era, when "Reine" was used to signify respect and admiration for a woman. The tone is continued with the choice of a verb, "acquiescez," that connotes deference and esteem.

The poet requests a lock of hair, a physical attribute that constitutes an erogenous zone in some nineteenth-century poetry – Baudelaire's "La Chevelure" is a well-known example – and his choice of words suggests that he is referring to an ample coiffure. "Boucle" is a lock of hair, but the verb "déferler," meaning "to unfurl," has a grand, majestic ring to it, as in unfurling a sail or a flag, giving the impression that the amount of hair is quite substantial (and hence more highly charged erotically). The poet's lightness of touch reveals itself in line 2 in the play on the two meanings of "lames," a word that can refer to the blades of the scissors that will cut her hair as well as to the waves of the sea, used metaphorically here for the waves of her mane. Like Baudelaire, he is enchanted by the smells of the hair that synesthesically recall the song of a bird and a night of love.

While the first stanza is a question, the first two lines of the second quatrain constitute an affirmation. The poet explains that the woman's soul (note the change in perspective from the physical "cheveux," to the spiritual "âme") sings ("a fait chanter sa flûte de roseau") in his heart, much like the birds in a small grove of trees. It is unclear whether the silk-like flower with rose scents referred to in line 9 is the woman or the lock of hair, but the poet does in any event pledge himself to restore the lock to her, even in another life. If necessary, he affirms, he would return it in Eden (by which we assume some pleasant afterlife) on the day they both sail off on the ideal sea (not an unusual image in nineteenth-century poetry). Significantly, this is a sea "où l'ouragan se ferle," that is, where hurricane winds *are not* unleashed.

LOVE AND ANXIETY

The storms that have quieted in "Placet pour des cheveux" are raging, however, in one form or another in most of Nelligan's poems touching on the question of love. The disquiet that surrounds his sensuality in his poetry is best approached through the prism of Nelligan's spirituality, for his religious belief imposes a behaviour that would countermand his sexual yearnings. Armand Laroche, in his play *Nelligan blanc* (1981), suggested that Nelligan was a homosexual, a condition that, if true, would be sure to heighten his anxiety in matters sexual. The suggestion has since been repeated by others, notably by Aude Nantais and Jean-Joseph Tremblay in their play, *Nelligan déchiré*. There is, however, no textual, biographical, or historical evidence for such a hypothesis, and it has not been endorsed by any scholar of Nelligan. Since homosexuality would not have been a subject of discourse in late nineteenth-century Quebec, the absence of such evidence is not, in itself, proof of the absence of the fact.[3] While acknowledging the possibility of homosexuality, I have chosen to remain close to Nelligan's poetic texts, where there are no indications that the love mentioned is not heterosexual. The anxiety found in them is not lessened for that, since in order to be enjoyed, sensual desire, condemned by his religious culture, would require that he detach himself from his formative community. On the other hand, there is no reason to posit, as has Pierre H. Lemieux, that Nelligan loved three specific women in his adolescence. A reliance on "le sens littéral et obvie des poèmes" (16) has led Lemieux to identify a German shepherdess named Gretchen as one of these objects of Nelligan's love. Not only does this methodology confer upon the poems the status of true representations of the historical life of the poet, it is totally unnecessary and distracts from the important tension between faith and sensuality.

Such tension is evident in one of his first poems, "Cœurs blasés," whose title evokes semes of love and satiety. Perhaps there has been so much love (sex?) that it has become uninteresting, boring. The number of persons alluded to is not specified, but can be presumed to be a couple, who have just died, perhaps in a final night of lovemaking ("dans la dernière Nuit"), never having been able to find the true source of life ("la vraie et bonne sève"). The reason for this failure is already perceivable in line 3, "Pour leurs cœurs blasphémants d'où l'espoir toujours fuit" (95), which stresses their disrespect for religion and morality. The second and final stanza makes clear the depths of their depravity and its costs:

> En vain ont-ils tué l'âme dans la débauche,
> Il reste encore, effroi! les tourments du Remords.
> L'Ange blême se dresse et se place à leur gauche,
> Leur déchire le cœur râlant jusqu'à la Mort. (95)

Debauchery can mean any number of excesses, but in nineteenth-century Quebec culture it most often connoted illicit sexual activities.[4] This is what has led to their destruction. In a rare instance of Gothic horror, Nelligan has a pale angel rip out their hearts. In the first of Nelligan's poems in which sexuality is evoked, it is associated with sin and depravity, an attitude wholly consonant with the religious discourse of the time.

That the sensual might coexist with the spiritual, or even that the spiritual might grow from the sensual, as Baudelaire seems at times to intimate, were insights to which Nelligan was culturally closed. Hence, whether sin or guilt are evoked or not, love in Nelligan is frequently associated with sadness and even a yearning for death.

Consider, for example, the two-stanza poem "Vasque," which, after evoking "une / Brise triste emmi l'ombre," concludes thusly:

Or les aimés s'en vont pleureurs au blanc de lune,
Le faune jase à la nuit qui dort,
Et leur vertige est tel qu'ils voudraient mourir d'une
Mort de Cygne, noyés au glauque de la lune
Enlacés dans la Vasque d'eau d'or. (145)

The final syntagm, "d'eau d'or" [dodɔr], which is also used in the first stanza, evokes through its phonetic similarity with *dodo* [dodo], connotations of the sleep of death, recuperating as well the semes of the first ("La vasque somnolente") and final ("la nuit qui dort") syntagms of the first stanza. Intimacy rarely seems to be an option for Nelligan.

A similar conjunction of love and death is found in "Hiver sentimental," a poem that, while less than successful as a whole, contains some of Nelligan's strongest individual lines.

Loin des vitres! clairs yeux dont je bois les liqueurs,
Et ne vous souillez pas à contempler les plèbes.
Des gels norvégiens métallisent les glèbes,
Que le froid des hivers nous réchauffent les cœurs!

Tels des guerriers pleurant les ruines de Thèbes,
Ma mie, ainsi toujours courtisons nos rancœurs,
Et, dédaignant la vie aux chants sophistiqueurs,
Laissons le bon Trépas nous conduire aux Érèbes.

Tu nous visiteras comme un spectre de givre;
Nous ne serons pas vieux, mais déjà las de vivre,
Mort! que ne nous prends-tu par telle après-midi,

Languides au divan, bercés par sa guitare,
Dont les motifs rêveurs, en un rythme assourdi,
Scandent nos ennuis lourds sur la valse tartare! (148)

The title of the sonnet, evoking the familiar Nelliganian image of winter, also announces its intimate side. "Sentimental," which Nelligan uses in two other titles ("Jardin sentimental" and "Thème sentimental"), alerts the reader that the poem will deal with love/intimacy/emotion. This is confirmed in the first line in which the poet addresses himself directly to a woman (the addressee's gender is identified in line 6), and not without a touch of sensuality. Drinking from her eyes assumes at least a minimal physical encounter, although this is the only real note of intimacy until the final tercet.

The two quatrains and the first tercet focus instead on a commingling of themes of winter, death, and misunderstanding. The first words of the poem, "Loin des vitres!", addressed to the woman, are unambiguous: the poet wishes her to distance herself from the window. The reason for this command, however, *is* ambiguous. It is not clear whether he wishes her to do this because of the intense cold she would feel through the windows (see line 3, with its strong imagery: "Des gels norvégiens métallisent les glèbes") or whether he wishes to protect her from a public that misunderstands them ("ne vous souillez pas à contempler les plèbes," line 2). Of the two, the conflict with society (expressed here as a tension between purity and impurity) seems the more important, since the couple's rancour will be evoked in line 6. Yet there are puzzles in this first quatrain. Why does the poet address this woman with the formal "vous"? What is the meaning of the last line, "Que le froid des hivers nous réchauffe les cœurs"? The image is certainly striking, but why do their hearts need warming? Because their love is waning? There is no textual evidence of that. Because of the hostility of the crowd? Possibly. Because they are near death? They, or he, to be precise, wants death, but there is no reason to believe that either is dying. Indeed, the desire for their hearts to be re-warmed would indicate a wish contrary to death.

The second quatrain, however, provides the focus for a coherent reading. While the classical simile with which it begins would seem to have little place here, it does introduce semes of heroism and grandeur in the face of defeat, semes which the poet needs in order to appeal to the woman to join him in invoking death. The idea is not to forgive or forget. On the contrary, he and his lover are to pay court to, flatter even, their rancour for an offense that is unspecified, but which we assume has something to do with the public. He calls for the two of them to disdain "la vie aux chants sophistiqueurs." The adjective "sophistiqueur," non-existent in French and an invention of Nelligan, could by analogy with the adjective "sophistiqué" refer to false or devious arguments or thinking, to a world that thinks differently than they (and hence wrongly). The choice of "chants" would indicate a repeated discourse, a refrain of prevailing wisdom. In the face of their own rancour and a false and devious world, the poem's solution is to call for the end of their earthly existence. Death is not seen as threatening, since the word "bon" in "le bon Trépas" contains semes of both goodness and familiarity. The choice of "Erèbes," retrieving at the rhyme the classical allusion of line 5, is far less threatening as their destination (it signifies the realm *before* Hades) than would have been the hell of the Christian tradition.

While the quatrains are addressed to the woman, the tercets are addressed to death, capitalized both in "Trépas" in the final line of the second quatrain and in "Mort" in the tercets. The capitalization does not carry, in this instance, any ominous semes, since "Trépas" is qualified by "bon" and since death is addressed by the familiar "tu" (in contrast to the woman loved, who is formally *vouvoyée*). Nevertheless, the image of death in the first line of the tercets is certainly not a comforting one: "comme un spectre de givre." The tension between horror and comfort surely betrays the poet's own uncertainty. Yet, evoking the *taedium vitae* that is the stock and trade of much nineteenth-century poetry ("Nous ne serons pas vieux, mais déjà las de vivre"), he calls on death to deliver them both. Significantly, he asks death to take them in a moment of vague sensuality on an afternoon when, "languides au divan," they lazily listen to the muted rhythms and the dreamy motifs of a guitar. The image, however tritely romantic, reemphasizes the link in Nelligan between love and death.

Death is sought after not only to flee "la vie aux chants sophistiqueurs" (line 7) but also to escape having to contemplate the ravages of time. In "Roses d'octobre," a rondel laden with Renaissance echoes, the poet invites the woman not, as did Ronsard, to come see whether the roses have lost their petals, but rather to die with him so that they will *not* have to see the roses wilt. Although the poet presents the two lovers as now dead to love, his poem remains, in the Renaissance manner, a strategy of seduction nevertheless. His invitation is to "Cloître ton cœur mort en mon cœur tué" (161), yet the tone of affection is evident in the evocation of their joint grave where "Nous y dormirons tous deux, ma mignonne." What is particular about this poem is its deliberate upsetting of the Ronsardian project, replacing sexual union with a common grave as the goal. Death brings permanence to love, which in Nelligan's poetic universe is incompatible with life.

WOMEN AND PURITY

A counterpoint to the sex/sin syndrome is the idealization of the woman who is pure, a notion thoroughly ingrained in traditional French-Canadian culture, which, following the strong Mariological tendencies of the French school, as well as the teachings of the Jesuits and the Oblates in the nineteenth century, proffered Mary as a model for women. Moreover, the attraction of Saint Cecilia, noted earlier, does not derive solely from her status as the patroness of music, but also from her being a particularly unusual virgin: she actually married, but convinced her new husband to respect her virginity. Such an idealization of virginity is already noticeable in one of Nelligan's first poems, "Béatrice." Written in 1896 in honour of his cousin's first communion, the poem, not unexpectedly, contains semes of purity. Yet there are qualities about this young girl that astonish. That she is "bonne et charmante" (line 7) is banal enough, as is the reference to her as "pleine / D'innocente candeur" (7–8). But she is also curiously "insensible au plaisir" (4). The tercets call upon the young girl to cherish her current life and express the hope "Que ces courts refrains soient tes plus belles chansons" (line 11). The poet seems to wish that there be no other songs for her, presumably no songs of love. The final tercet exalts her purity:

> J'élève mon regard vers la voûte azurée
> Où nagent les astres dans la nuit éthérée,
> Plus pure te trouvant que leurs plus purs rayons. (98)

Poems such as this one led Nelligan's first European critic to emphasize the chaste quality of his work. Indeed, the only Canadian trait that ab der Halden was willing to recognize in Nelligan's verse was its innocence: "l'ouvrage dont nous parlons," he writes, "pourrait être lu par la jeune fille la plus chaste" (351). Compared to Baudelaire, whose love poems frequently imply a physical relationship, Nelligan certainly does appear chaste. As we've seen in "Mon Âme," he highly valued purity in himself and on numerous occasions he reveals its attraction, such as in "Rêve d'artiste" in which, as noted in the previous chapter, the woman he desires is represented as completely disincarnated. This desire for a pure, spirit-like woman, part of a pervasive thematics of angelism in Nelligan, coheres with the discourse of a society that associated the body with evil and was given, in the words of Jean Le Moyne, to "d'arbitraires exhortations à la pureté" (63). The catechism of the diocese of Montreal published in 1888 (unrevised until 1951) taught that "une affection déréglée pour les plaisirs de la chair" (#61) was a capital sin and that "les pensées et les désirs impurs sont toujours des péchés mortels" (#452). The catechism here encapsulates Catholic teaching on sexuality for which, to quote one of its French spokesmen from the previous century, Father Joseph Lambert, "En matière d'impureté, il n'y a presque point de petits péchés" (qtd by Delumeau 489). This statement expresses standard pastoral teaching in Quebec that well into the twentieth century included impure thoughts among the transgressions forbidden by the sixth commandment.[5] The nostalgia for childhood, which appears so frequently in Nelligan, masks a desire to return to a time when impure thoughts did not exist. Hence the regret for the undifferentiated sex of early childhood, expressed by the common clothing then worn by both boys and girls ("nos robes frippées," 107; "mes robes d'enfant," 117).

Nelligan's constant quest to conjoin love and purity is reflected in the title "Amour immaculé," which he chose for a poem first published in *La Patrie* in 1899. "Immaculé," which etymologically means "spotless," signifies "pure" in general usage. It also has religious connotations, since its most frequent use in nineteenth-century Catholic cultures was in the collocation "Immaculée Conception," the theological doctrine proclaimed by Pius IX in 1854 affirming that Mary was conceived without sin (in one of Nelligan's transcriptions of this poem during his internment, he titled it "L'Immaculé [*sic*]-Conception").

The first quatrain describes a stained glass window that portrays a blue-eyed saint (the original title, as published in *La Patrie*, was "Les Saintes au vitrail"). Critics have identified the window as one representing Saint Cecilia in Notre-Dame Church in Montreal (Lemieux 206; RW 455), but given that only the detail of blue eyes is given in the poem, it is more likely that Nelligan did not wish to make a specific identification of the church or of the saint. What interests him is the supernatural quality of the window, which is termed "merveilleux," an epithet that translates easily as "marvelous" but one that retains here the semes of the supernatural that attend the substantive, "le merveilleux." The artist, inspired by an archangel, we are told, painted this figure "d'une façon mystique" (line 3). The second quatrain presents the poet who, in a strangely exalted state ("l'esprit hanté de rêves nébuleux," line 5), comes to pray before this saint's window. The tercets, however, transfer the focus to the woman he loves:

> Telle sur le vitrail de mon cœur je t'ai peinte,
> Ma romanesque aimée, ô pâle et blonde sainte,
> Toi, la seule que j'aime et toujours aimerai; (205)

Clearly, the purpose of the quatrains is to establish the terms of a comparison. The poet has painted the woman he loves on the window of his heart, much as the saint is painted on the window of the church. It is important to retain the full comparison and particularly the mystical semes that derive from the painting in the first quatrain. "Ma romanesque aimée" (line 10) might indicate that the woman is imaginary, but "romanesque" could also refer to the church's architecture, further strengthening the link between the woman he loves and the saint in the window. Love is once again envisaged on a spiritual rather than physical level, for the object of his affection remains a "pâle et blonde sainte" (line 10) to whom he is pledging perpetual fidelity: "Toi la seule que j'aime et toujours aimerai" (11).

Yet this woman remains indifferent:

> Mais tu restes muette, impassible, et, trop fière,
> Tu te plais à me voir, sombre et désespéré,
> Errer dans mon amour comme dans un cimetière! (205)

The accusation is severe. Not only does she not respond to his love ("muette, impassible"), she is too proud and even takes pleasure in his pain; she is hardly a saint, then, as he had imagined her to be. The final simile, in which he sees himself wandering aimlessly through his love as one might wander through a cemetery, illustrates well the macabre side of his impulses.

The valorization of purity is strengthened by an idealization of the poet's mother, who is at the centre of several of his poems. Much has been written about the important role of the mother in the French-Canadian imagination, in which she overwhelms all other manners of imagining womanhood.[6] In a poem specifically entitled "Ma Mère," the mother is associated in the first distichs with purity: "Quelques fois sur ma tête elle met ses mains pures, / Blanches, ainsi que des frissons blancs de guipures" (112). The signifiers "pures," "blanches," and "blancs" present a mother who is untainted. Indeed, in all the poems in any way dealing with his mother, she is presented as pure (since the father is never mentioned in his poetry, the mother comes close to being a *virgo mater*). Yet, in this poem as in some others, he uses language that one might expect from a lover to his loved one: "Ô toute poésie, ô toute extase, ô Mère" (line 6). Such imagery has led one critic to suggest that "dans ce drame religieux se glisse ... le tabou de l'inceste" (Beaudet 101). There are other hints that Nelligan's love for his mother may have been more than filial. In a curious poem entitled "Devant deux portraits de ma mère," the poet reacts to two photographs of his mother that, according to Robidoux and Wyczynski, actually existed: one dating from 1876 when Nelligan's mother was twenty, and the other, from 1896, when she was forty (RW 369). The poet, who would have been nineteen at this writing, is quite taken with the portrait of his mother when she was his own age:

> Ma mère, que j'aime en ce portrait ancien,
> Peint aux jours glorieux qu'elle était jeune fille,
> Le front couleur de lys et le regard qui brille
> Comme un éblouissant miroir vénitien! (112)

The second portrait, however, disconcerts him:

> Ma mère que voici n'est plus du tout la même;
> Les rides ont creusé le beau marbre frontal;
> Elle a perdu l'éclat du temps sentimental [.] (112)

His sadness ("Aujourd'hui je compare, et j'en suis triste ...") could be read as a reflection on the ravages of age, but there are no signs in the historical record that Mrs Nelligan was prematurely aging. One is led to wonder whether his fascination for his mother at his own age might translate into unconscious desire. At the very least, the process of individuation from the mother does not appear to be complete. He himself seems to be aware that something inexplicable is going on, alluding to a "mystère du cœur qui ne peut pas s'éclairer" (line 12). In "Ma Mère," however, he is careful to stress that his is a respectful and filial relationship, ("A l'autel de ses pieds je l'honore en pleurant," line 7).

The immaculate mother emerges as a guarantor against her son's errant behaviour ("Premier Remord"), but especially against his sexuality. The sonnet "Le Talisman" is important in this respect:

> Pour la lutte qui s'ouvre au seuil des mauvais jours,
> Ma mère m'a fait don d'un petit portrait d'elle,
> Un gage auquel je suis resté depuis fidèle
> Et qu'à mon cou suspend un cordon de velours.
>
> « Sur l'autel de ton cœur, puisque la Mort m'appelle,
> Enfant, m'a-t-elle dit, je veillerai toujours.
> Que ceci chasse au loin les funestes amours,
> Comme un lampion d'or, gardien d'une chapelle. »
>
> Ah! sois tranquille en les ténèbres du cercueil!
> Ce talisman sacré de ma jeunesse en deuil
> Préservera ton fils des bras de la Luxure,
>
> Tant j'aurais peur de voir un jour sur ton portrait,
> Couler de tes yeux doux les pleurs d'une blessure,
> Mère! ... dont je mourrais, plein d'éternel regret. (113)

The poet's mother clearly dominates this poem: the first stanza describes her activity, the second is a quotation of her words, and the tercets are addressed to her. She is to play an important role in protecting her son from the perils of sexuality. The first line of the poem makes clear that the poet is at a crucial temporal juncture, "au seuil des mauvais jours." He is to enter a new life, the post-pubertal life of sexual desire that is already labeled as evil ("mauvais") and requiring a struggle ("la lutte qui s'ouvre"). Having evoked this situation succinctly in the opening line, he then places "Ma mère" in the initial position in line 2 and makes her the subject of the main verb of the stanza. "Elle" refers to the mother and its phonemes supply the dominant rhyme of the quatrains. Not only does [ɛl] appear four times, as would be expected and as does [ur], but it is echoed twice internally: "portrait d'elle/Un gage auquel ..." (lines 2–3); "la Mort m'appelle, / Enfant m'a-t-elle ..." (5–6). "Mère" is also in the initial position in the last line of the poem, thereby framing its content.

The mother who occupies the space of the poem stands between the poet and the "mauvais jours" evoked in the first line. There are hints, however, that the poet might be uncomfortable with that protection. The line relating the gift of her picture, for example, is not without harshness at the phonetic level. The phrase, "don d'un petit portrait d'elle," with a string of consonants [d ... d ... p ... t ... p ... rtr ... d ... l] that includes five dentals and two bilabials, lacks the euphony of the other verses. Similarly, the fourth line, which reveals that he is wearing this portrait tied to his neck, might, by repeating the velar [k] ("qu'à mon cou suspend un cordon"), elicit semes of cutting, "coupes." Could this tiny portrait be cutting his neck? He affirms that he has remained faithful to his mother's admonitions, but the verse making that affirmation, "Un gage auquel je suis resté depuis fidèle" (line 3), and the verse reassuring his mother, "Ah! sois tranquille en les ténèbres du cercueil!" (9), are the only lines of the poem that do not follow the traditional rules of the alexandrine: there is no caesura after the sixth syllable. This deviance from the regularity of the sonnet may be another clue that the poet is not entirely comfortable with this situation. Significantly, the mother refers to him as a child, addressing him as "Enfant" (line 6). He, however, refers to himself as her son, "ton fils" (11) and speaks not of his childhood but of his youth, "ma jeunesse" (10).

The mother's warnings, expressed in the second quatrain, contain no direct religious references, but her metaphors rely on religious vocabulary: "l'autel de ton cœur," "lampion d'or" (an image she uses as descriptive of her own portrait), and "gardien d'une chapelle." Her portrait is the vigil candle that guards the chapel that is his heart. The mother attributes to herself the function of a guardian angel ("je veillerai toujours"). Religious vocabulary frames the mother's main desire that the portrait might drive away love that is dangerous, even fatal: "Que ceci chasse au loin les funestes amours" (line 7). In the original version published in *La Patrie* in 1899, the line reads as "je veux qu'il luise en toi, gardien de tes amours," while in the version in *Les Soirées du Chateau de Ramezay* in 1900 we find "Que ceci te protège des vaines amours." Neither is as forceful as the one I have quoted, which all editions of Nelligan's poetry have reproduced since Dantin's version of 1904. While the possibility of tampering by Dantin cannot in this instance be excluded, the word "funestes" applied to love does cohere with the moral discourse of the period and the ethos of Nelligan's poetry. In its stronger meaning, "funeste" is that which brings death.

The poet's aim is to reassure his mother. He does so in part by identifying her portrait as a talisman, an object which, strictly speaking, has supernatural powers. He then pleonastically modifies "talisman" with "sacré," thereby linking it with the religious semes prominent in his mother's speech. Since it is hung from a neck on a velvet string, the portrait serves as a scapular, a tiny holy picture (usually the Virgin on one side and the Sacred Heart on the other) traditionally hung from the neck and kept beneath the clothing. This pious practice, popular in Nelligan's time, was believed by some to preserve the wearer from hell at the time of death. The mother's picture is assimilated to that of Jesus and Mary, themselves models of chastity, and associated with protection from hell, the punishment for those who yield to their sexual temptations.

The portrait/talisman will protect him, then, from "les bras de la Luxure" (line 11), i.e., pleasures of the flesh. Notably, the only other reference to arms as being dangerous occurs in "Gretchen la pâle" where it is applied to Anadyomena who uses her arms to kill. Pleasures of the flesh lead to death. Significantly, the two capitalized substantives in the poem are "Mort" and "Luxure" whose link at the graphemic level supports their linkage at the level of meaning. The dying mother, it needs to be noted, is not a datum of Nelligan's life, for his mother was neither dying nor even ill at the time this poem was written. Nelligan is using a worn literary topos – the dying person uttering final words of wisdom – to stress the importance of the mother's admonition, but also, and perhaps more importantly, to insert connotations of death ("Mort," "cercueil," "deuil," "mourrais") into the poem as a context for the warning against sexuality. Sex, "les funestes amours," leads to death, and death following illicit sex leads to hell.

The centrality of the struggle against the flesh, which informs so many of Nelligan's poems, resurfaces in "Châteaux en Espagne" where we find the poet in despair because he has been unable to "soutenir le combat des vieux Anges impurs" (156). The latter image, found neither in Nelligan's European sources nor in his Canadian predecessors or contemporaries, is common in the discourse of Catholic moral theology of the nineteenth century where "les vieux anges impurs" are the fallen angels who, having become demons, seek to attract us all towards sins of impurity. In "Le Talisman," however, he insists that he will not yield to the flesh for fear that this would grieve his mother, something that would cause him eternal remorse. The guilt envisaged would derive not from his having sinned against God, but rather against his mother. She has replaced Christ and the Virgin on the scapular, becoming in their stead his protector against sensuality. Curiously, she is envisaged not as being in heaven but in a dark coffin.

Nelligan's friend Joseph Melançon claimed that his fellow poet wrote "Le Talisman" after reading Rodenbach's "Le Coffret" (Filteau 87). While there is no reason to disbelieve this assertion, Robidoux and Wyczynski expand the link between the two poems further than necessary when they assert that Rodenbach's poem contains "une méditation semblable" (RW 370) to Nelligan's sonnet. Indeed, what is striking is how dissimilar the meditations of the two poems are. To be sure, Rodenbach's poem, from his collection *Les Tristesses* (1879), does feature a mother and a son. But Rodenbach's mother limits herself to showing her son the hair of his ancestors, which she keeps safely in a small chest, to which has been added the golden hair of his deceased sisters. The poet's meditation consists of his wish that his mother's hair will be grey by the time it is added. The question of sexuality, so central to Nelligan's poem, is totally absent from Rodenbach's, as is the notion of the mother as a protectoress against moral turpitude. Nelligan may have been inspired by Rodenbach's poem, but there are few transtextual relations between it and Nelligan's text, whose coherence derives from his sexual anxieties.

In "Tristesse blanche," in which the poet addresses a woman with whom he is clearly in a relationship, the semes of sensuality are considerably muted. The poem is framed by the statement that he and his loved one suffer from a deep sense of emptiness: "Et nos cœurs sont profonds et vides comme un gouffre" (116) provides both the first and last lines. That their hearts are deep implies a substantial capacity for being filled, a fulfillment that has, however, eluded them. In the face of such emptiness, the poet wants to flee with his beloved not only from everyday reality but from matter itself. The verse "Oui, fuyons la Matière aux yeux encorcelants" appears twice, as lines 4 and 12. That matter, capitalized and thus set in opposition to the also capitalized "Idéals," should be described as having bewitching eyes may imply that by "matter" he means "flesh." Where he wants to flee is also repeated twice: "Fuyons vers le castel de nos Idéals blancs" (line 3; line 11 repeats the verse while substituting "château" for "castel"). The Rodenbachian accent detectable in the title does not detract from a Baudelairean thrust: the flight is away from this world towards a "pays d'or plein de lieds et d'oiseaux" (line 7), where they will be able to rest from what he refers to as their "intimes désastres" by listening to the rhythms of the flute playing the waltz of the stars. The escape is necessary, for both suffer ("tu souffres et je souffre," repeated twice, lines 2 and 13), leading the poet to suggest a joint suicide. This poem, though filled with worn topoi, asserts once again Nelligan's greater comfort in the realm of purity than in that of sensuality.

A similar perspective is discernible in "Jardin sentimental," a poem that appears on the surface to be idyllic and serene. Two young lovers, holding hands, linger in a natural setting on a beautiful evening as they watch Venus rise in the sky. The poem closes with their imagining themselves being raised up to the planet of love. Their intimacy is emphasized by the frequent repetition of "nous" (seven times) and the predominance of verbs in the first person plural. The night is not to be feared, for it is broken by the light of the fireflies, the red and purple of the setting sun, and the light of Venus itself: "Nous sentions se lever des lumières d'espoir" (125).

Yet, even in such surroundings, love is not without anxiety. The second stanza in this poem of six tercets is conspicuous in being the only one whose perspective is not in the first person plural. Indeed, it features the only appearance of *je*: "Je tenais, tremblants, / Tes doigts entre mes mains, comme un nid d'oiseaux blancs" (lines 5–6). This sentence is of some interest, both from the point of view of the poet-lover and that of the loved one. The woman's trembling fingers suggest that the serenity of the scene has not assuaged a certain anxiety on her part. As for the poet, he holds her trembling hands as he would a bird's nest, hence very gently. Why the trembling? Why the hesitation on the part of the poet who dares not grasp the hand more firmly? While strong emotion could be inferred – perhaps the reticence of adolescent love – the answer seems to lie, rather, in line 9, which is the centre of the poem and is striking in its seeming discontinuity with the rest of the poem. The poet speaks of the effect of their gazing at Venus and the hope that rose up "En notre âme fermée ainsi qu'un donjon noir." Why are their souls closed as a dark dungeon? Piercing through this poem, I would suggest, is the familiar notion that somehow love is associated with sin. The dark dungeon evokes semes of hell, and the closed souls may be those that have been separated from God because of sin, perhaps the sin of love. This is why Venus, not God, gives them hope, why in spite of the evocation of the angelus in line 13 – its unpleasant sound ("voix grêle") is not intended to be comforting in any case – their dream is to rise up "aux astres de Vesper," that is, to Venus itself.

THE GRETCHEN CYCLE

These contradictions are highlighted in four poems frequently referred to collectively as the "Gretchen Cycle," in which a girl/young woman named Gretchen figures prominently. Some critics have argued for an expansion of the Gretchen Cycle to include poems in which she is not named but which are thematically related. Gérard Bessette adds three poems to the group (Bessette 55–6) and Pierre H. Lemieux adds another eight (Lemieux 123–4), considerably – and unnecessarily – stretching the category. The debate over inclusions of poems in this group is not fruitful unless one accepts Gretchen's historical reality. Her existence was first affirmed by Luc Lacourcière when he stated in his influential edition of Nelligan that Gretchen was "une jeune Allemande qui demeurait dans le voisinage de Nelligan, qu'il admirait comme une sorte d'Aurélia, mais à qui il n'osa jamais parler" (1952, 290). Although taken as fact by most subsequent critics, this statement, for which Lacourcière gave no source, is certainly open to challenge, particularly since no member of Nelligan's family nor any of his acquaintances has ever testified to her existence. While Gretchen's existence is historically possible, since there was a small German community in Montreal at the time, comprising about one per cent of the population (Linteau 162), no contemporary verification of this "fact" has yet come to light.[7]

It is much more likely that Gretchen is a creation of Nelligan's imagination. Robidoux and Wyczynski, who do not challenge Lacourcière's assertion (indeed, they repeat it), point out the frequency of the name Gretchen in imaginative literature since Goethe's *Faust* and note the appearance of a short story entitled "Gretchen" in the Montreal magazine *Le Monde illustré* in 1899 (Wyczynski 1960, 113; RW 153), where she is described as "très pale," a trait that Nelligan retains for his loved one. In his biography of Nelligan, Wyczynski adds that "Gretchen est l'héroïne de plusieurs contes parus dans les journaux montréalais et les jeunes connaissaient la 'Gretchen-Polka' dansée avec entrain" (1987, 209). Banville's "Le Sabbat," which Wyczynski believes Nelligan read, contains an allusion to Gretchen and is a probable source for Nelligan's "Lied fantasque," in which Nelligan evokes Gretchen for the first time (1987, 208–9). While these poems may very well be based on amorous feelings that the poet might have had towards a young woman, or even several young women, positing, as has Lemieux, a specific person who answers to the details of the poems is not helpful.

"Lied fantasque," the only one of the Gretchen poems to be relatively free of anxiety, opens with the evocation of a cold Parisian night, represented by a brilliant set of images by which the snow-covered roof-tops and their chimneys resemble old soldiers trying to keep warm while on sentry duty. The scene is focalized from the inside of a dwelling, and it is to that interior that the sonnet shifts its attention ("Restons en intime pourpris," 152) as the poet asks Gretchen to put down her guitar so that he might contemplate her eyes and let his imagination roam without distraction ("ne distrait le bizarre / Rêveur ... ," 152). The preference for interiors is prevalent in Nelligan, but the contrast here is intended to valorize the world of the imagination as against the harsh world of reality. The woman's eyes – a not infrequent figure in love poetry – call not so much to love-making as they do to image-making. To pick roses from her eyes may have an erotic dimension, but the poet specifies that these are "roses de ta Westphalie." Her presence calls forth images of Germany (evoked as well by the poem's title and her own name). The word "fantasque" in the title, then, seems closest in meaning to its etymological root in the Greek "phantastikos," which is applied to that which governs the imagination.

In "Five o'clock," a poem imbued with "un charme troublant et bizarre" (Dantin 1997, 98), it is Gretchen herself who seems anxious. The poet creates an atmosphere of pervasive sadness, beginning the poem with the line "Comme Liszt se dit triste au piano voisin," which, given the assonant connection between Liszt and "triste," emphasizes a dysphoria that will be repeated in lines 7 and 13 where Haydn and Mozart replace Lizst respectively. In this poem, Gretchen is evoked by name only in the final line where she is asked to pour tea. Amorous or sensual themes are absent from this text which focuses on the contrast between a cold, stormy exterior and the inner scene of the five o'clock tea. Yet the poet notices that tears are forming in Gretchen's eyes as her eyelashes "s'amalgament de perles" (line 14). Unlike what is frequently the poet's situation, there is a specific cause for her sadness, for she is reflecting on the death of blackbirds in the bitter cold. The poet's reaction strikes the reader as insensitive, however, since it is limited to his singing scales and telling her to serve tea. Anxiety surfaces in another poem featuring Gretchen, although she is now seen as its remedy rather than its source. "Frisson d'hiver" likewise takes place on a cold winter night and again the poet and Gretchen are indoors. This time, however, it is he who is in a state of high anxiety. Suffering greatly, but for an unspecified reason, he speaks of his sobs, his "névrose," and his "âme inconsolée." The poet plays on the word "frisson," a shiver normally caused by the cold. Indeed, this would seem to be its meaning, given the cold described in the title. But it is not altogether clear that his shudders are caused solely by low temperature, for the sobs, the disconsolate soul, and the neurosis of which he speaks appear determining as well. Gretchen, whose name is called out at the end of each stanza (her name alone, followed by an exclamation point, constitutes the fourth line of every stanza), is seen as a source of comfort and warmth: "Chauffe mon cœur" (lines 2 and 25); "Prends-moi le front, prends-moi les mains" (line 9).

"Rêves enclos," in which Gretchen is not mentioned by name, is sufficiently related thematically and lexically to "Frisson d'hiver" for the poem to be considered part of the same cycle. In this poem as well, the woman is seen as someone who will save the poetic persona from his anxiety:

Enfermons-nous mélancoliques
Dans le frisson tiède des chambres,
Où les pots de fleurs des septembres
Parfument comme des reliques.

Tes cheveux rappellent les ambres
Du chef des vierges catholiques
Aux vieux tableaux des basiliques,
Sur les ors charnels de tes membres.

Ton clair rire d'émail éclate
Sur le vif écrin écarlate
Où s'incrusta l'ennui de vivre.

Ah! puisses-tu vers l'espoir calme
Faire surgir comme une palme
Mon cœur cristallisé de givre! (165)

The title of the poem is paradoxical, if not oxymoronic, for dreams are precisely phenomena that transcend barriers. "Enclos," on the other hand, refers to an area that is fenced in. Fred Cogswell has appropriately translated this title as "Walled-in Dreams" (20); "enclosed dreams" would capture it as well. The poet's dreams are those he hopes to realize in the enclosed space of intimacy.

The strong imperative verb of the first line of the poem confirms the poet's firm desire to close himself and his companion off from others. The initial verse also contains a given, the melancholy that both of them share (or rather, that the poetic voice assumes they share), although what might have led to this condition is not revealed. The poet asks that they confine themselves "dans le frisson tiède des chambres," presenting the reader with a daunting catechresis. "Frisson tiède" would first appear to be oxymoronic, since "frisson," in its primary meaning, refers to the muscular tremors that are part of the body's response to cold. More likely, "frisson" is to be taken figuratively, referring to shivers that are the result of strong emotion. But why are these lukewarm? And who is shivering? Grammatically, it would have to be the rooms: "le frisson tiède *des* chambres." If we accept a catechretic metaphor, we can conclude that the line refers to the emotion that would derive from being closed in together.

The pleasant odour of autumn evoked in the two final lines of the quatrain add a sensual dimension to the private, warm enclosure, although the comparison in these same distichs of the smell of the flowers to that of relics also introduces a troublesome note. The word "reliques" adds not only a religious seme to the stanzas but a lugubrious one as well, since relics by definition are the remains, of body or clothing, of a saint. One wonders whether they have odours and, if so, how they could be pleasant. Yet, the reference to relics may serve as a moral admonition for the couple while in their private space, for saints have merited canonization because they have been able to resist temptation.

As we've seen in "Placet," female hair is erogenous in Nelligan, as in nineteenth-century French poetry generally. The second quatrain is devoted exclusively to the woman's hair, evoking its sensuality while inserting religious semes that may help guard against that very sensuality. The constituent phrases of the stanza, when placed in a normal syntactic order, would read as follows: "Tes cheveux sur les ors charnels de tes membres rappelent les ambres du chef des vierges catholiques aux vieux tableaux des basiliques." Line 8, then, is a complement of "cheveux" in line 5. The image is that of the woman's golden hair flowing over the golden flesh of her upper body. "Charnel," which derives etymologically from the Latin for flesh, refers to that which is related to the senses, most commonly in the expression "plaisirs charnels." The sensuality of the image is heightened by the unstated but suggested possibility of the woman being unclothed. "[L]es ors charnels de tes membres" assumes flesh that can be seen. This sensuality is counterpointed, however, by another set of images drawn from religious iconography, for the woman's hair is compared to that of Catholic virgins found in old paintings in churches. The use of "chef" for head is a deliberate recourse to an old French substantive not then in current use but whose meaning was still recognized by French readers. Its usage inserts medieval semes that concur with those found in ecclesiastical paintings. Virgins, of course, are those women who have not yielded to the temptations of the flesh.

The commingling of the spiritual and the sensual in the quatrains sets the stage for a different kind of blend in the sestet. Sensuality returns even more strongly; spirituality is not evoked, but weariness is. The first tercet constrasts the erotic and *ennui*. Its first line is the most carefully crafted line of the poem, phonetically [tɔ̃klɛrirədemajeklat], balanced between beginning and end ([t̲ɔ̃k̲l̲ … k̲l̲at̲]) with internal phonetic equilibria as well ([ɛrirə], [emaje]). The polished nature of the line may be a clue to the importance of its image, that of a laughing mouth revealing white teeth. The second line extends the image to red lips ("écarlate") and to the oral cavity they form: "le vif écrin." The mouth is proposed as a jewel box ("écrin"), a living ("vif") repository of precious things. This sensual representation of the woman's mouth does not seem to calm the disquieted poet. In the tercet's last line, "l'ennui de vivre" is depicted as having been encrusted on her lips. But whose *taedium vitae*? Her own? In the first line of the poem, the poet has used "mélancoliques" in the plural to indicate a mutual condition – yet a "clair rire d'émail" would not seem to belong to someone weary of living. Perhaps she has overcome her dysphoria? The past definite, "incrustra," suggests something that has come and gone. One wonders whether the "ennui de vivre" might have been the poet's rather than hers. Could she be laughing at his ennui? At his anguished kiss? The final tercet expresses the poet's wish, or his dream, that she might, in this enclosed space, draw his heart, now crystallized with frost, towards a serene hope.

Gretchen, who is hardly minatory in such contexts, does become a threat as she becomes sexually attractive. One of Nelligan's better-known poems, "Gretchen la pâle," makes this clear:

> Elle est de la beauté des profils de Rubens
> Dont la majesté calme à la sienne s'incline.
> Sa voix a le son d'or de mainte mandoline
> Aux balcons de Venise avec des chants lambins.
>
> Ses cheveux, en des flots lumineux d'eaux de bains,
> Déferlent sur sa chair vierge de manteline;
> Son pas, soupir lacté de fraîche mousseline,
> Simule un vespéral marcher de chérubins.
>
> Elle est comme de l'or d'une blondeur étrange.
> Vient-elle de l'Éden? de l'Érèbe? Est-ce un Ange
> Que ce mystérieux chef-d'œuvre du limon?
>
> La voilà se dressant, torse, comme un jeune arbre.
> Souple Anadyomène ... Ah! gare à ce démon!
> C'est le Paros qui tue avec ses bras de marbre! (153)

The opening quatrain, rich in its evocation of Gretchen's beauty and subtle sensuality, draws first from the environment of art, comparing her beauty to Rubens' female figures. Nelligan's first editor pointed out that Rubens' somewhat heavy women are not an appropriate comparison for the woman Nelligan is here describing (Dantin 1997, 79). Yet Nelligan, whose knowledge of painting was limited, utilizes a cultural reference to activate semes of sensuality that remain important throughout the poem. The question of resemblance to the model evoked is not crucial, since his point is that Rubens' figures pale before the superior beauty that is Gretchen's ("Dont la majesté calme à la sienne s'incline"). Drawing next from the realm of music, he evokes a rich, sensuous voice. The image of a golden voice and the associations with mandolins and Venetian balconies are trite enough, but the atmosphere of the stanza recalls the "Luxe, calme et volupté" of Baudelaire's "L'Invitation au voyage." The slowness of song (the beautifully assonanced "chants lambins") introduces a sensual languor, though with some discretion, which will not be the case in the second quatrain.

The following stanza is, in fact, quite startling in the context of late nineteenth-century French-Canadian poetry, for nothing quite like it had been written previously. The closest was probably Alfred Garneau's "La Jeune Baigneuse de l'album de Lady Belleau" published in *Le Journal de Québec* several decades earlier. Garneau had been criticized for this depiction of a joyful female bather, even though he presented it as the depiction of a figure in a painting (see the text in Grisé et al., 10:73–6). When Nelligan's poem appeared in *Les Débats* in 1902 after his internment, there seems to have been no scandal at all. Either Nelligan's readers did not understand the image of the first two lines (she is nude and wet, with her ample hair unfurling on her body), or they mistakenly took her for a mythological figure (not an unexpected assumption, since she is compared to Venus in the final tercet), or were reassured by the conclusion of the poem which depicts the woman as a demon. Moreover, a number of signifiers in this quatrain contain semes of purity that, in other poems, Nelligan associates with women: "chair vierge," "soupir lacté," "fraîche mousseline," "chérubins." Whiteness in Nelligan and in the Western imagination is associated with goodness. Yet, the key word here, "vierge," does not, in this context, refer to her "virgin flesh" but rather to her body unadorned by clothing ("vierge de manteline").

Faced with such a woman, the poet is led in the first tercet to question her provenance and nature, drawing, once again, from the paradigms of his culture. Is she from Eden or hell? Rather than envisage this woman in her humanity, he asks himself whether this beautiful body ("ce mystérieux chef-d'œuvre du limon") could be that of an angel. Before he can answer these questions, the erotic image returns with full force. As Gretchen straightens herself, emphasizing her chest ("torse"), the poet imagines a young Venus ("souple Anadyomène"). It is here that three suspension points indicate the pause that permits the poet to answer the question he had raised in the first tercet. No, she cannot be an angel. She is, rather, a demon who kills with the very arms she would use to embrace. Feeling threatened by the sexual desire that had seized his imagination, he retreats to the belief of his culture that desire is evil. Baudelaire, having asked a similar question of beauty, had preferred not to resolve it: "Que tu viennes du ciel ou de l'enfer, qu'importe, / O Beauté" (52). For Nelligan, more faithful to the exigencies of his religious faith, it does indeed matter. One cannot imagine Nelligan, a great admirer of Baudelaire, concluding a poem about a woman in the way that the French poet, who could both curse and celebrate womanhood, ended "Le Possédé":

> Sois ce que tu voudras, nuit noire, rouge aurore;
> Il n'est pas une fibre en tout mon corps tremblant
> Qui ne crie: *O mon cher Belzébuth, je t'adore!* (64)

The double nature of woman – angel and demon – is a commonplace of French symbolist poetry. Nelligan's distinction is that he is unwilling to accept such a coexistence.

In "Le Vaisseau d'Or," a poem I'll discuss in greater detail in the next chapter, the consequences of desire are clearly evident, as are the semes of sexuality: "La Cyprine d'amour, cheveux épars, chairs nues, / S'étalait à sa proue, au soleil excessif" (312). What is significant here is that "la Cyprine d'amour," that is, Venus, is not represented as the idealized goddess of love but rather as the alluring temptress who, her hair disheveled, exposes herself naked under an excessively hot sun. This eroticism is associated with the wreck of the ship which strikes "le grand écueil / Dans l'Océan trompeur où chantait la Sirène" (312), the siren being, of course, the symbol of the seductive woman. The result is the fall into the "profondeurs du Gouffre" (312): sexuality leads to the abyss of hell. Nelligan's view of women, then, stands in contrast with that of his Québécois contemporary, Albert Ferland, who in *Femmes Rêvées* (1899) presented women as creatures of charm, grace, and goodness. Rather than the seductress who leads men to evil, she is "Toi dont l'amour élève et fait l'homme plus fort" (12). While Nelligan is obsessed with knowing whether the woman is from heaven or hell, Ferland merely wonders what faraway city or country she is from. Ferland, who is comfortable with the Church's teachings on sexuality, even penned a poem in imitation of the style of the commandments where we find such precepts as "Vierge ton corps tu garderas / Jusqu'à l'hymen jalousement" (44). For him, there is no tension between feelings of love and the prevailing moral discourse.

Nelligan's view of sexuality, however, can lead only to guilt. Because Nelligan had spoken of Satan in a humorous way in "Rondel à ma pipe," ab der Halden concluded that "visiblement, il n'y croit guère" (350). Whether Nelligan believes in Satan or not, he is clearly cognizant of the reality of sin which for him and for his coreligionists is one of the realities of the human condition. The catechism used in Montreal at the time affirmed that we are all "participants [du] péché et de [la] punition de nos premiers parents" (#45). Guilt, experienced at a level of anxiety rarely found elsewhere in verse written in French, dominates Nelligan's poetry. The first remorse he describes is that of having one day played truant rather than attend school, and we notice in this young poet a sense of guilt that is completely out of proportion to this innocuous offense. Yet, the discourse of the French school of spirituality often blurred the distinction between minor and major transgressions, as in Cardinal de Bérulle's admonition, "vous ne devez tenir pour petit aucun des sujets pour lesquels le sang du fils de Dieu a été répandu" (2:901). In Nelligan, guilt, real guilt, comes from thoughts or pleasures of the flesh, from which the talisman given to him by his mother was to protect him.

We have only to return to "Confession nocturne," where the poet describes his soul as "le donjon des mortels péchés noirs" (281), to doubt the efficacy of this talisman. The nature of these mortal transgressions is not specified, but when, in another poem, the poet plaintively expresses the wish, "Je ne veux plus pécher, je ne veux plus jouir" ("Rêve d'une nuit d'hôpital," 208), we can conclude that the forbidden pleasure is that of the flesh, "la chair maudite descendue d'Adam," as Olier called it (188). The consequences of an infraction against purity are heavy, as I've noted in "Cœurs blasés," a poem with a clear message that debauchery leads to destruction.

As a way of dealing with his lack of success in love and with the culpabilization that his culture associated with succumbing to female charms, the poet occasionally fell back on another prevailing view of woman, namely her treachery. In Nelligan's discourse, kisses are described as mendacious, as in the first line of his "Le Tombeau de Chopin" where he enjoins the composer to sleep "loin des faux baisers de la Floriani" (257), la Floriani being a reference to George Sand. The alarm is sounded again in "Le Suicide d'Angel Valdor" in which the hapless bellringer has been lured by the "baisers trop menteurs d'une femme" (270). The image is further broadened in "Le Chat fatal" in which he muses that his own heart will continue to be eaten away "tant que mensonge / Engouffrera les jours, / Tant que la femme sera fausse" (276).

It is no surprise, then, that in one of his darkest poems, "La Vierge Noire," life itself is depicted as a treacherous woman:

Elle a les yeux pareils à d'étranges flambeaux
Et ses cheveux d'or faux sur ses maigres épaules,
Dans des subtiles frissons de feuillages de saules,
L'habillent comme font les cyprès des tombeaux.

Elle porte toujours ses robes par lambeaux,
Elle est noire et méchante; or qu'on la mette aux geôles,
Qu'on la batte à jamais aux grands fouets de tôles.
Gare d'elle, mortels, c'est la chair des corbeaux!

Elle m'avait souri d'une beauté profonde,
Et je l'aurais crue aimable et, sans souci du monde,
Nous nous serions tenus, Elle et moi par les mains.

Mais, quand je lui parlai, le regard noir d'envie,
Elle me dit: « Tes pas ont souillé mes chemins. »
Certes, tu la connais, on l'appelle la Vie! (302)

Like the woman of "Gretchen la pâle," abundant hair covers her shoulders. But something is fake ("ses cheveux d'or faux"), either the hair or the gold, and the hair covering the body is compared to the flora of sorrow ("saules") and death ("cyprès").

The harshness towards this black virgin may translate Nelligan's own anger toward women. He wants this evil woman jailed, but also severely flogged with whips of metal. The reason is that she has deceived him, having approached him with smiles and goodness, leading him to believe in her love. That the poet makes her into a metaphor for life at the poem's end ought not distract us from the fact that the woman described is a woman of flesh and blood, a point on which Bessette has insisted (55), and that she is deceptive, an assessment of women that has an ancient lineage. Bessette has conjectured that Nelligan, conscious of the audacity and ferocity with which he treats this woman, makes her into a metaphor for life as a way of stepping back from his anger (55). The negative view of women which sometimes surfaces in his poetry cannot be attributed solely to adolescent unrequited love but also, and perhaps primarily, I believe, to his association of sex with sin.

Aggravating his sense of culpability is the realization that his infractions are a violation of Christ's very body. As he contemplates the crucifix, the poet affirms, "j'entendais en moi des marteaux convulsifs / Renforcer les clous noirs des intimes Calvaires" ("Le Christ en croix," 189). The notion that a human being can by his sins inflict physical pain on the body of Christ was common coin among Nelligan's contemporaries, but he differs from them in the sense that he does not envisage forgiveness. If, in "Nocturne," the poet repents and asks for God's pardon, only one poem, "La Réponse du crucifix," transmits the message of forgiveness. While such verse was not uncommon in this period, this is for Nelligan an isolated text that was probably commissioned, since it was first published in *Le Petit Messager du Saint Sacrement*, a religious magazine Dantin was at that time publishing. Nelligan's work conveys a sense of guilt that would seem to surpass forgiveness. If few are chosen, Nelligan seems convinced that he is not one of them. This perhaps explains why in "Musiques funèbres" and "Soirs hypocondriaques" he envisaged the possibility of suicide.

The tensions between the spiritual and the sensual in Nelligan's poetry clearly link his sombre lyricism to the then dominant religious discourse in Quebec. To be sure, the conflict between the temptations of the flesh and the call to purity is not unique to Nelligan nor to French-Canadian Catholics. In the early 1890s, the decade of Nelligan's struggles, this same tension was a preoccupation of André Gide, who had a French Protestant upbringing. Nor should we assume, for the facts would contradict us, that private, impenitent infractions of the church's sexual teaching did not exist in Montreal of the 1890s. My reading of Nelligan's poetry, however, suggests that he assimilated the prevailing discourse of Quebec spirituality, one that invited what Delumeau, referring to the situation in France in the previous century, called a "superculpabilisation de l'impureté" (490). A pessimistic view of human nature as naturally inclined to evil had led to the implicit condemnation of man's "lower" nature. Nelligan's poetry is not immune from such a vision of mankind and the human condition. A spirituality of abasement that had as its goal the creation of authentic humility led in his case to a loss of self-esteem and a sense of being destined to failure. The bravado of "La Romance du vin" notwithstanding, he did not succeed in escaping the prevailing religious ethos that others were able to wear more lightly. Rather, the violation of its internalized standards was for him a source of profound anxiety. "Le Talisman," which can be read as a frantic effort to stave off the temptations of sin, dates from March 1899, only a few months before his mental collapse. Continuing to believe in sin while no longer believing in grace, he had locked himself into a world of depravity. Against ab der Halden's statement about Nelligan that "Le Canada lui est aussi indifférent que possible" (359), we should rather affirm that the religious ethos of French Canada constituted an important dimension of his interiority and that recognizing its interdiscursive presence in his poetry is essential to reading Nelligan.

3 The Poetics of Failure

Nelligan's poetry is permeated by semes of defeat. His earliest surviving text, "C'était l'automne ... ," focuses on a dying adolescent, and some of his earliest published poems tell of other persons who have been defeated by life. In "Silvio Corelli pleure," a poor orphan sadly plays a fiddle to survive, with no hope of ever attaining a modicum of happiness. "La Chanson de l'ouvrière," a little-known poem that constitutes a rare instance of social consciousness in Nelligan, depicts a weary working woman who has been so vanquished by her condition that she yearns for her life to end:

> Je suis lasse de cette vie,
> Je veux dormir, ô bonne amie,
> Laisse moi reposer, assez! (92)

Her sentiments in the face of her defeat are unusual in a late nineteenth-century French-Canadian context, for she is willing to render God responsible for her misery: "je blasphème ma destinée, / ... / Pourquoi donc Dieu me rend-il si malheureuse?" (93). If Silvio Corelli and the working woman could allege definite causes for their defeats, such specifics are not needed for a sense of failure to occur. In "Quelqu'un pleure dans le silence," for example, no reason is given for the poetic voice's sense of having been defeated. In "La Passante," he explains that his youth is like a woman in mourning whom he has fleetingly seen: others will have seen him, but none will love or understand him.

The stresses that developed in Nelligan from the incompatibility he perceived between his spiritual and sensual yearnings were accompanied, then, by a deep sense of failure. His conception of himself as deficient derives, however, not solely from the moral dilemmas he experiences but also from the fact that women are not receptive to his love. The only woman he records smiling at him is the one represented in "Thème sentimental," but she is distant (she inhabits "la planète des Bergers," hence, Venus) and clearly not of flesh, resembling in her composition of diamond and marble Baudelaire's enticing though impassive beauty in "La Beauté." This woman who makes him suffer ("fait mon martyr," 32) is no more accessible than the others. In "Bergère," the shepherdess he claims to have loved is, by the end of the poem, no more than a ghost at his window, leaving him in sadness. That the woman is not within his grasp is clearer still in "Beauté cruelle":

> Certe, il ne faut avoir qu'un amour en ce monde,
> Un amour, rien qu'un seul, tout fantasque soit-il;
> Et moi qui le recherche ainsi, noble et subtil,
> Voici qu'il m'est à l'âme une entaille profonde.
>
> Elle est hautaine et belle, et moi timide et laid:
> Je ne puis l'approcher qu'en des vapeurs de rêve.
> Malheureux! Plus je vais et plus elle s'élève
> Et dédaigne mon cœur pour un œil qui lui plaît.
>
> Voyez comme, pourtant, notre sort est étrange!
> Si nous eussions tous deux fait de figure échange,
> Comme elle m'eut aimé d'un amour sans pareil!
>
> Et je l'eusse suivi en vrai fou de Tolède,
> Aux pays de la brume, aux landes du soleil,
> Si le Ciel m'eût fait beau, et qu'il l'eût fait laide! (160)

In this poem, the poet expresses an ideal that he takes to be universal but which he makes his own, that of exclusivity and fidelity in love, an ideal also proffered in "Amour immaculé" ("la seule que j'aime et toujours aimerai," 205) and one that is consonant with his religious faith. His strong statement in this regard begins with an adverb of affirmation and contains a high level of redundancy: "un amour en ce monde / Un amour, rien qu'un seul" (lines 1–2). The repetition of "un" three times, strengthened twice (by "en ce monde" and "seul"), and the use of the adverbial locutions "ne que" and "rien que" establish the unassailability of the premise: we must have one love alone, one that rises above sensuality, that is "noble et subtil." He seeks this kind of love, but alas! it has brought him suffering as painful as a deep gash in the flesh.

The second quatrain sets up a contrast between the poet and an unnamed woman who has been the object of his exclusive love. She is, of course, beautiful, and the poet is careful to stress that beauty by rhyming the last word of the first hemistich with its opening word: "Elle ... belle" (in a version he transcribed in 1938, Nelligan gives the woman a name containing the same phonemes: Isabelle) Yet the [ɛl] contained in "belle" is also present in "cruelle" of the title, establishing a phonetic link that strengthens their semantic association. She is also haughty, perhaps a result of her beauty. He, being timid and ugly, can only approach this inaccessible woman in his dreams. Indeed, the more he approaches, the more she rises (semes of ascension and assumption are frequent in Nelligan) and disdains him, for she prefers another.

Given this situation, the poet is led to imagine a hypothetical situation. Like Proust's narrator who fantasized that his love object, Mme de Guermantes, became destitute while he became rich, the poet imagines their appearances having been reversed: if *he* had been handsome and *she* ugly, then she would have loved him and he would have followed her to the ends of the earth. The accusation is clear: the woman, seduced by external beauty, is interested in surfaces. His deeper love is attracted to the person, regardless of external appearance. Representing the woman as superficial helps him cope with his lack of success in love.

His love for cruel beauty ends in failure, but then, so do most of his attempts at love. In "Le Robin des bois," the poet reminds the woman of a scene in the woods where, moved by the singing of a robin, "j'ai saisi vos mains, j'ai saisi vos mains blanches, / Et je vous ai parlé d'amour ..." (164; lines 3–4). She was unresponsive: "vous êtes restée insensible à ma voix, / Muette au jeune aveu des affections franches" (lines 4–5). She was moved, though, by the sudden death of a robin, leading him to reflect that their love, like the robin, was now dead. The shepherdess in "Bergère" has likewise abandoned the poet, as has the woman violinist of "Le Violon brisé." Angel Valdor ("Le Suicide d'Angel Valdor") does succeed in love, but then commits suicide when his wife is unfaithful. Failure, particularly in love, is a major theme in Nelligan's work, and one that is crystallized in two poems in particular, "Châteaux en Espagne" and "Le Vaisseau d'Or."

"CHÂTEAUX EN ESPAGNE"

A repeated feature of Nelligan's poetry consists in the reversal of the opening of a text by its closure. About ten of his poems, including "Le Vaisseau d'Or," "Devant le feu," "Premier Remords," "Le Jardin d'antan," "Ruines," "Amour immaculé," "Potiche," and "Château rural," employ this structure. In all of these texts, closure is determined by a thematic structure that produces an antithetical relation between opening and ending. In a poem dedicated to Nelligan, his contemporary Albert Lozeau, himself a fine and sensitive poet, seemed to recognize one of these antitheses, ascent and fall, as emblematic of Nelligan's poetic trajectory:

Tu montais radieux dans la grande lumière,
Énivré d'idéal, éperdu de beauté,
D'un merveilleux essor de force et de fierté,
Fuyant avec dédain la route coutumière.

Tu montais emporté par ton ardeur première,
Battant d'un vol géant la haute immensité,
Et là, tout près d'atteindre à ton éternité,
Tu planais, triste et beau, dans la clarté plénière.

Mesurant du regard le vaste espace bleu,
Tu sentis la fatigue envahir peu à peu
La précoce vigueur de tes ailes sublimes.

Alors, fermant ton vol largement déployé,
O destin! tu tombas d'abîmes en abîmes,
Comme un aigle royal en plein ciel foudroyé! (*L'Âme solitaire* 193)

It has been pointed out (Brissette, passim) that the rise/fall paradigm is a constituent feature of the Nelligan myth as it has been played out in the Québécois imagination. Yet, neither its use within mythic discourse in Quebec nor its importance in both classical and Judaeo-Christian narratives of origin obviates the existence of something real, not only in Nelligan's biographical itinerary but in his imagination as well. His poetry sufficiently demonstrates how the dream "de monter aux astres de Vesper" (125) is counterbalanced by the conviction that "tout choit avec prestesse" (176). Lozeau's poem, Baudelairean in its thematics, vocabulary, and rhythm, captures Nelligan's ardent and defiant desire to rise above the common herd as well as the sense among his friends and acquaintances that he was destined for an inevitable fall.

In Nelligan's own poems this paradigm is nowhere more prominent than in his sonnet "Châteaux en Espagne," which becomes thereby an exemplar of the reversal poem:

Je rêve de marcher comme un conquistador,
Haussant mon labarum triomphal de victoire,
Plein de fierté farouche et de valeur notoire,
Vers des assauts de ville aux tours de bronze et d'or.

Comme un royal oiseau, vautour, aigle ou condor,
Je rêve de planer au divin territoire,
De brûler au soleil mes deux ailes de gloire
À vouloir dérober le céleste Trésor.

Je ne suis hospodar, ni grand oiseau de proie;
À peine si je puis dans mon cœur qui guerroie
Soutenir le combat des vieux Anges impurs;

Et mes rêves altiers fondent comme des cierges
Devant cette Illion éternelle aux cent murs,
La ville de l'Amour imprenable des Vierges! (156)

Unlike any of Nelligan's other reversal poems, "Châteaux en Espagne" displays a title that has no literal relationship with the body of the poem. Castles are not mentioned in the text, and Spain is evoked only by the word "conquistador." Recognition of the figurative meaning of the popular expression "castles in Spain," however, enables the title and thereby the text to be understood as referring to unrealizable projects. By preceding the poem and being set off spatially from its body, the words of the title gain a supremacy that signifiers within the poem proper cannot achieve. Semes of the unrealizable hover over this text from the beginning, influencing our reading of the poem and predicting the reversal.

The initial verse of the first quatrain sets the tone for a stanza brimming with confidence and hopes of conquest: "Je rêve de marcher comme un conquistador." The triple, successive, alliterative velars (comme, conqu ...) followed by two dentals (... tador) establish a tone of virility associated with military victory. The word "conquistador" itself contains the phonemes of conquest (conquis ...) and, by association with the Spanish conquerors of the Americas, the semes of conquest as well. Moreover, "comme," which introduces the extended similes of both the first and the second quatrains, is a prominent feature of epic style. A proleptic caution can be detected in the first two words, "Je rêve," however. Given the objects of the verb *rêver*, its meaning may be interpreted as being within the semantic range of "I desire," "I wish," "I yearn to," that is, we may legitimately interpret it figuratively in the first instance. The repetition and similar syntactic position of "Je rêve" in line 6 tend to corroborate this reading. But *rêver* has a primary meaning, referring to the free flow of imagination within sleep, that is, to the unreal, if not the chimerical. The primary semes of dream, with their clear links to the title, are present, though not fully operative within the first verse and quatrain, where the dominating semes are those of assurance and boldness.

The remainder of the stanza elaborates on the dreamed-of activity of this simulated conqueror who envisages raising up his "labarum triomphal de victoire, / Plein de fierté farouche et de valeur notoire." Nelligan's choice of the historically inappropriate "labarum" (Heredia uses "pennon" in similar contexts) is of some significance. The labarum, which was the imperial standard of Constantine, contains both religious and military semes. A Christian tradition claimed that Constantine *in a dream* saw the Chi-Rho monogram (the first two letters of the name of Christ in Greek) which he then had placed on his standards with the inscription *In hoc signo vinces* (By this sign you shall conquer). This anecdote, which brought together religion and military victory, would have been known to Nelligan and his intended readers since it was widely taught as historical fact in Catholic schools in Quebec until the 1960s. We now know that the Chi-Rho monogram existed long before Constantine's alleged dream, for it was also an abbreviation for the Greek word *chrestos*, which means "auspicious." As such, it was seen in ancient times as a good omen, and scholars today believe that it was in this sense that it was adopted by Constantine. It is reasonable to assume, however, that Nelligan intended to actualize the religious semes and to encode them within the concept of conquest,[1] for this labarum is "triomphal de victoire" (line 2). The poetic voice is not content with victory alone, for his activity stimulates his pride ("Plein de fierté farouche" [line 3] – the alliterative [f]s accentuate a flamboyant swagger) and his quest for fame ("et de valeur notoire" [4]). As he dreams of marching "Vers des assauts de ville aux tours de bronze et d'or" (line 4), he resembles Heredia's conquerors who were "ivres d'un rêve héroique et brutal" (135).

But what is this city of gold and bronze towers? While it might be tempting to see it as a Heredian city of the Americas (Heredia writes of "Une Ville d'argent qu'ombrage un palmier d'or" [140]), we might also recall that in Nodier's dream narrative, *Smarra* (1821), the protagonist attempts to penetrate into a city which also, coincidentally, has magnificent towers. As he approaches the city, he reflects:

> N'entends-tu pas au loin les cris de plaisir qui s'élèvent
> des murs de Larisse! ...
> Voilà, voilà les tours superbes de la ville de Thessalie,
> si chère à la volupté; et cette musique qui vole dans l'air,
> c'est le chant des jeunes filles.
>
> Qui me rendra d'entre vous, songes séducteurs qui bercez l'âme
> enivrée dans les souvenirs ineffables du plaisir, qui me rendra
> le chant des jeunes filles de Thessalie et les nuits voluptueuses
> de Larisse? (48)

The key collocations of Nodier's text, "cris de plaisir," "chère à la volupté," "songes séducteurs," "souvenirs ineffables du plaisir," "chants de jeunes filles," and "nuits voluptueuses," indicate rather clearly what this walled city contains. An influence of Nodier on Nelligan is not suggested here, but the thematic affinity is instructive nonetheless. As in Nodier, the walls and towers protect sexuality, a reading corroborated by the last lines of the poem, "... cette Illion éternelle aux cent murs, / La ville de l'Amour imprenable des Vierges!" (lines 13–14), to which I shall be returning. Interestingly, walls as symbols of interdiction appear as well in Nelligan's "Premier Remords," where the poet recalls a repeated offense of his youth: "Je montais à l'assaut des pommes et des prunes / Dans les vergers bordant les murailles des cours" (111). What might be seen as a minor adolescent infraction is pictured in that poem as a major sin, given the scene he encounters on arriving home: "Devant le crucifix où sa lèvre se colle / Ma mère était en pleurs!" (111). In "Premier Remords," the crucified Christ appears as a guarantor of the interdiction; in "Châteaux en Espagne," the poet attempts to co-opt Christ for his enterprise by appropriating the labarum as his standard.

The second quatrain continues the semes of confidence and conquest, but shifts to a different simile, based initially on ornithological imagery. The poet now compares himself to mighty birds: "vautour, aigle, ou condor." The species-specific identification is significant since birds, though a presence in Nelligan's poetry, are rarely so identified. The size and strength of the eagle and the condor are, of course, legendary and their place in the poetic tradition well established. Leconte de Lisle, to give but one example, celebrated the condor in "Le Sommeil du Condor" (the Latin-American semes of "condor" relate, in addition, to the semes of "conquistador"). The eagle, sacred to Jupiter, is an ancient symbol of power and victory. In Rome it was associated with nobles and patricians, a linkage that further activates the epithet "royal" (Lozeau refers to Nelligan as "un aigle royal"), and it was emblazoned on the standards of Roman legions (note the link with "labarum" in the first quatrain). The vulture, which does not enjoy the literary/mythological prestige of the condor and the eagle (although Hugo featured a vulture in *Dieu*), fits into the series by virtue of being a bird of prey, yet disrupts the scheme by evoking connotations different from those of the eagle and the condor. This disruption might be seen as another proleptic hint of the reversal to come.

Conquest is not abandoned as a desire in this quatrain, but the emphasis is on achieving great heights (the seme of height was already present in the participle "haussant" in line 2). The Romantic dream of flying high into the heavens ("de planer au divin territoire") – one is reminded of Baudelaire's "Élévation" – is joined by the Icarian attempt to reach the sun ("De brûler au soleil mes deux ailes de gloire") as well as by the Promethean impulse to steal from the gods ("A vouloir dérober le céleste Trésor"). The semes of pride and glory persist: "mes deux ailes de gloire" recall "Plein de fierté farouche et de valeur notoire" (line 3). Yet what is most striking about this stanza is that while it repeats the dream of victory ("Je rêve de ..."), it includes within the dream the semes of defeat: "De brûler au soleil mes deux ailes de gloire." The reader's cultural competence immediately relates this verse to the story of Icarus, who by flying too close to the sun, melted his wings of wax and plunged into the sea. A French poetic tradition, going back at least to the sixteenth-century poet Philippe Desportes, associates the Icarian myth with the poetic quest. In the nineteenth century especially, Icarus functioned as the archetype of the poet (Baudelaire: "Je sens mon aile qui se casse; / Et brûlé par l'amour du beau" ["Les Plaintes d'un Icare," 202]), but the poetic quest for the ideal does not appear to be the dominant seme in this poem. The story of Icarus, which functions here as a mediating text, is a story of defeat. Icarus's failure could be seen as an exemplary chastisement of the very *démesure* which the quatrains express (the poet has already identified himself as "plein de fierté farouche" and will characterize his dreams as "altiers" in line 12). Nelligan stresses Icarus's failure and seems even to seek defeat for himself. What kind of dream is this that *seeks* to burn its wings? Oneiric flight, Bachelard and others have maintained, can be associated with a desire for seduction (1943, 29). While the poet's dream is diurnal, we recognize the verb "to burn" as a common poetic metaphor for sexual desire and/or passion. "Je rêve ... / De brûler au soleil" might well contain such associations, for the sun, too, has connotations of sensuality in Nelligan. In "Le Vaisseau d'Or," for example, "La Cyprine d'amour, cheveux épars, chairs nues, / S'étalait à sa proue, au soleil excessif" (312).

Such a reading might help us deal with the last verse of the second quatrain: "A vouloir dérober le céleste Trésor." The poet dreams of burning in the sun in the process of stealing the heavenly treasure. But what is this "Trésor"? If we accept that there are Promethean connotations in this verse, then we might well conclude that the "Trésor" is fire, since that is what Prometheus is said to have stolen from the gods. Prometheus's fire is supposed to have been literally the heat and flame of burning substances, although since the Romantic period it has frequently been interpreted as the light or truth which the poet brings to mankind, an intuition concretized in the Rimbaldian depiction of the poet as a "voleur de feu" or in Fréchette's designation of him as a "nouveau Prométhée" (20). Since both Icarus and Prometheus have been associated in Western artistic tradition with the poetic quest, it would be possible to read this quatrain as an expression of that pursuit. Given what we know about the possible connotations of "ville" in line 4, however, it is legitimate to consider whether this fire represents burning passion. It might be argued that in this poem, the Promethean gesture translates a personal desire for that which is forbidden (fire is, in any case, one of the primary interdictions and a highly sexualized one at that, as Bachelard pointed out [1949, 28*ff*, 75]). The capitalized *T* in "Trésor" connects the word with the three other capitalized common nouns in this text, all of which are related somehow to sexuality: "Anges impurs" (line 11), "Amour" (16), and "Vierges" (16). Could the treasure being sought, then, not be the treasure of love?

Semes of reversal were already suggested by the title and proleptically encoded in the quatrains, particularly in lines 7 and 8 with the evocation of Icarus and Prometheus, both of whom were destroyed as a result of their quests. Hubris in the classical tradition leads only to disaster, as does pride in the Christian tradition. The reader is therefore prepared for this inevitability when reaching the formal volta, that turn in thought characteristic of the sonnet as a genre, which occurs in the first line of the first tercet. The possibility that the dreams expressed in the quatrains might become reality is now clearly denied: "Je ne suis hospodar, ni grand oiseau de proie," Nelligan writes, sweeping away in the first hemistich the conqueror simile of the first quatrain ("Je ne suis hospodar" negates the entire first quatrain), and repudiating in the second hemistich the mighty bird image of the second quatrain ("ni grand oiseau de proie" negates the entire second quatrain).[2] The confident "Je" of "Je rêve" of the quatrains becomes the diminished "je" of the first tercet: "A peine si je puis dans mon cœur qui guerroie / Soutenir le combat des vieux Anges impurs" (lines 10–11). The military semes have returned, but in a negative register. Neither the expected victories against walled cities nor the majestic flights are possible, for he can hardly contain the struggles within his own self. The combat becomes internal, or rather, it has been internal all along. As we have seen, within the popular Catholicism of the end of the nineteenth century, "vieux Anges impurs" could only refer to fallen angels, or devils, those devils whose purpose it was to tempt humans, especially adolescents, into what were then called "les péchés de l'impureté," the sins of the flesh. Louis Dantin, who knew Nelligan well, makes a discreet allusion to the poet's nocturnal dreams of "jeunes filles qui étaient à la fois des séraphins, des muses et des amantes" (70). In "Le Talisman" Nelligan evokes his conflict with the flesh as "la lutte qui s'ouvre au seuil des mauvais jours" (113). The struggles are presented in that poem as so difficult that he needs a picture of his mother to protect himself from "[les] bras de la Luxure" (note again the capitalization of a word associated with sexuality). His attempt to associate religion with victory by appropriating the labarum has failed. The devils are "vieux" perhaps because the fall of the angels antedates creation, but more probably because they have been fighting for his soul – or he has been fighting them – for what seems a long time. "Mon âme est le donjon des mortels péchés noirs" (281), he concludes in "Confession nocturne." Lozeau, in his poem of homage, misreads Nelligan by depicting him as having attained the great heights that are no more than a dream in Nelligan's own poem, and by attributing his fall to the fatigue required by the effort, rather than to the moral struggle within the poet.

The reversal is completed in the second tercet with the poet's admission that his haughty dreams, "mes rêves altiers," are melting like candles. In Western iconography, the candle is frequently a symbol for human life. At other times, it stands for joy and hope. But there are no semes of life, joy, or hope here, for a melting taper extinguishes itself. The erection of the labarum in line 2 is negated by the melting candles of line 12. Appropriately, Nelligan's choice of "cierges" contains, like "labarum," religious connotations, since in Quebec the word was used exclusively for large candles in churches. The opposition between "labarum" and the "cierges fondants" is all the more striking when we recall the well-known French expression *droit comme un cierge*. The image of melting wax was already implicit in the Icarian theme of verse 7; it reappears here not as a result of the sun but in the face of the impregnable city of love: "Devant cette Illion éternelle aux cents murs, / La ville de l'Amour imprenable des Vierges!" (in late medieval art, the castle of love is also defended by young virgins against the assault of youths). The closure of the poem takes up the assault on the city featured in the overture, but in a register of defeat. "Illion éternelle" is the eternal Troy that, unlike the legendary Troy, could never be taken. The city of love, the city of virgins, is not for him; with its hundred walls, it is "imprenable." The entire enterprise was an illusion. The exclamation point at the end of the last line stresses the finality of the failures and signals the impossibility of their reversal in the future.

The expression *châteaux en Espagne* has a long literary tradition dating back to the *chanson de geste*, and one of its early literary uses is of interest here. The expression occurs in the thirteenth century in Guillaume de Lorris's *Le Roman de la Rose*, a lengthy poem that is a dream narrative as well as an *art d'aimer.* A substantial portion of this text consists of the god of Love's elucidation of the mysteries of love to the narrator. At one point he explains to him that, when in love, he will be tormented at night and will tremble, shudder, and shake. Then he will remember the woman he loves:

Telfoiz sera qu'il t'iert avis
Que tendra cele au cler vis
Entre tes bras, tretoute nue,
Aussi cum s'elle fus devenue
Du tout t'amie et ta compaigne.
Lors fers chatiaus en Espagne. (101)[3]

Although *Le Roman de la Rose* is in part an apology for dreams, its use of *châteaux en Espagne*, possibly the first literary usage in relation to love, coheres with Nelligan's use of the expression: dreams of love are revealed to be just dreams. The next lines of Lorris's text make this abundantly clear:

Et avras joie de noient,
Tant cum tu seras solement
En la pensee delitable
Ou il n'a que mensonge et fable (101)[4]

Nelligan's dream, like the one evoked in Lorris's text, is revealed to be but "mensonge et fable."

"Châteaux en Espagne" is not Nelligan's only poem dealing with dreams, love, and *châteaux*. One other in particular unites all three – the little-known poem "Château rural":

J'eus ce rêve. Elle a vingt ans, je n'en ai pas moins;
Nous habiterons ces chers coins
Qu'embaumeront ses soins.

Ce sera là tout près, oui, rien qu'au bas du val;
Nous aurons triple carnaval:
Maison, coq et cheval.

Elle a les yeux de ciel, tout donc y sera bleu:
Pignon, chassis, seuil, porte, heu!
Dedans peut-être un peu.

Elle a les cheveux blonds, nous glanerons épis,
Soleil, printemps, beaux jours, foin, lys
Et l'amour sans dépits.

Sans doute, elle m'aura, m'ayant vu si peu gai
– Ne fût-ce que pour me narguer –
Un ange délégué!

This is so far an adolescent dream of romance with a farm girl – until the last stanza effects the expected reversal. It had all been literally a dream:

Brusque je m'éveillai. Mon coq au jour qui gagne
Pleurait là-bas dans la campagne
Son poulailler d'Espagne. (128)

[P]oulailler d'Espagne is Nelligan's own rejoinder to his *châteaux en Espagne*, which have revealed themselves to be *châteaux de cartes*.

"LE VAISSEAU D'OR"

"Le Vaisseau d'Or," which Dantin read as Nelligan's premonition of his impending insanity, was probably written in the summer of 1899 and remains among the best-known of his poems. Its theme has inspired Québécois painters and sculptors, and it has elicited the most commentary of any of his texts:

C'était[5] un grand Vaisseau taillé dans l'or massif.
Ses mâts touchaient l'azur sur des mers inconnues;
La Cyprine d'amour, cheveux épars, chairs nues,
S'étalait à sa proue, au soleil excessif.

Mais il vint une nuit frapper le grand écueil
Dans l'Océan trompeur où chantait la Sirène,
Et le naufrage horrible inclina sa carène
Aux profondeurs du Gouffre, immuable cerceuil.

Ce fut un Vaisseau d'Or dont les flancs diaphanes
Révélaient des trésors que les marins profanes,
Dégoût, Haine et Névrose, ont entre eux disputés.

Que reste-t-il de lui dans la tempête brève?
Qu'est devenu mon cœur, navire déserté?
Hélas! Il a sombré dans l'abîme du Rêve! (312)

While the trope of the boat wrecked at sea is an ancient one, the ship as representative of the poet's personal experience has a more narrow history. One of its earliest manifestations in French literature, Abraham de Vermeil's "Je m'embarque joyeux ...", which dates from the first decades of the seventeenth century, is worth noting in relation to Nelligan's poem:

Je m'embarque joyeux, et ma voile pompeuse
M'oste desja la terre et me donne les mers,
Je ne voi que le Ciel uni aux sillons pers
C'est le premier estat de mon ame amoureuse.

Puis je vois s'eslever une vapeur confuse,
Ombrageant tout le Ciel qui se fend en esclairs;
Le tonnerre grondant s'anime par les airs,
C'est le second estat dont elle est languoureuse.

Le troisiesme est le flot hideusement frisé,
Le mast rompu des vents et le timon brisé,
Le navire enfondrant, la perte du courage.

Le quatriesme est la mort entre les flots salez
Abbatus, rebatus, vomis et avalez;
Bref mon Amour n'est rien qu'un horrible naufrage. (132)

This voyage on a ship functions as a trope representing the four stages of the poet's experience of love. Illustrating the first stage is the joy on boarding the ship under a clear blue sky, which resembles the confidence expressed in the opening stanza of Nelligan's "Le Vaisseau d'Or," as well as the initial euphoria that marks Rimbaud's "Le Bateau ivre." However, this exuberance quickly yields to clouds, thunder, and lightning (second stage), as in the middle stanzas of Nelligan's poem, then to the wreck of the ship (third stage), and finally to death: "Bref mon Amour n'est rien qu'un horrible naufrage." The similarities between Vermeil's poem and Nelligan's are sufficiently clear. Both are sonnets featuring a shipwreck at sea, but more importantly, they share an analogous thematic structure – from exaltation to destruction. While Vermeil's poem is related in the first person by one who identifies the voyage as emblematic of the stages of his love, Nelligan's poetic voice, which likewise relates a sentimental adventure, itself becomes the ship. Both, however, are poems of failure, Nelligan's ending in madness, Vermeil's in a horrific death of the love relationship.

Vermeil, little known even to specialists, has never been evoked in any discussion of Nelligan, and it is highly unlikely that a late nineteenth-century Montrealer would have known this sonnet. One poem he probably did know, de Borelly's "La barge d'or," which appeared in *Le Samedi* in 1894, may very well have inspired Nelligan's title. As Wyczynski has pointed out (1960, 240), the poem is not without stylistic features in common with Nelligan's "Le Vaisseau d'Or":

C'était une nef, ou mieux une barge,
Caravelle un peu, galère à demi,
Faite pour tenir les gros temps du large
Comme pour voguer sous un ciel ami.
[…]
Cette barge était, carène et bordages,
Un bijou, miracle en or ciselé:
D'or, tout était d'or sauf quelques cordages
Et quelques haubans en argent filé. (qtd by Wyczynski 1960, 239–40)

While this poem does not follow the exaltation/destruction pattern, it could well have supplied Nelligan with the image of the title, the idea of a ship made of precious metal, and even the first clause of the poem.

For most readers, however, the likely poem of comparison would be Rimbaud's "Le Bateau ivre." Edmund Wilson may have been the most prominent critic to link Nelligan with Rimbaud (97), but the connection had been made as early as 1941 when, shortly after Nelligan's death, the Montreal newspaper *Le Jour* published an article, perhaps by Dantin, entitled "Celui qu'on pourrait appeler 'le Rimbaud canadien.'" Nor has there been a shortage of passing linkages between the two poets in the last six decades.[6] Most of these *rapprochements* have done little more than repeat the well-known biographical parallels, particularly the striking fact that both poets wrote practically all their poems between the ages of fifteen or sixteen and nineteen or twenty and then appeared to stop writing altogether, though for different reasons.[7] It might be possible to get a better perspective on Nelligan, however, if we were to compare their best-known poems rather than their lives.

A few critics have moved in this direction, emphasizing intellectual and artistic rather than biographical parallels between the two poets. Réjean Robidoux has suggested that Nelligan, without knowing Rimbaud's now famous "lettre du voyant," had put its directives into practice (1992, 163; Grisé et al. 138), a perspective that needs to be tempered by the recognition that Nelligan's understanding of subjectivity was quite different from Rimbaud's. Paul Wyczynski has proposed that "Le Vaisseau d'Or" was for Nelligan what "Le Bateau ivre" was for its author: "un résumé poétique de sa vie et son art" (1965, 101). Indeed, "Le Bateau ivre" and "Le Vaisseau d'Or" do lend themselves to a fruitful encounter. Rimbaud's poem dates from 1871, but was not published until 1883 in the review *Lutèce*. It was reprinted in Verlaine's *Les Poètes maudits* in 1884, in *La Plume* in 1890, in *Le Reliquaire* in 1891, and in the *Poésies complètes* in 1895. It is not known when Nelligan composed "Le Vaisseau d'Or," which he never published nor recited at the École littéraire de Montréal and which first appeared in its entirety in *La Revue canadienne* in 1903, but it was certainly not before 1897 and probably not before 1899.[8] It is possible, then, for Nelligan to have had access to Rimbaud's poem,[9] and indeed Jean Charbonneau, who knew Nelligan during his creative period, affirmed that "le 'Bateau ivre' emporte la préférence de notre poète" (1935, 122). There is, however, no corroborating contemporary testimony of this.[10] It is also possible that Nelligan had seen Rimbaud's *Une Saison en enfer*, which was included in the *Poésies complètes* of 1895 (it had been published though not circulated in 1873). *Une Saison en enfer* is of some interest because "Adieu," the final section of the book, evokes a vision that contains the title of Nelligan's poem: "Quelquefois je vois au ciel des plages sans fin couvertes de blanches nations en joie. Un grand vaisseau d'or, au-dessus de moi, agite ses pavillons multicolores dans les brises du matin" (140). "Vaisseau d'or" is an unusual enough collocation – Apollinaire would use "des vaisseaux d'or" in 1908 – that it might be tempting to see Rimbaud as a possible source for it. Neither *vaisseau* nor *or* is uncommon in Nelligan's poetry, however, and there is no evidence that Nelligan knew *Une Saison en enfer.* If there is a specific source for the title, it is, as we've seen, more likely de Borelly's "La barge d'or." Nelligan, who may have known Thomas Gray's "The Bard," as Alfred DesRochers suggested (195–6), may also have remembered the line "In gallant trim, the gilded vessel goes" (Gray 80). He used "nefs d'or" in "Potiche" and the verse "Ce vaisseau d'or qui glisse avec l'amour en poupe," in "Banquet macabre," a poem probably composed in April or May 1899 (see Wyczynski 1971, 119). The use of a ship as an image for a person – though not of gold – is, of course, present in Baudelaire as well as in Rodenbach. The possibility that Nelligan had direct knowledge of Rimbaud's poem needs to be acknowledged, but a familiarity with "Le Bateau ivre" does not imply an influence and does not in any case carry much interpretive potential. What is more interesting is how these two poems intersect and how they diverge.

The formal differences are clear enough. Although both texts are written in alexandrine verse, Nelligan's poem, like Vermeil's, is a sonnet, the form preferred in the nineteenth century by the Parnassians because of the discipline and condensation it imposes, while Rimbaud's is a lengthier poem containing twenty-five stanzas. Fourteen lines versus one hundred constitute clearly different dimensions requiring distinct poetic strategies. What invites a comparative study of the two poems is not their formal similarity but the fact that they are both structured around the central image of a ship at sea. In early Christian art, the ship was a symbol of hope, and semes of hope and especially of confidence are evident in the opening lines of both poems (as well as Vermeil's). Nelligan's poem depicts *ab initio* a large ship hewn from solid gold with masts touching the sky, clearly a vessel destined to inspire confidence. Rimbaud's opening features an escape from *les haleurs*, the boat-towers associated with authority figures, permitting the poetic narrator to venture boldly on his own.

Yet each poem attaches different values to the nautical craft. Not only is Nelligan's ship large (*vaisseau* is by definition a sizable vessel) and great ("Vaisseau" has a capital *V*), but its very designation as a *vaisseau* marks it positively. *Vaisseau*, as I have noted, is not an unfamiliar word in the lexicon of Nelligan's poetry[11] where it appears as a means of attaining the ideal. In "Placet pour des cheveux," he speaks of the day "que nous prendrons vaisseau / Sur la mer idéale" (151); in "Jardin sentimental" he declares that "dans un grand vaisseau vert, / Nous rêvions de monter aux astres de Vesper" (125). Moreover, *vaisseau* is associated with the voyage to adulthood. "La Fuite de l'enfance," one of many of Nelligan's poems tainted with precocious nostalgia, ends with the poet's invitation to his companion to follow him "devers les idéales côtes, / La fuite de l'Enfance au vaisseau des Vingt ans" (119). For Nelligan, then, *vaisseau* consociates the quest for the ideal and the passage to adulthood. Rimbaud's *bateau* conveys no such association. Ships, boats, or other sea craft do not occupy a central position in his poetry. Nelligan is a master at reworking about a dozen key images, some of which are prominent in this poem. Rimbaud, whose imagery is far richer, creates for the purposes of "Le Bateau ivre" what is for him a unique image: in no other of his poems does the boat appear in any significant way.

The modifiers in the titles present still other divergences. Nelligan's ship is of gold; Rimbaud's boat is drunken. "[T]aillé dans l'or," as Réjean Robidoux (23) and André Gervais (34) have reminded us, constitutes poetic license, since gold is not chiseled but cast from a molten state. Yet the image, present in de Borelly's poem ("en or ciselé"), carries more consciously artistic semes than would *moulé*. The careful, painstaking work associated with the act of chiseling further reinforces the precious character of this ship that is also a work of art. The word *or* as the substance or as the colour appears frequently in Nelligan's texts where it is most often a positive marker, as

I've noted in my discussion of his relationship to Parnassianism. The word *ivre*, on the other hand, is not particularly Rimbaldian: it occurs only three other times in Rimbaud's work, although its nominal form figures in the title of the prose poem "Matinées d'ivresse," an exaltation of the altered states of consciousness produced by hashish. The concept of inebriation does cohere with his call for a *dérèglement de tous les sens*, however, and *ivre* is connected to the body of this poem through a series of related signifiers: "tâches de vin blanc," "vomissures," "alcool," and "fermentent."

Thus Nelligan's title projects largely positive signifiers that are prominent within the corpus of his texts. Rimbaud's title does not resonate with salient signifiers from his other texts, but is perhaps more effective than Nelligan's title in telling us something about the poem. As a title, "Le Vaisseau d'Or" gives no hint that the self of the poet might be present in the text and might lead a reader unfamiliar with Nelligan to expect a glittering Parnassian description, something this poem decidedly is not. "Le Bateau ivre," however, suggests a prosopopoeia, so that the reader knows the text will not be a simple description of a nautical craft. This boat will clearly stand for a person. We have reached here a fundamental divergence between Nelligan's and Rimbaud's poems, one which the opening lines of each poem underscore.

"Comme je descendais des Fleuves impassibles": the first line of Rimbaud's poem introduces a first person consciousness that remains the voice throughout its one hundred lines. It is clear from the outset that the poem records a personal experience, be it imagined or not. The first person controls the text: the personal pronoun "je" occurs twenty-four times, "moi" six times, "me" four times. Ten of the twenty-five stanzas begin with a first person pronoun. Possessive adjectives are also in evidence: "ma" is used twice, "mon" twice, and "mes" four times. An iterative paradigm of first person signifiers explicitly controls the textual components of "Le Bateau ivre."

The poem narrates a break away from authority figures, an uncontrolled personal adventure which initially brings about great joy, exaltation, and exhilaration ("je me suis baigné dans le Poème / De la mer," lines 21–2) but turns to deception, suffering, horror, and, eventually, to a desire for self-destruction: "O que ma quille éclate!" (line 92). This verse, the ninth from the end, is only the second in the present tense, all the others having been in the past.

Ninety per cent of the poem relates a past adventure, one that began "l'autre hiver." Line 84 is the first in the present: "Je regrette l'Europe aux anciens parapets." This line and the last nine of the poem, also in the present, represent the feelings of the narrative voice at the moment of narration. This same voice has sustained the poem from "je descendais" in verse 1 to "je ne puis plus" in verse 97. The poem's closure represents the narrative voice's resignation to the *status quo ante*, to the situation before the beginning of the adventure that has just been narrated.

"Le Vaisseau d'Or" diverges sharply from "Le Bateau ivre" on a number of these points. While a first person poetic voice controls "Le Bateau ivre" from its beginning, the first person does not clearly emerge in "Le Vaisseau d'Or" until the penultimate line. The reader familiar with Nelligan's corpus might be able to make the association between the ship and the poetic voice earlier since the expression "mon cœur vaisseau" occurs in the poem "Je veux m'éluder" (308). Taken singly, though, the poem builds up to a recognition of the identity of the ship and the poetic voice. The first clue appears in the second line, where the text specifies that "Ses mâts touchaient l'azur." We easily perceive the vertical direction that marks the spatiality of Nelligan's poetry, but we recognize as well in "azur" a word that in nineteenth-century French poetry had very specific connotations. *Azur* in Baudelaire, Mallarmé, and countless others signifies the ideal. Familiarity with this connotation leads us to suspect that this golden ship may well represent a quest for the ideal "sur des mers inconnues," the latter syntagm evoking the sense of adventure and discovery, and perhaps also the originality, of his quest. In the next line, however, semes emerge that in Nelligan usually stand in opposition to the ideal, namely semes of sexuality: "La Cyprine d'amour, cheveux épars, chairs nues, / S'étalait à sa proue, au soleil excessif." "La Cyprine d'amour" clearly designates Venus, not a blue stone (!), as R.-S. Catta proposed in a mistaken attempt to deeroticize the verse (79), since Cyprine is one of the attested names for the Roman goddess of love. Nor is it excluded that Nelligan could have known that one of the meanings of "Cyprian" in English is a lewd woman or a prostitute and wished to activate these semes in this instance. Venus's presence here is appropriate since she was born from the sea. But this is not the idealized goddess of love; she is, rather, more of a Cyprian: a sultry temptress, naked like Gretchen/Anadyomène in "Gretchen la pâle," lying at the ship's prow, her hair disheveled. That she is sprawled in the sun, excessive sun specifies the text, completes the sensuality of the picture. The image also recalls "Banquet macabre," whose first stanza concludes with the image of "Ce vaisseau d'or qui glisse avec l'amour en poupe" (308) and may derive from Thomas Gray's "In gallant trim, the gilded vessel goes, / Youth at the prow, and Pleasure at the helm" (Gray 80; see DesRochers 195–6). While Rimbaud initially emphasizes the new sense of freedom he is experiencing, Nelligan's poem is marked by connotations of the sensual.

In "Gretchen la pâle," Venus is dangerous; she is "ce démon ... le Paros qui tue avec ses bras de marbre" (153). This stance differs considerably from that of Rimbaud's "Soleil et chair" in which the poet exclaims, "O Vénus, ô Déesse! / Je regrette les temps de l'antique jeunesse," only to repeat later in the poem, "Je crois en toi! je crois en toi! Divine mère, / Aphrodite marine!" (28, 29). In the second quatrain of "Le Vaisseau d'Or," it becomes evident that the sexuality Venus represents is associated with the wreck of the ship: "Mais il vint une nuit frapper le grand écueil / Dans l'Océan trompeur où chantait la Sirène." The shift from bright light ("au soleil excessif") to darkness ("une nuit") may signal the forthcoming victory of the forces of evil. An *écueil*, which means a reef or any dangerous obstacle, is here qualified as "grand," making it a worthy adversary to the "grand Vaisseau." In two manuscript versions, one dating from the 1920s and the other from 1935, Nelligan substituted "grave écueil" for "grand écueil," perhaps to emphasize the serious danger of the reef. The broader meaning of *écueil* is useful if we consider that bodies of water are common metaphors for life, especially in the French literary tradition since Chateaubriand and Lamartine. A line of Rollinat's verse that was certainly known to Nelligan expressed not only the well-known metaphor but much of the meaning of Nelligan's poem as well: "La Vie est un vaisseau dont le Mal est l'écueil" (2:257). "[L]'Océan trompeur" recalls, moreover, "ce monde menteur" of "Mon Âme." We can assume that the ocean – or life – is "trompeur" because of woman, a topos dating from Genesis. Sirens, who were said to attract sailors onto reefs, are also symbols of the seductive woman. The association of woman, water, and the destruction of a man reappears in "Le Puits hanté," a strange rondel in which a mad priest is drowned in a well by an unnamed woman. The age-old allegory – the pure man led to his death by the impure woman – haunted this young poet.

Wyczynski's suggestion that Nelligan's siren "appartient à ces océanides calmement peintes par Joseph Autran" (1960, 239) in "Les Océanides" is misleading, for Autran's sirens are not excessively threatening and, indeed, seem missed by the poetic narrator:

Que de nuits à nager près des plages sereines,
A folâtrer, tandis que nos sœurs les Sirènes
Attiraient à l'écueil par leurs voix souveraines
La barque désireuse et craignant d'approcher!

Cet heureux temps n'est plus. (1:86)

What for Nelligan is an *écueil* is presented in Autran more as an *accueil*. Nelligan's siren, moreover, is not a sister and she can be destructive: "Et le naufrage horrible inclina sa carène / Aux profondeurs du Gouffre, immuable cercueil." The experience narrated here is far removed from Leopardi's famous closing line of "L'Infinito" in which he proclaims "E 'l naufragar m'è dolce in questo mare" (1:132). Leopardi imagines a shipwreck in the infinite as pleasurable, but this is clearly not Nelligan's situation. Nor does the poetic persona's sinking represent a purifying entry into the maternal womb, as it does in some other poets, such as Saint-Denys Garneau. The verb *incliner*, which contains connotations of "bowing to" and "yielding to," suggests submission to a greater force. With "Gouffre," the abyss, the other pole of Nelligan's vertical spatiality is specified, but we encounter as well a word which in nineteenth-century French poetry from Hugo onwards evoked either hell or nothingness. Jacques Michon was certainly correct to place the Siren among the various "médiateurs infernaux" that can be found in Nelligan's poetry (1983, 43). Whether the sexual encounter was real, as Bessette proposed (59), or imaginary, the quest for the ideal has foundered on the reef of sexuality. The ship has been transformed into a coffin.

The two quatrains, which tell of the proud ship and its demise, are situated in the past. So is the first tercet, which reflects on the event. The opening verse of the first quatrain, "C'était un grand Vaisseau taillé dans l'or massif," is compressed into the first hemistich of the initial line of the tercet: "Ce fut un Vaisseau d'Or," its compression including a significant change of tense: the duration emphasized by the imperfect of the first line is replaced by a preterite finality. "Vaisseau" retains its capital *V* while "or" takes on the upper-case O it carries in the title. This would seem to be a reaffirmation of the solidity, and especially of the richness and precious value of the ship; the poet is stressing his own worth to underscore the pathos of his fate. But now, this ship made of gold is said to have diaphanous sides:

> dont les flancs diaphanes
> Révélaient des trésors que les marins profanes,
> Dégoût, Haine et Névrose, entre eux ont disputés.

Were this a mimetic text, we would be confronted with an absurdity: nothing could be of solid gold and be at the same time diaphanous. At the level of semiosis, however, it is clear that "or massif" now retains mainly the semes of richness and solidity while "diaphanes" retains the seme of revelation. Treasure lost at sea is common coin of much imaginative discourse. Joseph Autran expressed in his collection of sea poems the popular belief that the ocean is full of sunken treasures: "O mer! sinistre mer! N'as-tu donc pas assez / Enfoui de trésors sous ton onde entassés" (1:176). The treasures in Nelligan's poem more probably refer to the genius the poet contains within him. The first tercet, then, introduces another crucial element into the poem. This ship is not only a person with sensual yearnings; it is also a poet, a notion intimated in the second line when its masts were said to reach "l'azur." The revelation of these treasures is not, however, complete; diaphanous does not imply transparency. That they are revealed is also important because of what is done to them. The sailors, who should be responsible for the safe passage of the ship, had, instead, been fighting over its treasures. But who are these "marins profanes"? The syntax identifies them with "Dégoût, Haine et Névrose," which appear to be in apposition to "marins." The sailors embody disgust, hatred, and neurosis, and are thereby incapable of understanding the quest for the ideal.[12] They might well then represent society at large, a reading corroborated by one of Nelligan's transcriptions of part of this poem in 1938. In this transcription, he added after the last line the phrase "Le monde par ses soins ne changera pas" with, on the line below and to the right, the word "Alceste" (M 282). This quotation is of interest for several reasons. In the first place, the line is not by Alceste, but rather it is addressed *to* Alceste by Philinthe who, in *Le*

Misanthrope, is the voice of acceptance of society as it is. Secondly, Nelligan has slightly revised the quotation. In Molière's play, Philinthe says to Alceste: "Le monde par *vos* soins ne changera pas." Nelligan is not addressing Alceste but referring to him: the substitution of the second person possessive adjective by one in the third person is intended to be a reflection on the futility of Alceste's efforts to change society. After some thirty-nine years of internment for insanity, Nelligan was still recopying this poem and placing it within the context of society's hostility. An alternate reading might place "Dégoût, Haine, et Névrose" in apposition to "trésors," thereby attributing these qualities to the poetic voice. In this case, these might be the sentiments resulting from the encounter with the *Sirène*. As Bessette has reminded us, if there had in fact been a sexual experience, this would have caused in this Catholic adolescent disgust, self-hatred, and stress (59).

It is clear, though, that these treasures belong to the poetic voice and that this is his adventure, as we learn in the final tercet:

> Que reste-t-il de lui dans la tempête brève?
> Qu'est devenu mon cœur, navire deserté?
> Hélas! Il a sombré dans l'abîme du Rêve!

The abyss recovers the semes of "Gouffre" in line 8 to designate the depths of the poet's fall. "[L]'abîme du Rêve" can be read as the abyss caused by the world of dreams, by an excessive imagination. In one of his transcriptions during his internment, Nelligan substituted "les racines du Rêve" for "l'abîme du Rêve" (M 73), violating the rules of prosody but stressing further the roots of his tragedy. The hole or the abyss is a recurring image in Nelligan. From the "puits noir" into which the mad priest has been thrown ("Le Puits hanté") and the ditch where the idiot woman was found dead ("L'Idiote aux cloches") to the poet's desire in "Prélude triste" to "mourir dans mon trou" (241), the image expresses his sense of having already sunk into an abyss from which he cannot rise. His regret at this defeat is explicit in "Ténèbres" where the poet confesses: "Et je rêve toujours au vaisseau des Vingt ans, / Depuis qu'il a sombré dans la mer des étoiles." (311)

The semes of confidence and hope of the first lines of both Nelligan's and Rimbaud's nautical poems have disappeared. As Jacques Michon has reminded us, the world of dreams is not in this instance a "récupération symbolique du monde" (1983, 69). Indeed, the poet can no longer retrieve the world, symbolically or otherwise, and can only ascertain his condition in it. Nelligan's "Le Lac," a poem with clear Lamartinian resonances but without Lamartine's futile hope that somehow nature will retain the memory of human experience, confirms the boat as an object of destruction. After recalling the death of two lovers as their boat sinks, the poet affirms that life is like a body of water which conceals "De blonds rêves déçus, d'illusions noyées, / Où l'Espoir vainement mire ses astres d'or." (263) The ship, which in the history of Western signification has sometimes symbolized safety – the early Christian fathers spoke of the Church as the ship of salvation – has led instead to destruction. The fact that it is a ship made of gold that is wrecked renders its sinking all the more tragic, as Jacques Ferron astutely observed (1969, 89). The penultimate line of Philippe Desportes's sixteenth-century sonnet on Icarus encompasses the trajectory that "Chateaux en Espagne" and "Le Vaisseau d'Or" represent: "Le ciel fut son désir, la mer sa sépulture" (12), the first hemistich encapsulating the thrust of the former poem, the second, the ultimate failure of the latter. Desportes's positive inference, "Est-il plus beau dessein, ou plus riche tombeau?" (12), is contrary, however, to Nelligan's dejected outlook.

Nelligan's most direct poetic heir, Saint-Denys Garneau, appropriated the theme of the sinking ship at the age of eighteen, about the same age as Nelligan when he wrote "Le Vaisseau d'Or." Garneau's poem invites some reflection because it can be read as the logical continuation of Nelligan's poem and even as a reflection on Nelligan's poetic trajectory. Significantly, it is entitled "Sombrer":

Ah! cette volupté sans bornes de périr,
De sombrer dans la mer de la désespérance,
Dans un océan noir de morbide souffrance
Où la raison s'enlise et se comprend mourir!

Sentir, sentir qu'on disparaît dans l'ombre immense
Et puis, sombrer toujours, ne pas se retenir,
Entendre au fond de soi quelque chose frémir,
Croire que c'est la mort peut-être qui commence ...

Le navire a frappé quelqu'invisible écueil:
Penché dessus le gouffre noir comme un cercueil,
Il frémit dans la nuit qui l'environne; il sombre ...

Le capitaine est là, superbe, sur le pont;
Il n'a pas voulu fuir. Ivre, de son œil sombre,
Il regarde monter les abîmes sans fond! (112–13)

Garneau's poem exhibits not only a broad Nelliganian theme, the anticipation of death, but also shares with "Le Vaisseau d'Or" a number of lexical items (*sombrer*, *écueil*, *gouffre*, *cercueil*, *nuit*, *abîmes*) in addition to its structuring image. Garneau's choice to express death through the image of sinking, *sombrer*, engages his poem within the imagery of the Christian tradition in which sinking can also connote a fall from grace, but it links it as well with the strong vertical thrust of Nelligan's imagination. Like Nelligan's ship, Garneau's also hits a reef which, though not overtly sexual as in Nelligan's poem, represents something that, being invisible, could not be avoided. The Vignian ending, featuring a captain who refuses to abandon ship, cannot mask the strong persistence in French-Canadian letters of the Nelliganian conviction that sinking into the depths is part of destiny.

What can we conclude about Nelligan from the meeting of his text with that of Rimbaud? We note, first, that Nelligan, although a poet very much present in his poetry, is also capable of restraining the self's revelation, in this case until the end of the poem. We also have confirmation that Nelligan, who – unlike Rimbaud – refrains from revolting against Western civilization, is more likely to rework personal obsessional themes, reusing a limited number of images. One of these images is the ship, which in this poem he identifies with the poet, as does Rimbaud in his own poem. While Rimbaud's poem, however, is circular in that the poetic voice yearns to return to reduced dimensions, Nelligan's is linear since the voice in his text resigns itself to the world of uncontrollable dreams. "Et je voudrais rêver longuement, l'âme entière, / Sous les cyprès de la mort" (311), he confirms in "Ténèbres."[13] More important, however, is the manner in which both poets interpret their failure. Rimbaud clearly lays the blame on his own inability. His boat survived "l'assaut des récifs" (line 42) as well as the "échouages hideux" (line 54), so his powerlessness to continue is largely a result of his own incapacity. "Lassé" (line 61), diminished to a "planche folle" (line 78), he admits to his impotence: "j'ai trop pleuré" (line 89); "Je ne puis plus" (line 97). Nelligan, for his part, deflects the blame to forces outside himself. His ship does hit a reef but, unlike Rimbaud's boat, sinks.

Within the poetic texture of the poem, this reef is, we know, sexuality. His destruction is a result of sensual temptation, seen as something coming from outside rather than within him. Nelligan is attributing his ruin in part to the Siren's lures. But he is also ascribing his downfall to society at large, to the "marins profanes" who have not been able to understand him. The poet-*navire* is "déserté": he has been abandoned by the woman who displayed her seductive charms, and also by the community that refused to sustain him. Sexuality and society rather than his own inability account for his failure. Rimbaud's adventure, which is presented as having lasted longer than Nelligan's, was a learning experience ("Je sais," lines 29, 30; "j'ai vu," 32, 33; "j'ai rêvé," 37; "j'ai suivi," 41), and might have been an exemplary one ("J'aurais voulu montrer aux enfants ces dorades / Du flot bleu, ces poissons d'or, ces poissons chantants," lines 57–8). But there is nothing of the *Bildungsgedicht* in Nelligan's text. This is why, unlike Rimbaud, he does not wish to return to a simpler, smaller scale of things, why he accepts the dream-world of madness, why, in the end, this poem might also be an extended pun – why *le vaisseau d'or* might also imply that *le vaisseau dort*.

The sense of failure is not, for all that, less acute, nor, would it appear, less long-lasting. Jean Larose (106–7) casually reports that Nelligan's nephew, Gilles Corbeil, told him that he once witnessed Nelligan begin to recite "Le Vaisseau d'Or" and then suddenly veer into a recitation from Hugo's narrative of the battle of Waterloo in *Les Misérables*, and then return to complete the recitation of his poem. This anecdote led Jacques Michon to point out the logic of this detour: the narrative of Waterloo, the story of a major defeat, precedes a section of the novel entitled "Le Vaisseau l'Orion" (1981, 51). Nelligan's title, then, is embedded in Hugo's. Importantly, the ship in question, once a glorious warship, is now "un navire malade" (Hugo 1969, 11:300), a condition that could be attributed to Nelligan's "mon cœur, navire déserté." The Orion's narrative has led from greatness to illness. Interestingly, Hugo inserts into this chapter a discussion of France's war with Spain in 1823, a victory for the French that Hugo nevertheless discusses in a register of defeat. For Hugo, France's success against Spain marked the defeat of the ideals of the French Revolution. It is perhaps relevant to note as well that the last part of the chapter immediately preceding the Waterloo narrative is entitled "Tombeau convenable," a title that would resonate with Nelligan's imagination. The reference is to the burial of Fantine in a pauper's grave. When, in the account given by Gilles Corbeil, Nelligan begins reciting "Le Vaisseau d'Or," interrupts it to quote from Hugo's chapter on Waterloo, and then returns to the poem, he is placing Waterloo, a historic defeat, at the centre of the preoccupations of "Le Vaisseau d'Or," just as Hugo had placed this narrative between "Tombeau convenable" and "Le Vaisseau l'Orion," all three chapters dealing with different defeats of an ideal, in this case, that of the French Revolution.

"JE VEUX M'ÉLUDER ..."

The sense of failure associated with both sexuality and society and the acceptance of madness as an escape are even sharper in "Je veux m'éluder ... ," a poem that Nelligan never published nor recited publicly, but which appears to have been written about the same time as "Le Vaisseau d'Or" (see RW 538):

Je veux m'éluder dans les rires,
Dans des tourbes de gaîté brusque,
Oui, je voudrais me tromper jusque
En des ouragans de délires.

Pitié! quels monstrueux vampires
Vont suçant mon cœur qui s'offusque!
Oh! je veux être fou, ne fut-ce que
Pour narguer mes Détresses pires!

Latent comme un monstre cadavre
Mon cœur vaisseau s'amarre au havre
De toute hétéromorphe engeance.

Que je bénis ces gueux de rosses
Dont les hilarités féroces
Raillent la vierge Intelligence. (306)

The initial verses of this strange poem[14] appropriate a theme of "La Romance du vin," also from the same period, in which the poet evokes false laughter as an antidote to his sadness. What is particular in "Je veux m'éluder ..." is the poet's resolve, stressed by the initial

"Je veux" and repeated by "Oh! je veux ..." in line 7. Yet the excessive language signals the factitiousness of these outward signs of happiness: "tourbes de gaîté brusque" designates a kind of unforeseen mêlée (*tourbes* <Lat. *turba*: crowd) and transmits semes of tempestuousness that are echoed in "ouragan de délires." While "délires" figuratively and perhaps more commonly refers to the agitation associated with high emotion, the literal meaning of the abnormal mental condition of delirium is surely active here. The second quatrain makes clear the extent to which the poet is overwhelmed: the "monstrueux vampires" are sucking his heart. The prominence of the image of the heart, repeated in the tercets, suggests that this personal devastation is related to sensuality as well as to his status as a poet. In this situation, madness is the lesser of two evils, since it would allow him to thumb his nose at his distress (capitalized in the text). It is important to note the two meanings of "fou" at play in this context. The first and most obvious refers to the state of madness the poet wishes to appropriate. In doing so, he shares the vision of poetic madness that Jacques Blais has called the "vouloir-vivre-fou" (1999, 274) that was especially prominent among the Decadents.[15] But "fou" also means "fool" in the sense of buffoon, as in the expression *le fou du roi*. That Nelligan intended this meaning as well becomes clear when we take note of the fact that Nelligan never decided between two versions of line 7. The manuscript version, the only extant autograph copy (reproduced in RW 307), shows that "Je veux être fou" is actually written above the words "qu'on me fasse fou," which Nelligan did not strike out in any fashion. "Qu'on me fasse fou" carries the sense of being appointed to the position of fool, which would allow him to mock his own anguish. The ambiguity between the yearning for madness that would allow him to escape into his private world and the desire to pretend to be mad (as would a court fool) captures nicely Nelligan's own ambiguities regarding madness.

The first tercet is crucial, for it establishes an incisive, startling image: his heart becomes a ship ("Mon cœur vaisseau"), while being compared to a monstrous corpse ("un monstre cadavre"). His metonymic identification with his heart and his association with a cadaver suggests that his sentimental and perhaps sensual life, though anchored safely and protected from those who despise him, is now dead. In the second tercet, the poet effects a semantic shift to evoke the incomprehension and derision of society. The "vierge Intelligence" that is surely his own is the object of the ferocious hilarity of the "gueux de rosses," a designation that carries semes of viciousness. The poet, not sparing his irony, takes it as a mark of distinction that he is persecuted: "que je bénis ces gueux de rosses" (line 12). Their mockery and disdain confirm his status as other than what they are, while also confirming his need for illusion ("je voudrais me tromper jusque / En des ouragans de délires" lines 3–4) or even delusion. The beleaguered "cœur vaisseau," which in "Le Vaisseau d'Or" had let itself sink into "les racines du rêve," finds in this poem safe harbour only within madness or its pretense.

Nelligan's adventure at sea, like Vermeil's and Rimbaud's, is at odds with that of Victor Hugo, the nineteenth century's foremost optimist, whose poem "A M. de Lamartine" uses the trope of the ship at sea to evoke both a stunning success and the possibility of failure. This poem is of some interest, not because of its similarities with "Le Vaisseau d'Or," as Catta has maintained (80–1), but because of its radical difference from it. Hugo imagines both Lamartine, to whom this poem is offered in homage, and himself as ships at sea. Both are seekers of truth who are misunderstood and even hated by the masses. Both must battle with the storms at sea, but eventually Hugo's ship loses sight of Lamartine's and must fight the storms alone. Lamartine's ship, though, reappears on the horizon as a magnificent and triumphant vessel now acclaimed by the masses, while Hugo is still struggling at sea. He asks Lamartine to grieve over him if he should fail, as Columbus would grieve over La Pérouse (a French explorer killed by indigenous peoples). The reader has the clear impression, however, that Hugo does not really expect failure, but anticipates a triumphant return similar to Lamartine's. Indeed, from the first stanza he has insisted on the parallelism of their itinerary, using the word "même" three times in the space of five verses. This insistence on their similarity returns in the tenth stanza where the poet asserts that they had both wanted to "Doubler le même promontoire, / Remporter la même victoire, / Dépasser le siècle en courroux" (55). Hugo's understanding of the myth of the misunderstood, persecuted artist is subordinated to a confidence in his eventual success and glory.

This is clearly not the case for Nelligan, in whose poetry key elements of the Romantic myth of the artist merge with a deep sense of personal failure. Hugo set out on the sea of life with high goals, seeking to "devine[r] le mystère" (1970, 58) and comparing his own sense of purpose to da Gama's and Columbus's indomitable ambition (54). When exalted goals do emerge in Nelligan, such as in "Châteaux en Espagne," they are diminished by the poem's title and immediately destroyed in the tercets, for failure seems a given of his *Weltanschauung*. Nor is there, except perhaps fleetingly in "La Romance du vin," the defiance that we see Hugo depict in himself and Lamartine as they continue to proclaim their poetry undeterred by the storms around them:

Tandis que la foudre sublime
Planait tout en feu sur l'abîme
Nous chantions, hardis matelots,
La laissant passer sur nos têtes,
Et, comme l'oiseau des tempêtes,
Tremper ses ailes dans les flots! (55)

Only rarely, as in Fréchette (see his "La Poésie"), does such self-confidence surface in French-Canadian letters, where the prevailing mind-set is perhaps best exemplified by a weary Crémazie, writing in 1866 to abbé Casgrain from his exile in France that he had been "un mauvais marchand et un médiocre poète" (2:76). Crémazie's self-deprecation betrays a sense of low self-worth that is much in evidence in Nelligan and that would survive him. When Nelligan writes "nous nous sentons névrosés et vieillis, / Froissés, maltraités et sans armes, / Moroses et vieillis" (121), he is defining a world-view that Gaston Miron recognized as still thriving in the 1950s in the "nombreux silencieux raboteux rabotés / dans les brouillards de chagrins crus" (75). Indeed, Miron's virulent verse is an endeavour to exorcize a collective sense of alienation, to "tromp[er] l'attente hériditaire et misérable" (92) and thereby give birth to a collective rebellion against defeatism. Miron's is an attempt to reverse a traditional wisdom, expressed by Roseanna Lacasse in Gabrielle Roy's *Bonheur d'occasion* ("on ne fait pas comme on veut dans la vie; on fait comme on peut" [89]), that stressed the limited possibilities of human life and rendered concepts such as "victory" or "achievement" illusory. Unlike Baudelaire, Nelligan was incapable of seeing any greatness in being vanquished, of conceiving of himself as a "grandeur déchue," to borrow Pierre Emmanuel's formulation (96) of Baudelaire's self-conception. His sense of failure in both art and love partakes of a broader sense of defeat that has long seized the collective French-Canadian imagination, one that various critics have seen as derivative of the defeat of 1759, when the previous conquerors were themselves subjugated. The considerable impact of the British conquest, that "blessure toujours ouverte" (Bouthillette 13), on the Quebec historical consciousness, remained throughout the nineteenth century in an uneasy tension with the equally strong vision of French Canada as a morally superior culture with a spiritual and intellectual destiny. This vision is absent from Nelligan's verse, as is the new optimism associated with the economic expansion and the triumph of political liberalism that coincided with his period of productivity.

The sense of defeat that permeates his poetry needs to be subsumed within a broader explanation that would include the religious teaching of which I spoke in the previous chapter, which, in addition to its harsh strictures on the expression of sexuality, promoted a sense of profound humiliation of the self. As an illustration, we need only consider Jean-Jacques Olier's *Introduction à la vie et aux vertus chrétiennes*, in which he warns his readers that pride is "le vice qui déplaît le plus à Dieu," calling it an "horrible et malheureux péché" for which God has "aversion et haine" (27). Olier's spiritual manual is laden with adages such as "le chrétien se défie de soi" (132), and "le chrétien se méprise" (132), "le chrétien se retire et se cache" (132), "le chrétien s'estim[e] moins que tous" (133). Christian humility, Olier maintained, was based on the awareness "qu'on ne vaut rien, qu'on ne sait rien, qu'on ne peut rien" (32). To be fair, these constitute only one dimension of a broad and complex spiritual teaching, but such notions, which may well have been transmitted at the École Olier when Nelligan was a pupil there, were certainly part of the pastoral teaching in Montreal. The over-heated rhetoric of abnegation that attended this discourse instilled a sense not only that success and accomplishment were not possible but that seeking them was in itself sinful. Like the *felix culpa* of Adam and Eve, like the providential defeat that protected Canada from the evils of the French Revolution, failures in this life protect us from our baser selves. For Nelligan, such a view could only lead to a profound dysphoria and a nostalgia for an imagined personal prelapsarian existence, subjects to which I now turn.

4 The Poetics of Melancholy and Nostalgia

While the condition of melancholy was first described in Hippocratic writings, its nosography has remained historically fluid. In the form of pervasive and chronic sadness, it has, however, significantly informed the thematics of Western poetry, especially since the British graveyard school of the mid-eighteenth century. Yet melancholy did not become a major preoccupation of French-Canadian poetry. Its rarity was remarked by the French consul in Canada, A. Lefaivre, who observed in an essay in 1877 that Canadian writers "ne sont jamais sérieusement atteints de notre spleen" (20), a judgment with which it would be difficult to quarrel. The earliest verse in French Canada consisted largely of commentary on social, political, and historical events, establishing a tradition of circumstantial poetry that remained strong in the nineteenth century. Such verse, which constitutes nearly all of the work of the century's most prolific poet, Adolphe Marsais, and comprises much of Crémazie's poetic production as well, continued to dominate well into Nelligan's time and beyond. Moreover, beginning in the early decades of the nineteenth century, poetry increasingly focused on the geography, topography, flora, and fauna of Canada, and, from the 1830s, its history. Much of the verse, including Crémazie's, was nationalist and patriotic and emphasized traditional values.

While the prevailing conservative aesthetic frowned on the display of intimate emotion of any kind, some verse tinged with melancholy did begin to appear with the dissemination of French Romantic poetry in Canada in the fourth decade of the century. Napoléon Aubin's "Tristesse," originally published in *La Minerve* in 1835 (and republished in James Huston's *Répertoire national* in 1848), is representative of this poetry. Yet, its most deeply melancholic stanza reads almost like a literary exercise:

Ô mélancolie
Qui partout me suis,
Vois, mon âme se plie
Aux faix des ennuis!
Chaque doux prestige
A qui devant toi
Monde où tout m'afflige,
Que veux-tu de moi? (Huston 1:334)

It has been suggested that this poem represents a personal emotion derived from a lived experience (Bisson 82); in any case, our chief interest in the European-born Aubin is that he was one of the first to introduce sadness as a poetic theme.[1] Although authentic instances of melancholy do surface in some of Crémazie's patriotic verse, such as "Le Drapeau de Carillon," as well as in Alfred Garneau (much of whose poetry was published after Nelligan had ceased writing new verse), Pamphile Lemay (see his "Tristesse"), and Évanturel ("Le Secret," "Soulagement," "Tristesse"), it is Nelligan's generation that made melancholy an important poetic theme. In the 1890s, a number of poems expressing melancholy appeared in cultural magazines published in Montreal such as *Le Samedi* and *Le Monde illustré*. Some of these are unremitting in their sadness, especially those by Silvio, a pseudonymous poet whose identity has remained a mystery (see Renaud 335–51). His "Poitrinaire"[2] and "Sonnet Triste"[3] reveal a distress so deep that its author wishes for death. Nelligan's friend Arthur de Bussières, in "Choses Mortes," counsels a friend, "Eh bien, pleurez! puisque c'est l'ordre ici; pleurez," revealing that he, too, does the same: "Pour moi qui pleure ainsi de n'avoir pu saisir / Un frisson d'idéal entrevue dans notre être."[4] Yet much of the melancholy expressed in the poetry of the period is assuaged by the comfort to be found in religion[5] or the voices of nature.[6] Moreover, cultural magazines in Montreal also published poems that urged *against* melancholy.[7]

Some instances of authentic melancholy can be discerned in the work of Nelligan's contemporary, the ill-fated Albert Lozeau, whose role in establishing the primacy of subjectivity in Quebec poetry has only recently been recognized.[8] Yet, given his personal situation (he was paralyzed in his late teens and remained bedridden until his death at age forty-six), it is surprising how little of his verse is marked by sorrow. What little sadness obtains in his poetry is resigned and accepting of pain as a blessing, an attitude exemplified in the opening lines of "La Belle Souffrance":

Oh! la bonne douleur qui nous fait l'âme forte!
Quelle paix bienheureuse et durable elle apporte,
Comme un vase de miel rempli jusqu'au bord,
Pour endormir le mal qu'elle engendra d'abord. (*L'Âme solitaire* 204)

Moreover, suffering tests "le métal / De notre âme, et le fait luisant comme un cristal" (204). Lozeau, who does not consider himself unique and who practices what one critic called a "stoïcisme souriant" (Paul-Crouzet 141), cannot be considered a "melancholy" poet. The same could be posited of Nelligan's fellow member of the École littéraire, Albert Ferland, who expresses his anguish in *La Consolatrice* (1898), but who concludes this dialogue with his muse with a defiant acceptance of the sad fate that is necessarily that of the poet.

It was Nelligan, then, who, more than any of his contemporaries, played the dolorous chord that Nerval had oxymoronically identified as "le soleil noir de la Mélancolie" (239). Georges-André Vachon has gone so far as to claim that "chez Nelligan, la mélancolie est comme le fondement de tous les thèmes, de toutes les images, elle est de l'ordre de l'essence" (105). The deep sadness of Nelligan's poetry was clear to his contemporaries as well, and Jean Charbonneau, who knew him well, dedicated his own poem "Le Vase de Tristesse" to him. By 1919, the French critic Louis Arnould was referring to Nelligan as "le jeune 'René' du Canada" (343), associating him with Chateaubriand's hapless protagonist. Significantly, in Nelligan's most serene poem, "Fantaisie créole," the poet's persona does not appear – it is a creole woman, not he, who sleeps peacefully amidst the perfumes of flowers – and the geographical references are Louisiana and Egypt, not Quebec. Clearly, Nelligan's normal mood is suffused with dysphoria while fleeting moments of joy are – as in "Fantaisie créole" – relegated to the vicarious imagination. Indeed, melancholy dominates about three dozen of Nelligan's poems, almost a quarter of his production.

Only one of these poems, "Silvio Corelli pleure," makes the slightest allusion to socio-economic reasons for the sadness evoked. The name chosen for the poem's persona, Silvio Corelli, whose voice is heard throughout the poem although the name does not appear in the body of the text, recalls well-known historical names: Silvio Pellico, whose *Le mie prigioni*, translated into French, was widely read in the nineteenth century; and Arcangelo Corelli, a seventeenth-century musician and composer for the violin (RW 350). Yet the persona in this poem has not been imprisoned, nor is there any indication that he composes music. This name provides part of the screen that allows the poet to express the sense of abandonment he clearly feels without revealing himself too openly. The concealment is accomplished by attributing the poem to Emile Kovar (Kovar = cover),[9] who is ostensibly writing the words of an orphaned musician with a name unlikely to be found in late nineteenth-century Montreal. His status as a musician, as one who is creative, suggests a link with the position of the poet.

Robidoux and Wyczynski consider the poem, only the second published by Nelligan, as "une naïve imitation du 'Je suis venu, calme orphelin' de Verlaine" (RW 350), but in fact the only link between the two poems is that both poetic personas are orphans. Verlaine's poetic voice, Gaspard, is, to be sure, rejected by men, women, and even death, but he does not share the profound sense of deprivation that is the lot of Nelligan's orphan. In this respect, the first two stanzas of Nelligan's poem establish the situation that is Corelli's:

Je ne suis qu'un être chétif:
Tout jeune, m'a laissé ma mère;
Je vais errant et maladif:
Je n'ai pas d'amis sur la terre.

Seul soutien et seul compagnon
– Gagne-pain de mes jours très drôle –
Je n'ai qu'un rude violon,
Pour gîte, l'ombrage d'un saule. (90)

The entire poem is dominated by the adverbial locution "ne ... que," with which it begins. The poet is deprived of health ("qu'un être chétif," "maladif"); a mother ("m'a laissé ma mère"); friends ("pas d'amis," "Seul soutien et seul compagnon"); quality possessions ("qu'un rude violon"); and home ("Pour gîte, l'ombrage d'un saule"). A willow, the well-worn symbol of melancholy, provides his only protection. Hardly a roving knight of medieval lore seeking after adventures and wrongs to right, he is a dispossessed wanderer, forsaken by family and friends. The crucial abandonment, however, is surely that of the mother, a detail worthy of retention since psychiatric discourse has for nearly a century maintained that melancholy frequently derives from a sense of maternal loss of some kind. "Chétif," which refers to a weak physical constitution, also means "miserable" and "wretched," suggesting the loss of self-esteem characteristic of melancholiacs.

The poem's strong first person voice (the pronoun "je" is used seven times in the compass of a twenty-line poem, all but once in initial position, while the possessive "ma/mon/mes" appears four times) establishes a personality who, while capable of irony, is conscious of all that he lacks while being aware of the greatness of his heart and the happiness that life could have:

Grand comme les cieux est mon cœur;
Et bien que mon œil soit sans flamme,
Je lis dans la vie un bonheur
Comme lit le Christ dans notre âme. (90)

The allusion to Christ strengthens his sense of abandonment and persecution. Moreover, the qualities of his mind have not attracted friends, for in the next stanza only nocturnal birds and a few disconsolate lovers (who do not seem to acknowledge him) are identified as appreciating the sad music he plays at night. Unlike the situation in Vigny's "La Flute," no authorial voice intervenes to reassure the mediocre musician that the greatness of his soul surpasses the poor quality of his instrument.

The final stanza expresses his recognition that his past, now but a memory, also constitutes his tomb:

Ainsi rêvant à l'avenir,
Je songe à mon printemps qui tombe;
Mon passé n'est qu'un souvenir,
Mais, hélas! il sera ma tombe. (90)

The poet is trapped in his past, for his dreams of the future always revert to thoughts of his fading youth. Only at this point does the reader fully understand the title, "Silvio Corelli pleure," for nowhere are tears mentioned in the poem. They relate to his abandonment, to be sure, to the deficiencies of his condition for which he is not responsible, but the sadness he expresses is also greater than the sum of his deprivations and relates to the passing of time. The verbal play at end-rhyme position on the homonym "tombe," employed both as a noun signifying a tomb and as a verb whose semes connote the rapid fall of his youth, reinforces the point. The allusions to memory and the past will intensify and become more conspicuous in subsequent poems.

While a number of Nelligan's poems reveal a sense of anxiety and sometimes of sin and guilt regarding sexuality, only a modest proportion of his verse expresses the melancholy of unrequited love, that not uncommon theme of adolescent poetry. In "Soirs d'automne," one of his weaker poems, the final tercet seems at first to envisage the autumn evening as a balm for his suffering love ("Et mon amour meurtri, comme une chair qui saigne, / Repose sa blessure et calme ses névroses" 163), but it then concludes, in Lamartinian fashion, with ambient nature partaking of his sorrow. "Le Violon brisé," on the other hand, deals directly with an implied rejection by a woman for whom the poet has an "amour infini" (176). No details of her refusal are given except that she made it known on an evening she played a piece by Paganini on the violin. This allows the poet first to highlight the violin (while attempting to reproduce its sound: the poem's phonology contains 22 [i]s) and then to establish an extended analogy between the instrument and his own heart. The personified violin is sad, for it is broken: "Il s'est brisé plein de tristesse" (line 2). Significantly, it broke "Aux soupirs de l'archet béni" (line 1), suggesting again both the sensual ("soupirs") and spiritual ("béni") dimensions of both music and love. The second stanza immediately links his emotional state with the fate of the violin. Its initial line, "Comme tout choit avec prestesse!" (line 5), encompasses in its universal application both the violin, suddenly broken, and his love, now associated temporally with the instrument: "J'avais un amour infini, / Ce soir que vous jouiez" (6–7).

Now, the broken instrument "dort sous l'étroitesse / De son étui de bois verni" (line 10). The constraints of "étroitesse" negate the benign quality of "dort," evoking connotations of a body in a casket. So, too, does the poet's heart now "repose avec tristesse / Au trou de notre amour fini" (14). Here "tristesse" seriously mitigates the positive quality of "repose." "[N]otre amour fini," activating semes of both the finite and the finished, stands in contrast with the "amour infini" of line 6, which was his love for her. Once "amour" is modified by "notre" and refers to their mutual love, the prefix *in* vanishes to reveal the finite nature of the relationship. The substantive "trou" resonates with semes of the abysmal, the despondent, and the sepulchral, fulfilling the poet's statement in line 4, "Comme tout choit avec prestesse!" The harshness of "trou" is more comprehensible if we refer to the two stanzas that Nelligan copied in his hospital notebooks in 1931. In that text, which has few variants from the original, he changed line 11, which originally read "Depuis le soir où, blonde hôtesse," to "Il collapsa le soir Comtesse" (M 120). In a rare recourse to an anglicism, what happened to the violin and, metaphorically, to his soul becomes considerably more drastic: total collapse. Like the violin, his heart is broken; it has collapsed into the depths.

A similar situation occurs in a companion poem, "Violon d'adieu," where sadness is again associated with a violin. The first stanza, a lovely chiaroscuro piece, describes a pleasant domestic scene, an evening of music by the fireplace:

> Vous jouiez Mendelssohn ce soir-là; les flammèches
> Valsaient dans l'âtre clair, cependant qu'au salon
> Un abat-jour mêlait en ondulement long
> Ses rêves de lumière au châtain de vos mèches. (177)

This ambient comfort is shattered in the second quatrain by the sadness of the notes that emerge from the violin, which are compared to the bristling of dried flowers in an evening wind:

> Et tristes, comme un bruit frissonnant de fleurs sèches
> Eparses dans le vent vespéral du vallon,
> Les notes sanglotaient sur votre violon
> Et chaque coup d'archet trouait mon cœur de brèches. (177)

The allusion to Verlaine's "les sanglots longs des violons" is clear enough, but the metaphor of the final line of the quatrain is unexpected and brutal. The bow of the violin is now a deadly weapon wielded by the woman who uses it repeatedly to attack his heart.

The sadness of the music, as we might expect, intensifies his own heartache. After leaving her early that evening,

> ... jusqu'à l'aube errant, seul, morose, attristé,
> Contant ma jeune peine au lunaire mystère,
>
> Je sentais remonter comme d'amers parfums
> Ces musiques d'adieu qui scellaient sous la terre
> Et mon rêve d'amour et mes espoirs défunts. (177)

The synesthesic discourse – music as bitter smells – appropriately captures the harshness of his disillusion. The final word, "défunts" (recalling the "fleurs sèches" of line 5), stresses the demise of his hopes for love. It is now clear that the piece by Mendelssohn had been farewell music, as the poem's title had anticipated. Significantly, the image of the "trou," found in the last stanza of "Violon brisé," reappears in the final tercet of this poem as the musical adieu effectively seals the poet's dreams of love beneath the earth. Both poems are dominated by a sense of the irredeemable.

The sonnet "À une femme détestée," discussed in chapter 1, insists that it is *not* about unrequited love, yet ends with the words: "... expliquez-moi ce soir, / Cette tristesse au cœur qui me cause des larmes" (lines 13–14). The sadness described does, however, seem to be caused by unreturned love, even if the poet does not admit to it. He protests (too much!) that his love was for art alone. Yet, lines 2, 3, and 4 describe a woman who obviously appeals to him:

> Vous êtes pourtant belle et très noble d'allure,
> Les Séraphins ont fait votre ample chevelure
> Et vos regards couleur du charme brun des nuits. (158)

This depiction of an attractive, even seductive, woman is preceded by the line "Combien je vous déteste et combien je vous fuis," certainly one of the most aggressively harsh lines in all of Nelligan's poetry. She is later accused of being fickle (line 7), indifferent, and devoid of a soul (10). Such invective derives from her having offended him in some way:

> Depuis que vous m'avez froissé, jamais depuis,
> N'ai-je pu tempérer cette intime brûlure:
> Vous m'avez fait souffrir, volage créature,
> Pendant qu'en moi grondait le volcan des ennuis. (158)

The final line of the quatrain suggests both that the poet has contained his sorrow (the volcano has not erupted) and that he is on the verge of exploding (active volcanoes do erupt). Lines 11–12 seem to be a definitive resolution: "Vieillissons tous les deux pour ne jamais nous voir. / Je ne dois pas courber mon front devant vos charmes." The "nous" in line 11 is a correction by Nelligan's most recent editors, for the poet clearly wrote "se": "Vieillissons pour ne jamais *se* voir." The editors justify their correction by pointing out that "se" is a grammatical error, since the first person plural verb requires "nous" (RW 411). In doing so, they fail to recognize that the ungrammaticality may be deliberate. The poet's anger directed at this woman is so great (he addresses her six times as "vous") that he cannot bring himself to use a pronoun, "nous," that would encompass them both. The two following lines, the concluding verses of the poem, are those quoted above: "Seulement, seulement, expliquez-moi ce soir, / Cette tristesse au cœur qui me cause des larmes." The anger, so open and so resolute, dissolves into sadness by the end of the poem. Rejection in love *is* a cause for sadness, but there are a number of poems discussed in chapter 2 (for example, "Hiver sentimental," "Tristesse blanche," "Jardin sentimental," and "Lied fantasque") in which the woman does not reject the poet. Clearly his melancholy has other, deeper causes.

TEMPUS FUGIT: OÙ SONT LES NEIGES D'ANTAN

Since Villon's "Où sont les neiges d'antan" in the fifteenth century, an abundance of French poems have looked back with sadness on the passage of time. Though less prevalent in Quebec, the theme was not unknown, providing, for example, Pamphile Lemay with some of his better lines. It is no surprise, then, that Nelligan's poetry would draw from this tradition. What may set him apart – at least in the Canadian context – is the intense personal quality of his confrontation with temporality. In *À l'ombre des jeunes filles en fleurs*, Proust's narrator speaks of the shock of recognition he experienced after a remark by his father that he, the narrator, was no longer a child and that his current tastes were probably permanent. With great sadness the narrator now realized, he says, that "je n'étais pas situé en dehors du temps, mais soumis à ses lois" (1:482). Such consternation at being part of temporality, of no longer being a child, is a constant of Nelligan's poetry. In a poem such as "Le Regret des joujoux," he asks himself, "Où donc a fui le jour des joujoux enfantins" (107, line 9) as he mourns the death of a childhood friend, the passage of time, and the transition to adulthood: "Ah! de franchir sitôt le portail des vingt ans" (line 14). The poem's question, heavily dependent on the adverb "où," is echoed by the frequent repetition of the sound [u], iterated a dozen times (including the title). "La Fuite de l'enfance," likewise a poem steeped with nostalgia in which two persons return to the places of their youth ("Gagnons les bords fanés du Passé" 119, line 4), is replete with melancholy and even despair ("nos cœurs pavés de désespoirs," 7), and ends with a sad allusion to "La fuite de l'Enfance au vaisseau des Vingt ans" (14). The past is to be regretted not only because the conditions of his existence were then different but also because *he* was different. As we shall see later, he mourns not only a lost time but a lost self.

In Nelligan, meditations on the passage of time usually occur in the context of a reflection on death. I've discussed Nelligan's earliest piece of writing, "C'était l'automne ... et les feuilles tombaient toujours," in the context of his spirituality. Mortality, the text's central theme, is emphasized by the conscious framing of the text between the identical title and last line. This enclosure replicates the framing of human life, which always ends in death, a finality echoed by the last word, "toujours." Mortality, moreover, was a frequently articulated theme within the discourse of nineteenth-century French-Canadian Catholicism, and, not unexpectedly, it provided the subject matter for a number of contemporary poems. The poetry it informed tends to conform to cultural expectations. Crémazie's well-known poem "Les Morts," which appeared in the *Journal de Québec* in 1856 on the eve of All Saints Day, the Church's traditional day of mourning for the dead, is addressed directly to the deceased. Its themes all lie within the expectations of the genre. The dead are alone, immobile, and cold, have neither the miseries nor the joys of the living, and seek only to be remembered as they briefly leave their graves on All Soul's Day. The poem ends with about forty verses calling on the faithful to pray for the deceased.[10] Poems of this type, though considerably shorter than Crémazie's, were not uncommon around 1 November. Rémi Tremblay's "Le Jour des Morts," for example, published on 2 November 1895, begins by linking the season (the death of nature) with the theme of human death, proceeds to offer prayers for the deceased, but ends on a note of hope:

> Dieu grava dans nos cœurs un sentiment suprême
> Qui survit au trépas:
> Au delà du tombeau, comme ici bas, l'on s'aime
> Car l'amour ne meurt pas.

The dead who have left their tombs are not at all threatening, for they are on their way to pray in the heavens.[11] Even Jacques Soulary's deeply sombre "Élégie" ends on a comforting religious note.[12] Nelligan's poetry, however, is of a very different stripe.

Although a poem such as "La Fuite de l'enfance" is not itself a reflection on death – indeed, death is not mentioned – nostalgia occurs within a linguistic field that is highly connotative of mortality: "jardins anciens" (119, line 1); "deux spectres tristes" (2); "Villa d'antan" (3); "bords fanés du Passé" (4); "râles / De sa joie" (4); "il expire" (5); "robes spectrales" (6); "soirs révolus" (10); "la fuite de l'Enfance" (12). More conspicuously, "Le Salon" opens with a stanza suffused with semes of death and decay:

> La poussière s'étend sur tout le mobilier,
> Les miroirs de Venise ont défleuri leur charme;
> Il y rôde comme un très vieux parfum de Parme,
> La funèbre douceur d'un sachet familier. (182)

The pronominal verb ("La poussière s'étend") and the impersonal pronoun ("Il y rôde") stress human helplessness in the face of the passage of time. Moreover, dust, the symbol of death (sanctioned as such by the Church in its Ash Wednesday liturgy) is rendered all the more sinister by the alliteration of [s]s in the first line. The preponderance of the phoneme [r] (twelve times in four lines), which also provides the initial consonant of "rôder," a signifier that includes semes of evil intent, further sustains the menacing tone of the stanza. Within this atmosphere, a marked silence reigns:

Plus jamais ne résonne à travers le silence
Le chant du piano dans les rythmes berceurs,
Mendelssohn et Mozart, mariant leurs douceurs,
Ne s'entendent qu'en rêve aux soirs de somnolence. (182)

The tercets identify the persona as "le poète." Wringing his hands, "hagard et solitaire," he wanders about "sous son massif ennui," imagining "Un grand bal solennel tournant dans le mystère, / Où ses yeux ont cru voir danser les parents morts" (lines 13–14). Unlike Vigny's Moïse, who is "puissant et solitaire," this poet is exhausted and alone, "hanté par des remords" that remain unspecified. Nelligan seems to be fulfilling Kierkegaard's definition of the poet as "an unhappy being whose heart is torn by secret sufferings"(1987, 1:19).

Robidoux and Wyczynski have linked the tercets of this poem with "Somnium," a poem by Nelligan's friend Joseph Melançon which he knew by heart (RW 434; see also Wyczynski 1960, 85). Yet the differences with Melançon's poem are more instructive than the similarities. Melançon's vision of the ghosts of his ancestors occupies the entire sonnet, not just the last line as in Nelligan, and clearly takes place in a dream ("quand le sommeil obscurcit ma prunelle" [Rainier 61]), whereas Nelligan is awake and conscious, allowing his imagination to evoke his dead ancestors in the final stanza. His vision of the ancestors caps a meditation on death. Moreover, Melançon's poem draws from the frenetic tradition (the ancestors have "vieux os livides" and he trembles "dans l'effrayante horreur de leurs orbites vides" [Rainer 62]), while Nelligan eschews such imagery, for his emotion in reflecting on the passage of time is not fright but sadness.

In "Le Regret des joujoux," the nostalgia for childhood we have already noted in that poem occurs within the context of a reflection on death. The playthings he regrets were those he shared as a child with a now deceased playmate, Lucile, whose death has left him deeply saddened:

Toujours je garde en moi la tristesse profonde
Qu'y grava l'amitié d'une adorable enfant,
Pour qui la mort sonna le fatal olifant,
Parce qu'elle était belle et gracieuse et blonde. (107)

The last line of the quatrain introduces the implication that the universe itself may be malevolent, a notion that recurs in Nelligan's poetry and is virtually absent from the verse of his Canadian contemporaries. The polysyndeton ("belle et gracieuse et blonde") suggests that it is *because* of these qualities that the young girl died. His reaction is sadness ("tristesse profonde" [line 1]; "navré du regret dont je suis étouffant" [7]) that results in self-isolation, a closing off from the world: "Or, depuis je me sens muré contre le monde, / Tel un prince du Nord que son Kremlin défend" (lines 5–6) The wall is self-constructed, a necessary protection in a universe in which there is little hope. Lucile may be "montée au fond des cieux latents" (line 12), but this vague and weak hint of an afterlife clearly offers no consolation. Unlike most teenagers who look forward to their twentieth birthday, this young man regrets "de franchir si tôt le portail des vingt ans" (line 14).

"La Sorella dell'Amore" similarly evokes Lucile's death and likewise suggests the presence of a hostile agent at work in the universe. In this instance, the malevolent force is identified more clearly as death itself, which the poet now addresses directly:

Mort, que fais-tu, dis-nous, de tous ces beaux trophées
De vierges que nos feux brûlent sur tes autels?
Réponds, quand serons-nous pour jamais immortels
Aux lumineux séjours des célestes Riphées? (108)

Death is here perceived in a pre-Christian context. The "beaux trophées / De vierges que nos feux brûlent sur tes autels" (lines 1–2) recall sacrifices made to appease the gods, and the "lumineux séjours des célestes Riphées" (line 4) situate the afterlife in a vaguely pagan Greek environment. No Christian prayer for the salvation of the loved one is offered; no hope of seeing her again in heaven is expressed. Rather, the poet feels helpless and alone: "Lucile est morte hier, et je sanglote, étant / Comme une cloche vaine en une solitude" (lines 13–15). Similar sentiments are expressed at about this time by Fleury Desjardins in his poem "Mortua," with the important distinction that Desjardins makes no reference to a malevolence inherent in the structure of the universe itself.[13] In evoking the near phonetic equivalence between the Italian [lamore] of the title and the French [lamɔr], Nelligan stresses the tragic irony intrinsic in creation.

Brooding on death includes reflecting on, and even wishing for, his own death. "Devant mon berceau," which reaffirms the prevalence of misfortune ("ce monde mauvais"), begins with obsessive, suffocating sobs as the poet recounts how, on the previous day, filled with bitterness, he had contemplated his childhood crib. The second stanza, describing the room in which he was born, is dominated by a series of signifiers related to death and decay: "chambre ancienne; moire ... flétrie; brocart fané; mobilier de deuil" (lines 5–7). The concluding third and fourth stanzas, which explain the bitterness of the first, are addressed to the crib, which the poet, echoing the sentiments of Kierkegaard's young man in *Either/Or* who dared to affirm that "happiest is the one who died at birth" (1:221), reproaches for not having transformed itself into a casket:

> Quand je n'étais qu'au seuil de ce monde mauvais,
> Berceau, que n'as tu fait pour moi tes draps funèbres?
> ....
> Ah! que n'a-t-on tiré mon linceul de tes langes[.] (109)

The moment of his birth had been one of joy, a moment "Alors que se penchait sur ma vie en tremblant / Ma mère souriante, avec l'essaim des anges" (lines 15–16). D.-L. Haineault has noted the homophony of *l'essaim* and *les seins* (115), a link that recalls the mother's early nurturing and specifically the "douceur maternelle" evoked in line 3. The poet regrets a neonatal paradise in which the newborn remains in an undifferentiated relationship with his mother. His life has since become one of darkness and error: "Ma vie est un blason sur des murs de ténèbres, / Et mes pas sont fautifs où maintenant je vais" (lines 11–12). The semes of guilt contained in "fautifs" may be related to an emerging lifestyle of which his mother disapproves, leading to an estrangement from the mother, whose "douceur" is evoked in the first stanza and whose smile is recollected in the last. His despondent nostalgia for childhood includes a grieving for a mother no longer willing or able to be unconditionally "souriante" towards him.

"Marches funèbres" (a title Maurice Rollinat had used in *Les Névroses*) illustrates what this brooding on mortality has done to the poet: he has internalized the concept of death to the point that he can *hear* it within himself. The poem opens with the declaration "J'écoute en moi des voix funèbres / Clamer transcendantalement." The reprise of the first line in lines 7 and 13 alters the verb to "j'entends," that is, "I listen." The initial "j'écoute," which connotes wilful listening, indicates Nelligan's own complicity with his melancholy, a subject to which I shall return. The second stanza confirms the link between the funereal voices within him and his deep sadness:

> Au frisson fou de mes vertèbres
> Si je sanglotte éperdument,
> C'est que j'entends des voix funèbres
> Clamer transcendantalement. (259)

The image of madly shivering vertebrae seeks to translate the physical effect of this experience. Yet "transcendantalement," which is conspicuous by furnishing six of the eight syllables of the verse (as it did in line 2), suggests that the crying out he hears, though inside him, is outside the range of human cognition. The experience is both horrific and inescapable:

> Tel un troupeau spectral de zèbres
> Mon rêve rode étrangement;
>
> Et je suis hanté tellement
> Qu'en moi toujours dans mes ténèbres,
>
> J'entends geindre des voix funèbres. (259)

While "hanté" means obsessed, it also carries the meaning of being visited by ghosts, assuming semes contained in "troupeau spectral." The helpless poet is inhabited by the incessant moaning of death, also suggested phonostylistically by the repetition of adverbs ending in [mã] five times in rhyming position. In this and other poems, the linearity of time remains a source of profound anxiety.

LOST PARADISE

> Ainsi les souvenirs, les regrets et l'amour,
> Et la mélancolique et douce rêverie,
> Reviennent vers les lieux chers à l'âme attendrie,
> Où nous fumes enfants, amants, aimés, heureux.
>
> – Jacques Delille, *L'Imagination* 1:254

If the poet is now obsessed with death, it is because he has lost a paradise that cannot be regained. "La Fuite de l'enfance" records the slipping away ("Dans les râles / De sa joie il expire," 119, lines 4–5) of a past represented as ideal: "la Villa d'antan" is said to have a "seuil immaculé" (3), an image that may be read as a metonymy for the sinless existence of childhood. The poet and his companion, now ghosts of their past selves, are returning to a site of their childhood, "nos cœurs pavés de désespoirs" (line 7), but they can only observe their past fading in the distance: "Suivons là-bas, devers les idéales côtes, / La fuite de l'Enfance au vaisseau des Vingt ans" (line 12). The capitalization of both "Enfances" and "Vingt" in this closing line emphasizes them as opposing categories. Sadly, the pensive young adults recognize that they can never regain their childhood. In a number of Nelligan's poems, Eden represents the world of his pre-adolescence rather than the garden of Adam before the Fall. Nelligan may thus be situated within a long line of writers, especially since the advent of Romanticism, who have indulged in nostalgia for childhood. Wordsworth, as Champigny has pointed out, intimated that "in the child, the original Paradise is still alive" (Champigny 126–7). In Nelligan, it lives only in a memory that serves to make the present all the more distressing. While nostalgia refers etymologically to a grieving for one's home (<Greek *nostos*: return home), for Nelligan, it is not so much a place as a time for which he yearns. We know that, except for a few escapades during which he stayed with friends, Nelligan continued to live at home during his creative years. The loss that

troubles him is not spatial but temporal. Nelligan would have concurred with Proust's affirmation that "les lieux que nous avons connus n'appartiennent pas qu'au monde de l'espace," but that "le souvenir d'une certaine image n'est que le regret d'un certain instant" (1:427). The time grieved for is very much present in his mind, even in detail, and the absence that is so present is the innocence he has lost in stepping beyond the immaculate threshold. The religious myth of Eden has become a private myth that articulates his personal sense of loss. As Jankélévitch has shown in his discussion of strictly defined nostalgia, the regretted object is not always the cause of nostalgia but rather its effect. Strong attachment to the past embellishes the past (see Jankélévitch 288). Nelligan's desire to hold on to the innocence of his childhood erases all blemishes from that period of his life. Whatever sibling rivalries might have occurred, whatever punishments he might have received from a stern father, whatever reprimands might have been meted out by teachers disappointed with his academic performance are occulted by what Jankélévitch would call a "mirage rétrospectif" (289) in which innocence alone is reflected.

The association of childhood with paradise is most clearly stated in one of Nelligan's more finely crafted poems, "Clavier d'antan":

Clavier vibrant de remembrance,
J'évoque un peu des jours anciens,
Et l'Eden d'or de mon enfance

Se dresse avec les printemps siens,
Souriant de vierge espérance
Et de rêves musiciens ...

Vous êtes morte tristement,
Ma muse des choses dorées,
Et c'est de vous qu'est mon tourment;

Et c'est pour vous que sont pleurées
Au luth âpre de votre amant
Tant de musiques éplorées. (105)

The keyboard of yesteryear is revealed to be the poet himself. *He* is the "clavier vibrant de remembrance," a richly sonorous metaphor

(2 [v]s, 2 [b]s, 3 [r]s, 2 [ã]s, 2 [ə]s within seven syllables), embracing a poetic archaism ("remembrance") of which Nelligan seems to have been fond. Like a keyboard vibrating with memories, he evokes his past, fulfilling a wish expressed in "Mon Âme" ("… retournons au seuil de l'Enfance en allée," 295). Within those "jours anciens" was "l'Eden d'or de mon enfance" (line 3), a phrase pregnant with meaning within the Nelliganian universe. The seemingly redundant modification of Eden, the perfect paradise, by gold, always a positive signifier in Nelligan, secures a collocation of the highest value. The phonetic link through the dental [d] only strengthens the bond further.

However banal its association with youth, spring remains a precious season in Nelligan's poetic world, and one that he evokes rarely, speaking more frequently of autumn with its connotations of sadness. Rare as well is his use of the verb "sourire," here a figurative act of his childhood Eden. In the context of Nelligan's multiple and frequent use of the verb "pleurer" and the noun "pleurs," this attachment of smiles to his childhood, attributed to a "vierge espérance" and "rêves musiciens," is to be noted. The "virgin hope" recalls the purity Nelligan sometimes identified with himself, as in "Mon Âme" where he suggested that his soul was endowed with "la candeur d'une chose étoilée / D'une neige de février" (295). Childhood is the pre-moral period before one gets sullied by life, when one can still hope, when one can still have musical dreams.

The suspension points at the end of the second tercet signal, as P. Bissonnette and J.-P. Bouchard have pointed out, the transition from *rêverie* to facing of reality (600). Indeed, the last two stanzas burst the poet's nostalgic dream with the brutal "Vous êtes morte" addressed to his muse, who has by now died in sadness. She was the muse of golden things, "de choses dorées," by which we can infer that she drew her inspiration from "l'Éden d'or." The death of his muse implies that he is losing his ability to retrieve his lost childhood poetically, while the suspension points at the end of the second stanza also indicate a fading away. The muse, then, becomes a source of his distress, for the poet is now left to producing tearful music. Or, rather, tearful music expresses itself *through* him. The use of the passive "sont pleurés," as Laure Hesbois has noted (102), stresses the primacy of the wailing melodies over the poet who produces them.

"Vieux Piano," published in *Le Monde illustré* in 1897 and hence one of Nelligan's earlier poems, associates a piano with melancholy.

The poem's epigraph, which reproduces the second quatrain of Catulle Mendès' sonnet "L'Absente," portrays a piano in mourning over the death of the musician, identified as female. In his poem, a reflection on an old, unused piano now relegated to a back room, Nelligan muses sadly on a recurring event of his childhood:

> Je me souviens encore des nocturnes sans nombre
> Que me jouait ma mère, et je songe, en pleurant,
> À ces soirs d'autrefois, passés dans la pénombre,
> Quand Liszt se disait triste et Beethoven mourant. (169)

In the quatrain's closing line, the poet stresses the dolorous quality of this music by establishing semantic and phonetic links between the composers and the sounds their music produces (Liszt = triste; Beethoven [pronounced with a concluding nasal] = mourant). This is one of the very few instances when the poet evokes any sadness at all during childhood and may be a clue to his early sensitivity. Yet his tears derive not so much from the memory of the sad music of Liszt and Beethoven as from the regret that he can no longer listen to the nocturnes being played in the evening. Significantly, the person playing the piano is his mother, frequently associated with the joys of childhood in Nelligan. There is no hint here of the death of the pianist (an essential element in Mendès' poem), but rather an insistence on the piano's abandonment. The unused piano becomes the image of the poet, from whom happiness has fled:

> Ô vieux piano d'ébène, image de ma vie,
> Comme toi du bonheur ma pauvre âme est ravie,
> Il te manque une artiste, il me faut l'Idéal. (169)

While its semantic parameters are not identified, "Idéal," a word he uses on several other occasions, is clearly not to be found in his present life now that the piano, his only source of joy (line 12), is silent. The description of the abandoned piano as "Ce misanthrope aigri de son isolement" in the final line of the first quatrain betrays his own bitterness at having been abandoned.

Nelligan's Eden is sometimes associated with a natural setting, as in one of his best-known poems, "Le Jardin d'antan." Nelligan's friend Joseph Melançon later reported that Nelligan had been inspired to write this poem after reading Fernand Gregh's *La Maison de l'enfance* (1897), a linkage noted by several critics (Wyczynski 1960, 237; Filteau 87). The deeply felt nostalgia for the joys of childhood clearly links the first part of Gregh's volume and much of Nelligan's poetry, as do specific images ("les jours dorés de l'enfance," Gregh 4) and contrasts ("j'habitais autrefois une maison heureuse [... / ...] Maintenant je suis triste, étonné, sans défense," 7). Nelligan's poem is, however, prosodically more interesting and his nostalgia deeper. His poem is also less sensual and ultimately more pessimistic:

Rien n'est plus doux aussi que de s'en revenir
Comme après de longs ans d'absence,
Que de s'en revenir
Par le chemin du souvenir
Fleuri de lys d'innocence
Au jardin de l'Enfance.

Au jardin clos, scellé, dans le jardin muet
D'où s'enfuirent les gaîtés franches,
Notre jardin muet,
Et la danse du menuet
Qu'autrefois menaient sous branches
Nos sœurs en robes blanches.

Aux soirs d'Avrils anciens, jetant des cris joyeux
Entremêlés de ritournelles,
Avec des lieds joyeux,
Elles passaient, la gloire aux yeux,
Sous le frisson des tonnelles,
Comme en les villanelles.

Cependant que venaient, du fond de la villa,
Des accords de guitare ancienne,
De la vieille villa,
Et qui faisaient deviner là,
Près d'une obscure persienne,
Quelque musicienne.

Mais rien n'est plus amer que de penser aussi
A tant de choses ruinées!

Ah! de penser aussi,
Lorsque nous revenons ainsi
Par sentes de fleurs fanées,
A nos jeunes années.

Lorsque nous nous sentons névrosés et vieillis,
Froissés, maltraités et sans armes,
Moroses et vieillis,
Et que, surnageant aux oublis,
S'éternise avec ses charmes
Notre jeunesse en larmes! (120–1)

This poem, which has elicited critical praise for its musical contours, sound repetitions, and rhythms (Wyczynski 1967, 47–8), opens with a nostalgic evocation of happy childhood, its poet seemingly blessed with an affective hypermnesia. The adverb "aussi" in the first line creates a past for the poem, for it supposes that the poet has already been involved in reverie and no doubt other nostalgic musings (Bessette 31). The first stanza expresses the sweetness of the return to nothing less than the "jardin de l'Enfance." Childhood, once again, is Eden. This is a place "fleuri de lys d'innocence," hence a place of purity. Gérard Bessette has remarked on this stanza's mix of concrete and abstract images that creates doubt as to whether what is represented is real or imagined. There is a road, but it is a road of memory; lilies, but they are lilies of innocence; a garden, but a garden of childhood. The suggestiveness of the stanza derives in part from the imprecision between the real and the imaginary (Bessette 35).

The three following stanzas recall the joy that reigned in this space. The first hemistich of line 7, "Au jardin clos, scellé," is not, however, without ambiguity. Since Nelligan has a clear affection for closed-in spaces, it would seem apposite to read the hemistich as indicating that the garden of childhood was indeed enclosed. This reading would cohere with the notion, found in Nelligan's other poems, of the home as a protected and protective place, and would situate its garden symbolically within the immaculate threshold mentioned in "La Fuite de l'enfance." We know, moreover, that the *hortus conclusus* is associated in some paintings with the Immaculate Conception. It is therefore appropriate that blooming along its path are lilies, long a symbol of purity and virginity and frequently associated with the Virgin Mary in iconography. Yet we cannot dismiss the possibility that the garden is now "clos, scellé," closed and locked, *to* the poet, signifying that he, like Adam, cannot re-enter paradise. The redundant "clos, scellé" pushes the concept of closure to the end of the hemistich, placing the important sixth syllable stress on the final syllable of "scellé." The most obvious reading of "scellé" is "locked" in reference to the gate of the garden, yet "scellé" has other connotations that may be at play here: it also refers to what is sealed by *le sceau de l'état* and suggests a powerful authority behind the locking of the gate, semes that confirm the impossibility of a re-entry. That the garden is also mute strengthens the reading of this verse as a description of the garden in its current state. The "gaietés franches," the uninhibited joys, have fled, as have the dances performed by his sisters who were, not surprisingly, dressed in white.

Once again, childhood is associated with springtime ("Aux soirs d'Avrils anciens") and, in contrast with the present "jardin muet," with sounds: "cris joyeux" (line 13), "ritournelles" (14), "lieds joyeux" (15), "villanelles" (18), and "guitare ancienne" (20). This jubilation, as joyful shouts of children blend with music, comes to a quick end as we reach the poem's volta in the first line of the fifth stanza, which provides the tone for the rest of the poem. The initial position of the conjunction "mais," immediately signifying a contradiction of what has previously been expressed, announces a negation: "Mais rien n'est plus amer" belies "Rien n'est plus doux." The poet realizes that all he has evoked in the first five stanzas has become "tant de choses ruinées" (line 26), that wilted flowers now line the pathways, and that he himself, having become old, morose, and neurotic, cannot reassume a childhood that is now but a "jeunesse en larmes" (line 36).

In "Ruines," the Edenic vision is associated with brightness ("or" [line 4], "blonds" [6], "feux" [6], "radieux flambeaux" [10], and "flammes" [11]), in contrast to the stark darkness of the poet's current situation under the dominance of "noirs maçons du Deuil" (13). The image of childhood cannot be more blissful:

Quelquefois je suis plein de grandes voix anciennes,
Et je revis un peu l'enfance en la villa;
Je me retrouve encore avec ce qui fut là
Quand le soir nous jetait de l'or par les persiennes. (243)

In this ideal state that is now relived imaginatively and is melodiously supported by triple labials and nasals ("l'enfance en la villa"), even the darkness of night produces light. For a moment, the past seems to come to life:

Et dans mon âme alors soudain je vois groupées
Mes sœurs à cheveux blonds jouant près des vieux feux;
Autour d'elles le chat rôde, le dos frileux,
Les regardant vêtir, étonné, leurs poupées.

Ah! la sérénité des jours à jamais beaux (243)

These days of bliss and serenity embodied in the playful sisters and the familial cat are, we learn in the rest of the poem, now "morts à jamais" (line 10) for "tout est défunt, enclos dans le cercueil" (12), the ultimate enclosure. The poem concludes with a strong image: "... sous les outils des noirs maçons du Deuil. / S'écroulent nos bonheurs comme des murs de briques!" (lines 13–14), hinting that forces beyond the poet's control have been at work. Imagery of light and movement gives way to images of darkness and hard immobility. Here Nelligan's poetic discourse coheres with the two metaphors that Stanley W. Jackson in his historical study of melancholy identified as standing out above others in the discourse of melancholiacs, namely being in a state of darkness and being weighted down (396). A sense of being under a heavy weight is clearer still in "Le Soulier de la morte," in which the poet declares himself "Broyé sous un fardeau de fer" (245). Darkness obtains here, too, internalized in his "cœur plein de noir" (246).

"Devant le feu," a good summary of Nelligan's "lost Eden" poems, follows the expected sonnet pattern, establishing a sharp contrast between the quatrains and the tercets. The quatrains, for their part, portray an unalloyed joy:

Par les hivers anciens, quand nous portions la robe,
Tout petits, frais, rosés, tapageurs et joufflus,
Avec nos grands albums, hélas! que l'on n'a plus,
Comme on croyait déjà posséder tout le globe!

Assis en rond, le soir, au coin du feu, par groupes,
Image sur image, ainsi combien joyeux
Nous feuilletions, voyant, la gloire dans les yeux,
Passer de beaux dragons qui chevauchaient en troupes! (298)

The sense of security in being seated with a group in the round, noted by Donald Smith (114), is negated in the tercets by the sombre bitterness of the present in which the poet is alone:

> Je fus de ces heureux d'alors, mais aujourd'hui,
> Les pieds sur les chenets, le front terne d'ennui,
> Moi qui me sens toujours l'amertume dans l'âme,
>
> J'aperçois défiler, dans un album de flamme,
> Ma jeunesse qui va, comme un soldat passant,
> Au champ noir de la vie, arme au poing, toute en sang! (298)

The contrasts between the quatrains and the tercets, predicted by the phrase "hélas! que l'on n'a plus" in line 3, are clear at the thematic and lexical levels. The words "frais, rosés," of line 2 yield to "noir ... sang" of line 14; "joyeux" in line 6 yields to "ennui ... amertume" in lines 10 and 11. More importantly, the past is represented as a group past, a time shared with friends and siblings. While the quatrains speak in the first person plural, the voice of the tercets is in the first person singular. Solitude marks the present as the poet remains alone. Moreover, in childhood, all was possible: "Comme on croyait déjà posséder tout le globe" (line 4). As a child, the "grands albums" provided the excitement of dragons passing by. Now, his only "album" is constituted of the flames through which his youth passes, "arme au poing, toute en sang" (line 14). He has been bloodied up by a life characterized by blackness, the traditional metaphor of melancholy.

In none of this poetry is there any expression of hope for happiness in an afterlife, for a future Eden that might compensate for the one he has lost. To the contrary, three of Nelligan's nostalgic poems regret a loss of the faith or religious fervour that he associates with a childhood past. "Les Communiantes," apparently written on the occasion of his cousin's first communion (RW 445), is quite unlike Rimbaud's anti-clerical and sacrilegious "Les Premières Communions," being closer to the sacramental poetry published in Montreal at the time.[14] Faithful to the requirements of this sub-genre, it is respectful both of the ceremony and its participants. His is, however, the only example of the genre in Canada in which the poet, "Plein de l'ardent regret des ferveurs en allées" (line 4), is conscious that he no longer shares the fervour of the communicants. A similar regret surfaces in "La Cloche dans la brume," a poem mentioned briefly in chapter 2, in which the poet addresses his own soul, summoning it to listen to the weeping sounds of a bell heard through the fog. He then wonders whether the cause of his soul's sadness might not be similar to that of the bell:

À quoi songez-vous donc? à quoi pensez-vous tant? ...
Vous qui ne priez plus, ah! serait-ce, pauvresse,
Que vous compareriez soudain votre détresse
À la cloche qui rêve aux angélus d'antan? ... (214)

"Vous qui ne priez plus" indicates a serious attenuation of religious practice, if not a loss of faith. His sadness, then, or to stay closer to the text, the sadness of his soul, comes from a sense of loss:

Comme elle vous geignez, funèbre et monotone,
Comme elle vous tintez dans les brouillards d'automne,
Plainte de quelque église exilée en la nuit,

Et qui regrette avec de sonores souffrances
Les fidèles quittant son enceinte qui luit,
Comme vous regrettez l'exil des Espérances. (214)

If hope has already gone, so too, perhaps, has faith. Further evidence of this emerges in "Mon Sabot de Noël," discussed in a previous chapter, which celebrates the arrival of Jesus who brings toys to children at Christmas. It differs considerably from the Yuletide poems published in Nelligan's own time, which maintain a celebratory, joyous, and religious tone throughout.[15] In its second part, Nelligan's poem – in defiance of the expectations of the genre – devolves into despair, for the poet now recognizes that Jesus will not come for the "fils errants de la Bohème" (226, line 15), such as himself. While this grief over the loss of his religious faith need not depict a persistent and chronic condition (that is, we need not posit that he had actually become a non-believer), it becomes part of a more generalized loss of self-worth. He can no longer believe as he once did. But this does not represent the liberation that some adolescents find in the rejection of faith, for religious belief was for him part of the Eden he was now mourning.

In his lucid essay on nostalgia, Sisto Vecchio has justly observed that it is impossible to speak of this condition without reference to a place (104). As we have seen, Nelligan's childhood home plays a role in his poetic imagination, representing a maternal and female space inhabited by his mother and sisters, but from which his father is excluded.[16] This space is clearly a metaphor for an idealized time and, moreover, an idealized self. Nelligan's Blakean and Wordsworthian view of childhood results in its representation as a state of wholeness and harmony between the "I" and the "we," between the self and the familial group consisting of his mother and sisters. His nostalgia, then, is not based on spatial distance from the loved object but requires that he imaginatively lengthen the temporal distance between his present and an idealized past. Only a few years separate this adolescent from his childhood, but the poetic voice of his verse is invariably much older, sometimes claiming to be near death. His situation is thereby more serious, for while space can be overcome, time cannot. The yearning for a past seen as static can only make the present, necessarily a state of becoming, all the more painful.

MELANCHOLY AS AN AESTHETICS

> Recollection has the great advantage that it begins with the loss, hence it is secure, for it has nothing to lose.
>
> – Kierkegaard, *Repetition* 12

In 1902, Louis Dantin made the following observation about Nelligan's melancholy:

> Car alors, ce qui est son fond essentiel, c'est une tristesse sombre et désolée. Non la tristesse qui flotte, vaporeuse et douce, sur l'âme des purs mélancoliques; – non celle qui s'amollit, comme chez Rodenbach, de la suaveté des souvenirs; – non plus celle qui se justifie et se raisonne, comme chez les grands pessimistes; – mais la tristesse sans objet, sans cause et dès lors sans consolation; lame implacable et froide enfoncée jusqu'au vif du cœur; torture aigüe, amère, enfiévrée et desséchante, n'ayant pas même l'orgueil de la force stoïque ou le soulagement des larmes (1997, 85).

While our previous discussion has substantiated that "la suaveté des souvenirs" does indeed play a significant role in Nelligan's dysphoria, Dantin's observation that his melancholy seems without a precise cause – an attribute of this condition recognized by Galen in the second century – is borne out in more than a dozen poems. The ground seems to be life itself or, more precisely, an existential condition which is the poet's own. Many of his poems are statements of melancholy, not explanations of the condition. The short, early poem "Quelqu'un pleure dans le silence," for instance, accentuates the poet's weeping ("Quelqu'un pleure" is repeated three times in the compass of six lines) but identifies no causality. A good example of melancholy with no specific cause is Nelligan's well-known rondel "Potiche," whose quatrains depict an oriental vase:

C'est un vase d'Égypte à riche ciselure,
Où sont peints des sphinx bleus et des lions ambrés:
De profil on y voit, souple, les reins cambrés,
Une immobile Isis tordant sa chevelure.

Flambantes, des nefs d'or se glissent sans voilure
Sur une eau d'argent plane aux tons de ciel marbrés:
C'est un vase d'Égypte à riche ciselure
Où sont peints des sphinx bleus et des lions ambrés. (237)

Egyptian vases also figure in "Fantaisie créole," but this one is no ordinary container: it is richly engraved in hues of blue and gold, depicting sphinxes, lions, golden ships on silver waters, and especially a profile of Isis, the mother-goddess seen as the source of all fecundity by mystery cults. She is wringing her hair, a characteristic of ancient depictions of Venus Anadyomène, to whom Nelligan alluded in "Gretchen la pâle." One might be tempted to read this conjoining of exoticism and sensuality as a Parnassian exercise, until one reads the rest of the poem:

Mon âme est un potiche où pleurent, dédorés,
De vieux espoirs mal peints sur sa fausse moulure;
Aussi j'en souffre en moi comme d'une brûlure,
Mais le trépas bientôt les aura tous sabrés ...

Car ma vie est un vase à pauvre ciselure. (237)

Paul Wyczynski has correctly noted that by the poem's closure "tout l'exotisme du début se pénètre des tourments d'une âme angoissée"

(1967, 55). The vase to which the lyric "I" compares his soul reveals itself to be quite unlike the richly painted Egyptian one of the first two quatrains. His hopes have had their gilt rubbed off, in contrast to the golden ships of verse 5. They are "mal peint sur sa fausse moulure," clearly the opposite of the "riche ciselure" of line 1. He suffers this contrast as he would a burn, a bodily injury, just as, in "Beauté cruelle," he suffered from a cut. The feeling of inferiority usually characteristic of melancholiacs surfaces in the conviction that he has been poorly made ("un vase à pauvre ciselure").

Non-specific melancholy receives a fuller expression in "Les Angéliques" and thereby merits a more detailed consideration:

Des soirs, j'errais en lande hors du hameau natal,
Perdu parmi l'orgueil serein des grands monts roses,
Et les Anges, à flots de long timbres moroses,
Ébranlaient les bourdons, au vent occidental.

Comme un berger-poète au cœur sentimental,
J'aspirais leur prière en l'arôme des roses,
Pendant qu'aux ors mourants, mes troupeaux de névroses
Vagabondaient le long des forêts de santal.

Ainsi, de par la vie où j'erre solitaire,
J'ai gardé dans mon âme un coin de vieille terre,
Paysage ébloui des soirs que je revois;

Alors que, dans ta lande intime, tu rappelles,
Mon cœur, ces angélus d'antan, fanés, sans voix:
Tous ces oiseaux de bronze envolés des chapelles! (171)

The poem's landscape, which does not derive from the geography of Nelligan's childhood, is obviously literary. Nelligan was born not in a hamlet but in Montreal, by then a sizable city that was not bordered by heaths or by forests of sandalwood. Nelligan often has recourse to the literature and especially the poetry of others to provide him with a vocabulary that can organize a discourse through which his melancholy can be expressed. As is his wont, he begins by describing a past to which, later in the poem, he will compare his present. He focuses on a repeated activity, a wandering in the countryside that occurred on more than one evening. The verb *errer*, meaning to wander aimlessly with no specific direction or purpose in mind, describes a condition that is a staple of pre-Romantic and Romantic poetry, and one that befits one who has no responsibilities, a status usually associated with childhood and youth.

However literary its source may be, the decor is resplendent. In a rural setting, as the roses diffuse their aroma, a golden sunset ("ors mourant") turns the surrounding mountains pink. This is the angelic space to which the title refers (in one of the hospital manuscripts, Nelligan retitled this poem "Soirs Angélises"). Kathy Mezei has correctly observed that "Nelligan's clear play on the word 'angélus' and 'angéliques' suggests that the ringing of the bells becomes, in the poet's mind, the singing of angels" (1980, 90). Unlike the "lost Eden" poems, this sonnet does not evince a sharp contrast between a past Eden and a present hell, for the landscape of the past already contains an endemic sadness. The mountains may have been serene in their pinkish hue, but the sounds of the bells have "de longs timbres moroses" (line 3). At the very moment the poet was breathing in the prayer of the angels through the aroma of the roses, "mes troupeaux de névroses / Vagabondaient le long des forêts de santal" (lines 7–8). The quatrains already express the poet's melancholy, so the expected sharp contrast between the quatrains and the tercets does not occur.

Significantly, the poet's own condition as a *névrosé* is associated not with his being a poet but with his being *like* a poet. The recourse to a simile is important: a direct statement such as "C'est en berger-poète" would equally have maintained the required meter. Situating himself analogically to a poet, "Comme en berger-poète" (line 5), assimilates him to the inner loneliness he attributes to the condition of the poet without claiming for himself poetic genius. In one of the hospital manuscripts, Nelligan transcribed the fifth line as "Comme un ange poète épris de récital" (M 148). The older Nelligan raises the level of the analogy from that of "shepherd-poet" to that of an "angel-poet," a not altogether surprising revision since the shepherd has religious connotations in the Judaeo-Christian tradition. What is perhaps more important is the change from "poète au cœur sentimental" to "poète épris de récital," thereby stressing an inner compulsion similar to that of the poet.

The quatrains, which mention no companions, had already assumed his solitude, a condition confirmed in the first line of the first tercet where he specifies that he wanders alone. He continues to do what he did in the past, having now internalized the landscape of his previous wanderings. The "lande hors du hameau natal" of line 1 becomes a "lande intime," as he shifts from the third to the second person in the final tercet in order to address directly his own heart, specifying that the reason for this internalization is to ensure that his heart not forget these voiceless, wilted sounds of the angels of yesteryear, which he compares to bronze birds having escaped from chapels.

Why seek to internalize a past marked by sadness? Here it is useful to draw attention to Nelligan's cultivation of his own melancholy, a trait observed by several of his adolescent friends. Louvigny de Montigny wrote of him that "il se laissait complaisamment pénétrer des névroses de Rollinat; ... il aurait souhaité être aussi triste que Rodenbach" (317). Another friend, Lucien Lemieux, told Luc Lacourcière that Nelligan "cultivait sa mélancolie" (1969, 32). Freud noted the "pleasurable" quality of the self-torments of melancholiacs (172); more pertinent, perhaps, is Kierkegaard's description in *Either/Or* of what he called the "aesthetic state," that is the condition of a person completely turned in on himself and absorbed in his own feelings. Such is the state of the young man who is the first person narrator of Part 1 of Kierkegaard's text. He suffers from a deep despair, confessing that "over my inner being broods an oppressivness, an anxiety that forebodes an earthquake" (1:29). Yet for him melancholy is to be treasured: "I say of my sorrow what an Englishman says of his house: my sorrow *is my castle*" (1:21; Kierkegaard's italics). "I love my sorrow" (1:33) adds this young man of evidently misanthropic disposition. His older friend, Judge William, the narrator of the second part, offers a searching critique of this attitude. For him, his young friend has created an image of himself as an exceptional man because of his melancholy and then has used that melancholy as an excuse for not rising to his obligations, that is, for not attaining the next level of existence, the "ethical state" in which the will engages itself in choice and in which the subject attains a level of self-transparence. While Nelligan's mental condition, little understood at the time,[17] could today be controlled to a certain extent by psychotropic medication, he, who differed in significant ways from Kierkegaard's young man, particularly regarding the concept of love and the role of conscience, appears like him to have needed his melancholy in order to maintain a certain image of himself, thereby remaining imprisoned in Kierkegaard's aesthetic state.[18]

The poet's willingness to blame his existential despair for his inability to act or, in Kierkegaardian terms, to engage himself in the ethical state, is evident in the deeply brooding poem "Ténèbres." Here, the word "ténèbres," signifying the total darkness (the traditional image of melancholy) that has engulfed the poet's soul, constitutes both the poem's title as well as its last word, thereby framing a text in which an active but undefined malevolent force is alleged to be afflicting him. "La Détresse," the capitalized and personified signifier of abandonment, takes concrete action inimical to the poet:

La Détresse a jeté sur mon cœur ses noirs voiles
Et les croassements de ses corbeaux latents;
Et je rêve toujours au vaisseau des Vingt ans,
Depuis qu'il a sombré dans la mer des étoiles.

Ah! quand pourrai-je encor comme des crucifix
Étreindre entre mes doigts les chères paix anciennes,
Dont je n'entends jamais les voix musiciennes
Monter dans tout le trouble où je geins, où je vis?

Et je voudrais rêver longuement, l'âme entière,
Sous les cyprès de mort, au coin du cimetière
Où gît ma belle enfance au glacial tombeau.

Mais je ne pourrai plus; je sens des bras funèbres
M'asservir au Réel, dont le fumeux flambeau
Embrase au fond des Nuits mes bizarres Ténèbres! (311)

The action of "la Détresse" described in the first two lines implies both its wilfulness and its strength as an agent. Distress has both subtracted and added: she has thrown a blank veil over his heart, depriving it of sight while at the same time assailing it with sounds. These sounds, the cawing of crows (generally negative symbols in modern Western cultures), are, moreover, unpleasant. Their harshness is reproduced phonetically through the alliteration of the velar [k] ("croassement de ses corbeaux"), and in the phonetic structure of "croassement" itself, with its velar followed by an [r], then a hiatus of two vowels [oa], normally frowned upon in French verse, followed by a hissing [s]. The disharmony at the phonetic level is meant to represent a harshness being imposed on the poet. The choice of the crows links the poem to one of Nelligan's most splenetic texts, "Les Corbeaux," in which crows pick away at the poet's body and soul.

In "Les Corbeaux," the crows' consumption of the poet is complete and entire, for they have taken not only his flesh but also his soul, "Déchirant à larges coups de bec, sans quartier, / Mon âme" (273). His response in "La Détresse" is to wish to continue dreaming, to continue recalling his youthful idealism, represented as a "vaisseau des Vingt ans" which has, however, already sunk. The image of drowning or sinking, which we saw in "Le Vaisseau d'Or," has remained a constant in depressed people, as David A. Karp reports from his interviews with persons suffering from depression (28–9). The power of the word "détresse" is heightened by the image of the sunken ship, since in French the established expression for a ship in difficulty is "navire en détresse." Not only was his condition of distress not responded to, distress itself becomes a malevolent force intent on his suffering. The poet's response is, once again, nostalgia. Lines 5, 6, and 7 evoke the "chères paix anciennes" (line 6) that have completely disappeared. Line 8 expresses well his situation, "tout le trouble où je gémis, où je vis," with the alliterative [t]s and [ʒ]s again producing a phonetic equivalent to his inner state. The phrases "où je gémis" and "où je vis," situated consecutively and paratactically, imply that for the poet, wailing and living are inextricably linked.

The tercets begin with another nostalgic foray as the poet "moves through dream into a landscape of his soul," as Kathy Mezei has aptly put it (1979, 154). Again he would like to recapture his "belle enfance," but significantly, he wants to do his dreaming in a space associated with death: "sous les cyprès de mort, au coin du cimetière / … au glacial tombeau" (lines 10–11). Yet he recognizes his incapacity: "Mais je ne pourrai plus" (line 11). The arms of death are tying him to a reality he does not want and with which he cannot cope. If his past is in ice ("au glacial tombeau"), reality's smoking torch is engulfing "au fond des Nuits mes bizarres Ténèbres" (line 14). His present suffering has incapacitated him. The semes of hell contained in "ténèbres" ("le prince des ténèbres," "l'empire des ténèbres") end the poem on a note of utter despair. The poet's self-absorption, by which he remains in Kierkegaard's aesthetic state, is made manifest in the strong presence of the first person pronoun, "je," which appears eight times in the poem, with its consonant [ʒ] making an additional fivefold appearance.

"Sérénade triste," based on an initial analogy between "larmes d'or" and "feuilles de mes bonheurs," confirms the poet's lack of control over his depressive state:

Comme des larmes d'or qui de mon cœur s'égouttent,
Feuilles de mes bonheurs, vous tombez toutes, toutes.

Vous tombez au jardin de rêve où je m'en vais,
Où je vais, les cheveux au vent des jours mauvais.

Vous tombez de l'intime arbre blanc, abattues
Ça et là, n'importe où, dans l'allée aux statues.

Couleur des jours anciens, de mes robes d'enfant,
Quand les grands vents d'automne ont sonné l'olifant.

Et vous tombez toujours mêlant vos agonies,
Vous tombez, mariant, pâles, vos harmonies.

Vous avez chu dans l'aube au sillon des chemins,
Vous pleurez de mes yeux, vous tombez de mes mains.

Comme des larmes d'or qui de mon cœur s'égouttent,
Dans mes vingt ans déserts, vous tombez toutes, toutes. (117)

The image of leaves falling like tears had been used by Charles Vellay in a prose poem, "Feuilles Mortes," published in 1895: "... les feuilles mortes tombent, tombent comme des larmes. Comme des larmes de souffrance, elles tombent les feuilles mortes ..."[19] Vellay's conclusion, that the loss of the leaves is necessary for new ones to be born, differs wholly from that of Nelligan, whose leaves, seen as tears of gold, represent the happiness that is leaving him piece by piece, as leaves drop from a tree. The place of gold in stress position at the end of the first hemistich further valorizes this signifier that we already know to be positive in Nelligan's work. The tears are golden because they are falling leaves, hence leaves whose colours have begun to turn. But gold also signifies the precious nature of what is being lost: "mes bonheurs." The prosodically unnecessary plural signals the disappearance of *all* pleasures, and is further strengthened by the echoic "toutes, toutes" at the end of the first distich, which effectively mimics repetitive drops of water. The most prominent signifier of the poem is "tombez," used seven times, in every distich except the fourth. Its repetitiveness increases the sense of loss while at the same time absolving the poet of responsibility for that deprivation. The agent that causes the leaves to fall – metaphorically the wind – is outside him, and its action in the poem is both minatory and capricious. An impersonal force is ripping away an important part of the intimate self, for these leaves are falling from "l'intime arbre blanc" (line 5), a key metaphor for the self of the poet. The unexpected epithet "blanc" may suggest that this tree has lost all life, that it will not, like other trees, regenerate itself in the spring. "Blanc" further recalls the virginal purity of the poet, proclaimed many times throughout his verse. The banal topos of falling leaves, which is featured in numerous French poems, including some by Millevoye, Lamartine, and Verlaine that Nelligan knew well, as well as in poems appearing in Montreal magazines, served Nelligan in his first piece of writing and is here redefined and personalized in an original way.

For a French-speaking readership, the "olifant" which appears at the centre of the poem is associated with hopelessness, for in *La Chanson de Roland* it is the horn that the dying Roland blew, too late to secure Charlemagne's assistance. The repetition of the opening distich as the closing couplet provides a circular structure, closing off hope of escaping the condition of loss. Yet, in repeating these distichs, Nelligan made one change, substituting "Dans mes vingt ans déserts" for "feuilles de mes bonheurs" in the last line. This substitution emphasizes the poet's relative youth (the falling leaves are not a metaphor of aging and death) and especially the barrenness of his life as the semes of sterility contained in "désert" are activated.

The topos of falling leaves reappears in "Tarentelle d'automne" in which the first two stanzas establish an analogy between the foliage falling to great depths ("dans les ravines / Dans les ravines") and the loss of the poet's illusions. The lyrical subject's unnamed companion is invited to observe these leaves cascading and then his/her attention is directed to the poet's illusions, which are so wilted that they are dropping like leaves:

Vois-tu sur le coteau des années
Choir mes illusions fanées,
Toutes fanées? (174)

A tarantella, normally a lively dance or its music, becomes the melody of melancholy, as "la bise de nos tristesses / De mes tristesses" (lines 8–9) creates a lugubrious mood, to which the poet himself contributes:

Ma sérénade d'octobre enfle une
Funéraire voix à la lune,
Au clair de lune. (174).

There is a sense in the poem that the loss is beginning to touch the inner core, for it seems to him that the trees are losing not only their leaves but their bark as well: "chaque arbre divorce / Avec sa feuille et son écorce, / Sa vieille écorce" (lines 25–7).

Such a psychological context can assist us in reading "Salons allemands," a piece that Nelligan contributed to a collection of poems assembled by members of the École littéraire de Montréal to honour their colleague, Louis-Joseph Béliveau, on the occasion of his marriage (RW 421). A decidedly odd contribution for a miscellany celebrating nuptials, this poem depicts old, decaying persons and things and even imagines wall portraits of the deceased asking, "Vivants, pourquoi tant rire?" (line 7), not the kind of question one should be asking at a wedding. The poem is, however, revelatory of Nelligan's self-preoccupation: "Mais surtout je pleure et ne sais que résoudre ... " (line 12; the suspension points are Nelligan's). "Mais surtout," which begins the line, is a particularly strong adversative, for as Claude Filteau has pointed out (27) it breaks the pattern established in the preceding three stanzas, all of which begin with "Je": "Je me figure" (line 1), "Je repense" (5), and "J'évoque" (9). Written in 1897 and therefore one of his earlier poems, "Salons allemands" exposes a young man incapable of empathy, so taken with his own melancholy that he is oblivious to the happiness around him – unless it is that very happiness that makes him sad. How different, then, is Nelligan's poem from "Soirée allemande" that his friend Arthur de Bussières published a few months earlier in *Le Monde illustré*.[20] Bussières' poem is dysphoric, to be sure, but his text, one of his best, is entirely descriptive, consisting of a third person poetic presentation of the coming of nighttime to an imagined German landscape. Nelligan, ever the poet of interiors, restricts himself to rooms inside a building, compulsively interjecting himself into the ambient sadness by having recourse to the first person pronoun "je" five times in the course of a sonnet. Such self-absorption, not an infrequent characteristic of depressed persons, constitutes the heart of the aestheticism criticized by Kierkegaard's second narrator. Weeping and indecisive ("surtout je pleure et ne sais que résoudre"), he remains, like a Kierkegaardian aesthete, "engrossed completely in mood" (2:229), incapable of the act of choice. This leaves him standing apart from the festivities in an isolating self-enclosure.

The poet's inability to experience even momentary relief from his dysphoria is reinforced in "Mazurka" where, as in "Tarentelle d'automne," joyful music is associated with a state of melancholy. Here, a comfortable, carpeted, and well-lit living room, in which someone is playing a piano, provides the environment for the poet to take delight in his own melancholy, to fully partake of Kierkegaard's aesthetic state. The first two lines of the poem constitute its key phrase: "Rien ne captive autant que ce particulier / Charme de la musique où ma langueur s'adore" (lines 1–2). The suggestion that Nelligan might take pleasure in his own despondency is nowhere stated more clearly than here. The second stanza elaborates further on the curious relationship between the poet and his moral fatigue:

> Que j'aime entendre alors, plein de deuil singulier,
> Monter du piano, comme d'une mandore,
> Le rythme somnolent où ma névrose odore
> Son spasme funéraire et cherche à s'oublier! (181)

He *enjoys* this somnolent rhythm in which his neurosis can actually smell its own funereal spasms. We ought not be misled by the final hemistich of line 8, "et cherche à s'oublier," for it represents not an attempt to lose or even forget his neurosis but rather a desire to merge his depression with what has become for him sombre music. The tercets make this clear:

> Gouffre intellectuel, ouvre-toi, large et sombre,
> Malgré que toute joie en ta tristesse sombre,
> J'y peux trouver encore comme un reste d'oubli,
>
> Si mon âme se perd dans les gammes étranges
> De ce motif en deuil que Chopin a poli
> Sur un rythme inquiet appris des noirs Archanges. (181)

In "Chopin," the poet had conceded that this composer's music "m'entraîne / Et m'a rendu malade et fou!" (180). Yet the poet believes he can perhaps find a respite in this intellectual abyss, "Malgré que toute joie en ta tristesse sombre" (line 9). In his desire to lose himself in a disquieting music perhaps of demonic origin ("des noirs Archanges"), this poet, who takes delight in his own sadness, seeks to remain one with his dysphoria.

In "Prélude triste," a dark, morbid (and considerably unfinished) poem written in 1898, the poet once again alludes to a past in which there was hope: "Aux jours où je vêtais des chasubles d'espoirs / Jouant près de ma mère en ma chambre angélique" (lines 3–4). The religious semes ("chasubles," "angélique," following "basilique" and "encensoir" in the opening couplet) in the proximity of maternal ones ("près de ma mère") suggests that the serenity of his childhood derives somehow from a harmony among his religious beliefs and practices, maternal approval, and himself. But the shift in this case comes early, with the first lines of the second quatrain: "Maintenant oh! combien je suis mélancolique / Et comme les ennuis m'ont fait des joujous noirs!" (lines 5–6). The poem is striking in its strange premonition of what would befall him a year later: "soudain par des causes étranges / Je surgirai mal mort dans un vertige fou" (11–12), including his death in an asylum: "Afin de retourner et mourir dans mon trou" (14).

The relationship between the poet and his sorrow is indeed intimate, and one from which it is not certain that he wants to escape. The imagery and discourse of "Sous les faunes" (296) is that of two lovers, and the vocabulary used stresses their embrace: "nous nous serrions" (lines 1 and 14), "rêvassions-nous, longuement enlacés"

(3), "nos cœurs s'emplissaient" (12). Only in the last line does the reader learn that the other person included in "nous" is "ma Douleur morne," although the adjective "hagard," used to describe the couple, had already introduced a cautionary note. The lover embraces not a woman but sorrow itself. The poet here joins Kierkegaard's young man who freely admitted that "My depression is the most faithful mistress I have known – no wonder, then, that I return the love" (1:20), a statement similar to one made by Kierkegaard himself.[21] In this poem, the persona's lengthy embrace suggests that for this poet sorrow likewise fulfills a desire. The return of the first hemistich of the first verse ("Nous nous serrions, hagards") as the first hemistich of the final verse – a wilful trangression of the rules of the sonnet – stresses his sense of being confined in his sorrow.

Cold appears as a significant correlative image of the poet's melancholy in two particularly dysphoric poems. "Frisson d'hiver,"discussed earlier in a different context, begins by noting that the gas heaters are almost closed. No explanation is given for these faulty heaters, but since gas is supplied by public authorities, their deficiency might indicate that warmth cannot come from society. As a result, "le givre ... s'éternise / Hivernalement" (lines 13–14), and the poet experiences chills. The ambient coldness reflects the conditions of his heart "dont les sanglots / S'épanchent" (lines 2–3), and to which he refers as "ce clavecin de mes névroses" (6). Again, the cause of the melancholy is not specified, but what is particular to this poem is that he sees a consolation in Gretchen, for she could warm him in the cold that envelops them. Like large Persian cats who show "des yeux reconnaissants" (lines 18–19), he, too, is seeking warmth that will mitigate not only the cold temperature but also the sadness in his heart. He seeks a solace that would result from physical contact: "Prends-moi le front, prends-moi les mains, / Toi, mon trésor de rêves maints" (lines 9–10). The lyric persona is not expressing his love for Gretchen, but rather, much like Persian cats, he seeks to *receive* affection, not give it. Like Kierkegaard's first narrator, he is given to wishing, not willing. It is important, then, not to read this text as a love poem. The reference to Persian cats, felines known for their reluctance to be affectionate, is telling. There is no suggestion that Gretchen could cure him of his sadness, that a response from her could heal his pathological melancholy.

The poem is constructed in such a way as to make the poet's appeal to Gretchen a haunting one. Each of the seven stanzas consists of three octosyllabic lines containing a single rhyme followed by a two-syllable line, composed in each case of the single word "Gretchen." The first stanza,

Les becs de gaz sont presque clos:
Chauffe mon cœur dont les sanglots
S'épanchent dans ton cœur par flots,
Gretchen! (154)

is repeated as the last stanza:

Chauffe mon cœur dont les sanglots
S'épanchent dans ton cœur par flots.
Les becs de gaz sont presque clos ...
Gretchen! (154)

By inverting the order of the lines so that the first line of the original tercet becomes the last of the poem, Nelligan creates once again a circular closure, not leaving much hope for an escape. Tellingly, we are not apprised of Gretchen's response or even if she had any.

The strongest metaphoric connection between winter and the poet's *ennui* occurs in "Soir d'hiver," a poem singled out by Dantin for its original "agencement musical" (1997, 6), and one of Nelligan's most successful pieces:

Ah! comme la neige a neigé!
Ma vitre est un jardin de givre.
Ah! comme la neige a neigé!
Qu'est-ce que le spasme de vivre
À la douleur que j'ai, que j'ai!

Tous les étangs gisent gelés,
Mon âme est noire: Où vis-je? Où vais-je?
Tous ses espoirs gisent gelés:
Je suis la nouvelle Norvège
D'où les blonds ciels s'en sont allés.

Pleurez, oiseaux de février,
Au sinistre frisson des choses,

Pleurez, oiseaux de février,
Pleurez mes pleurs, pleurez mes roses,
Aux branches du genévrier.

Ah! comme la neige a neigé!
Ma vitre est un jardin de givre.
Ah! comme la neige a neigé!
Qu'est-ce que le spasme de vivre
A tout l'ennui que j'ai, que j'ai! ... (299)

The strong phonetic presence of the phoneme [ʒ], the opening consonant of "givre" and "gelé" and the final consonant of "neige," locks the poem into its wintry scene. The initial distich is, first, an observation of how much it has snowed and how cold it is. And, clearly, "Ma vitre est un jardin de givre" (line 2) can be read literally: the cold and the storm have frosted over the panes of his windows. But metaphorically, as becomes evident further in the poem, "vitre" is also his soul, whose windows to the outside have iced. For, already in line 4, the poet has shifted the focus to his own condition, referring to "le spasme de vivre," a condition he mimics phonetically in "que j'ai, que j'ai."

While the second stanza also begins with a description of the weather, specifically noting that the swamps are frozen, the following line immediately refocuses on the poet's own condition, thereby retaining the link between the impersonality of the climate and his personal suffering. His soul is black, sharply contrasting with his white surroundings. Thus a sense of disorientation is evoked, an inability to know where he is and where he is going. In making the analogy between his state and the conditions outside him, he repeats the verse "Tous les étangs gisent gelés." The expression "gisent gelés" carries with it the sense not only of being frozen and its attendant semes of immobilization but also of being "dead frozen." All hope is dead, "l'Espoir, / Vaincu, pleure," as Baudelaire famously put it in "Spleen LXXVIII." Then, in two of his most beautiful verses, Nelligan transforms himself metaphorically into a country whose winters are virtually without daylight: "Je suis la nouvelle Norvège / D'où les blonds ciels s'en sont allés" (lines 9–10). Norway has reconstructed itself in him. His dark soul is left without light.

The thematics of the poem broadens in the third stanza where the poet implies that his plight may be the result of the nature of things, the "sinistre frisson des choses" to which he alludes in line 12. Just as he has invited the birds to weep at this existential condition, so too, in a recourse to polyptoton, does he invite them to weep over his own tears ("Pleurez mes pleurs," line 14). The final stanza repeats the first while changing one word, "douleur" to "ennui." His reflection on the sadness inherent both in him and in the very condition of human existence has led him to darken the description of his own situation. "Ennui," as Alain Masson has remarked (114), adds connotations of duration to the poet's suffering. The physical phenomenon of snow and ice has become a correlative to a moral morass bordering on despair. With one exception, "Caprice blanc," a playful poem on the whiteness of winter, Nelligan's winter verse differs sharply from the verse published on this subject at the time. To be sure, poems that depicted the harshness of winter did exist, but these more frequently had as their purpose exhorting people of means to come to the aid of the poor.[22] Other poems made light of winter,[23] or openly celebrated it, as did Augustin Lellis: "O splendide saison, sois donc la bienvenue!"[24]

Nelligan clearly borrows much from the European tradition of melancholy verse that dates from the middle of the eighteenth century. Nevertheless, the differences between his poetry and that tradition are more telling than the borrowings. In the tradition, especially as it was established in England, melancholy is a point of departure for a reflection on the human condition, and the individual poetic voice becomes a spokesperson for the human race in the face of the sadness of things. But this is not at all Nelligan's point of view; only occasionally does melancholy lead to philosophical musings in Nelligan. Unhappiness may be the lot of all men, but what concerns him is his unique experience of it. Indeed, he conceives of sadness as a constituent part of his being, repeating the collocation "Je suis tel" three times in "Soirs d'octobre" (297). Few lamentations on the misfortunes of human existence reverberate in this poetry dominated by the expression of a deeply personal sorrow. Hence, he draws few general conclusions, and his poetry contains none of the didacticism associated with the origins of melancholy verse in Europe. Nor does Nelligan participate in the long tradition, dating from Aristotle's *Problemata*, that sees a connection between melancholy and genius. While Nelligan occasionally links his sadness and his status as a poet, he is not given to exploiting a causality between the two. Melancholy in Nelligan is the expression of a personal sorrow in the face of a universe to which he does not belong.

Conclusion: Nelligan and Decadence

In the literary and intellectual history of Europe, the decade 1880–90 is distinguished by a thematic convergence that came to be known as decadence. Marked by pervasive sadness and pessimism about the self and civilization, decadence is associated with the thematics of fatigue and anxiety, with a rebellion against the materialism of both industrialism and positivist science, and with a rejection of the naturalist aesthetic. Drawing inspiration from nineteenth-century writers of the previous generation such as Baudelaire, Flaubert, Gautier, and Poe, and from selected later works of Verlaine, writers and artists in France sought to articulate the sense of decadence that pervaded intellectual milieus after the defeat of 1870, the trauma of the Commune, and the problems besetting the new republic. They formed a community of perspective rather than a school of any kind, even if Anatole Baju, the founder and editor of *Le Décadent littéraire*, did publish in 1887 a pamphlet entitled *L'École décadente*. Contemporaries identified various writers of the time as being decadent. Among these were figures who are little known today, such as Baju, Rollinat, and Francis Poictevin, as well as writers who are still read and discussed a full century later and whose stature continues to grow: Huysmans, Villiers de l'Isle-Adam, and Laforgue, especially.[1]

Since Nelligan wrote nearly all his poetry in the decade following the high point of decadence in Europe, since he was more acutely aware of European writing than almost any other poet of his time in Canada, and given the preceding discussion of his melancholy, it is legitimate to ask to what extent his poetry might be said to participate in the decadent ethos.[2] It is useful to recall that Dantin was already stating in 1903 that "On s'est habitué à voir en lui un *décadent*, un tenant de l'école dont Rimbaud, Mallarmé, Verlaine furent les coryphées, et qui, de Rodenbach à Viellé-Griffin, a compté depuis d'illustres représentants" (see 1997, 92). Nelligan clearly drew much from the decadents, not a specific syntagm or lexeme as he did from the Parnassians, but rather a whole semic field. I will demonstrate that he absorbed much of the discourse of decadence, but I will then propose that he uses it in a different ethical space from that of its texts of origin.

When Nelligan laments his having to live "En ce monde menteur, flétri, blasé, pervers" (295), he adopts an anti-social discourse common to both Romantic and decadent poets. As my discussion in chapter 1 demonstrates, one of his best-known poems, "La Romance du vin," illustrates the sense of isolation from society that haunts his poetry. In this poem, the opposition between the poetic self and his community is highlighted by a semic axis that reflects the attitude of society towards the poet, an axis containing semes of ill-will, disdain, and mocking laughter. In the face of a hostile crowd, this distressed poet will follow the pattern of retreat set by decadents in France. He has become, he tells us in "Le Regret des joujoux," "muré contre le monde / Tel un prince du Nord que son Kremlin défend" (107). In contrast to the movement of isolation practiced by the Romantics, the retreat sought by the decadents involves not only a withdrawal from society but a retreat from nature as well (Rollinat is the notable exception in this respect). Every critic of the decadents has noted a strong anti-natural current in the movement, but other than Gérard Bessette (225, 243–5), few critics of Nelligan have recognized the implicit rejection of nature in his poetry. It is noteworthy that whatever nature subsists in Nelligan is either conventional, indifferent, or hostile. The companion pieces "Presque Berger" and "Petit Hameau," for example, can be read as literary exercises, prosaic renditions ("le chien jappe. / Je me couche") devoid of Nelligan's usual musicality and imagery and manifesting none of the inner-life constellations that mark the rest of his poetry. Lines such as "Que vous êtes heureux, hommes bons des campagnes, / Loin du faubourg qui pue et des clameurs de bagnes" ("Petit Hameau" 127) represent a conventional and fleeting Rousseauism. But even here, I would maintain that

Nelligan is not romanticizing rural life as much as imagining a freedom in that life that he associates with his own childhood. "Oui, c'est délicieux ... d'être ainsi libre," he affirms in "Presque Berger," before concluding: "au temps de l'enfance, ma vie / Coulait ainsi, loin des sentiers, blanche et ravie" (126). He yearns not for nature but for the less restrained life of the child. In his poetry, nature does not represent a refuge for the present but rather is folded into his personal myth of childhood.

Some elements of nature, such as the wind, the most frequent meteorological condition in Nelligan, can be sinister. Moreover, in most of what might be called the "winter verse," nature in general is often represented as hostile. This is particularly so in "Paysage fauve," which Nelligan published in *Le Monde illustré* in 1897. In this poem,

> Les arbres comme autant de vieillards rachitiques,
> Flanqués vers l'horizon sur les escarpements,
> Tordent de désespoir leurs torses fantastiques,
> Ainsi que des damnés sous le fouet des tourments. (264)

It is, of course, winter, and a bitter one, as the second quatrain, which begins with "C'est l'Hiver, c'est la Mort," makes clear. This is a threatening nature, for we learn in the last five lines of the poem that

> ... voici que soudain se dessine dans l'ombre
> Un farouche troupeau de grands loups affamés;
> Ils bondissent, essaims de fauves multitudes,
> Et la brutale horreur de leurs yeux enflammés
> Allume de points d'or les blanches solitudes. (264)

These two and one-half stanzas are filled with signifiers containing semes of terror. The nature here evoked is not one to which one would go to seek refuge.

Most decadent writing is situated in urban settings, and much of Nelligan's verse is identified as urban as well. Even the garden which figures prominently in "Le Jardin d'antan" appears to be an urban garden, for it is "clos, scellé" (120). Cities are not, however, adequate refuges either. "Ô mornes et mortes cités!" he calls them in "Les Vieilles Rues" (249). "[J]e suis hanté, c'est la nuit dans la ville" (281), he adds in "Confession nocturne." The poet's advice to his loved one, "Fuis la ville" (136), is an invitation not to return to nature but to enter a vague afterlife. And so Nelligan goes a step further, as did Rodenbach in some of his texts, and retreats from nature to interiors, that is, to the inside of buildings: "Enfermons-nous mélancoliques / Dans le frisson tiède des chambres" (165). No other poet in Quebec prior to Nelligan situated as many of his poems specifically indoors.[3] The closed quality of interiors is preferred: to the openness of nature: "j'ai toujours adoré plein de silence, à vivre / En des appartements solennellement clos" (287). Interiors offer protection from the other and thereby the freedom for reverie. Yet, how morose are most of these dwellings, "ces grands salons muets / Pleins de velours usés et d'aïeules pensives" (170). Or, consider that in "Le Salon," "La poussière s'étend sur tout le mobilier, / Les miroirs de Venise ont défleuri leur charme" (182). The closed-in space that is the predilection of decadents may protect from the outside, but neither in Nelligan nor in decadent poetry does it assuage the despair that arises from within.

The nature rejected by the poet is seen as having abandoned man in any case. Most of the vegetative life in Nelligan's poetry is dead or dying, but this is just one instance of what seems like a universal decay. Withering, wilting, and fading are not attributed only to flowers and leaves. We also find in Nelligan "lèvres fanées" (112), "angélus ... fanés" (171), "brocart fané" (109), "bords fanés" (119), "guipure fanée" (221), "illusions fanées" (174), "amour fané" (271), and "pierres fanées" (286). Even the stones in Nelligan's universe, as in Rodenbach's, are wilting. *Fané*, used several times even by Fréchette, was a favoured adjective of decadent poets to the point that the celebrated pastiche of decadent poetry, *Les Déliquescences: poèmes décadents* by the fictitious Adoré Floupette (1885), contained the lines "Vous avez le flou / Des choses fanées" (50). If *fané* is the most prominent adjective of decay in Nelligan's work, it is not the only epithet so used. In his verse, watered silk has lost its colours, chapels are decaying, violins are broken, pages are yellowing, steps are crumbling, velvet is worn. "Comme tout choit avec prestesse!" as he puts it in "Le Violon brisé" (176). If Nelligan does not directly affirm, as do decadent poets and writers in France (except Baju!) that civilization itself is worn-out, aging, and dying, the reader of his poetry might well reach that conclusion.

As previous chapters have demonstrated, Nelligan's poetry is permeated with nostalgia for childhood and its innocence, and its author is clearly obsessed with the phenomenon of aging. References to his mother's growing old and to his own aging abound – this in spite of the fact that he wrote when still a teenager. What provides the decadent hue is that this aging of persons takes place within the context of a decaying environment. We find in Nelligan old streets in old cities, ancient chairs and old clocks in old living rooms, old villas, ancient corridors, old closets, old porcelains, old gardens, old oak trees, old books, old doors, old crosses, old kiosques, old pianos, old statues, old chapels, old monks, old artists, old angels, old voices, old moons, old minuets, and even old goat-keepers and old Hungarian tenors. To read Nelligan is to confront a semantic field connoting decrepitude that rivals any found in the decadent poets in France.

A similar obsession with death – "Je suis hanté tellement" (259) he writes in a reference to death – goes far beyond the thematics of mortality found in Charles Millevoye, whose early nineteenth-century elegiac verse had appealed to Nelligan. For the young poet, the sounds of death have been internalized: "J'écoute en moi des voix funèbres / Clamer transcendantalement" (259). "J'ai grandi dans le goût bizarre du tombeau" (252), he writes in "Le Cercueil." "Je suis de ceux pour qui la vie est une bière" (288), he adds in "Musiques funèbres." Some two dozen poems deal with someone's passing away. As he tells us in "Ruines," "tout est défunt" (243). But still more pronounced is his obsession with his own demise, "le trépas bientôt," as he puts it in "Potiche" (237).

Nelligan's is not, however, a Baudelairean vision of death as the ultimate meeting with the desired absolute, but simply a relief from the sufferings of life: "la mort que j'anticipe / Va me tirer de cet enfer" (213). Or, as he put it in his first published poem, "Rêve fantasque,"

> Qu'il est doux de mourir quand notre âme s'afflige,
> Quand nous pèse le temps tel un cuisant remords,
> – Que le désespoir ou qu'un noir penser l'exige –
>   Qu'il est doux de mourir alors! (89)

We find him calling for his own demise, envisaging his own body in a casket, toasting death, stating that his life is like death, and even alluding, twice, to the possibility of suicide. We recognize the morbid discourse of Rollinat and Rodenbach and the "mortelle fatigue de vivre" that Bourget detected in his contemporaries (xvii). It is no surprise that at least one-fourth of his poems, as Paula Gilbert Lewis has pointed out, are specifically described as nocturnal (230–1), nor is it a surprise that black, the colour of Des Esseintes's decadent banquet, should figure as prominently in his poetry as it does in Rollinat's. So dark is his poetry that Charles ab der Halden was moved to declare that next to Nelligan, "Schopenhauer lui-même n'est qu'un humouriste qui cherche à nous divertir par des boutades à l'emporte-pièce" (356).

Faced with a hostile, decaying world, obsessed with aging and dying, the decadent poets proclaimed their *névrose*, a condition they saw as particular to their generation which, coming too late in the course of history, could not hope for the robust health of more primitive peoples. They applied it to themselves in particular, and to artistic creation in general. Writing in 1883 on the poetry of his own time, Félicien Champsaur concluded with the remark, "Paris attend le grand poète de la névrose moderne" (Mianney 19). The literary journal *Le Scapin* proclaimed in its first issue in 1885, "place à la névrose!" (Marquèze-Pouey 181). Cesare Lombroso, who was not a partisan of decadence, stated flatly in his *L'Homme de génie* that "Le génie est une névrose" (xxii). Rollinat, a major source for Nelligan, titled one of his more successful volumes of poetry *Les Névroses* in 1883, and Nelligan himself had chosen "Soirs de Névrose" as the title for a section of his projected volume of verse. Interestingly, Dantin, commenting on Nelligan's internment, remarked that "La Névrose, cette divinité farouche qui donne la mort avec le génie, a tout consumé, tout emporté" (1997, 65). It could certainly be argued that Nelligan's claim to neurosis is more genuine than that of his French counterparts, but his neurasthenic discourse clearly draws from theirs.

Decadent neurosis most often subsumes a profound sadness, a thematics evident even in the titles of collections of poetry published in the period, such as *Les Tristesses* by Rodenbach. Jean Pierrot has correctly observed that the last twenty years of the nineteenth century in France witnessed a new wave of dysphoria more intense than that which had marked the Romantic period (61). Certainly, Nelligan, who willingly expresses his "ennui de vivre" ("Rêves enclos"), his "tristesse profonde" ("Le Regret des joujoux"), his "tristesse immense" ("La Cloche dans la brume"), his forehead "terne d'ennui" ("Devant le feu"), his being "sombre et désespéré" ("Amour immaculé"), and the darkness of his soul ("Soir d'hiver") suffers from a sadness that is more pronounced than, say, Lamartine's. As in some Romantic poetry, this condition leads to weeping. He writes of his suffocating sobs ("Devant mon berceau"), the fury of his sobs ("Banquet macabre"), and his tearful youth ("Le Jardin d'antan"). But Nelligan, like the French decadents, goes beyond Romantic melancholy whose physical symptoms were limited to tears and pallor. Decadent neurosis, which derives a great deal from Baudelaire, has more pronounced physical symptoms. Nelligan, who describes himself as *névrosé*, is afflicted with physical fatigue ("Je me sens ténaillé des fatigues physiques," 287) and shivers ("au frisson fou de mes vertèbres," 259; "au frisson glacé de mes vertèbres," 273). These shivers are sometimes accompanied by spasms. "[M]a névrose odore / Son spasme funéraire," he tells us in "Mazurka" (181). "[J]'eus ... / Des spasmes d'angoisse immortelle," he writes in "Le Chat fatal" (275). Life itself is likened to a spasm: "Qu'est-ce que le spasme de vivre / A la douleur que j'ai, que j'ai" (299), a verse whose ending, with its repetition of a voiceless velar followed by a voiced palatal ("que j'ai, que j'ai") effectively mimics spasm. Moreover, he seems acutely aware that his neurosis is leading him to the brink of madness, once referring to himself as "malade et fou" (180) and anticipating his being "mal mort dans un vertige fou" (241).

Decadent discourse allows for no solution to this sad state of affairs. As Paterne Berrichon, a collaborator of Baju, put it,

Dans le passé, rien que remords.
Pour le présent, pas une obole.
Le futur, c'est un discobole
Me visant de guignons le corps. (31)

Not even love is seen as a possible antidote to neurosis, for love, as Schopenhauer had taught, was but a ploy of nature to ensure reproduction. Nelligan's own discourse on love and sexuality is complex, as our previous discussion has shown. It is clear, however, that in his poetry the poet's quest for love is never realized, sometimes because of the rejection of the woman, sometimes because of his own timidity, but also because Nelligan judges his erotic desires to be evil. Significantly, Nelligan's sole use of the word "volupté" is modified by "sordide" (295). Nelligan's poetry evinces a discourse common to that of decadence, one that depicts woman as inherently evil, as the seductress and temptress who brings man to his downfall, a notion traceable to Genesis but made prominent by Flaubert's *Salammbo* and Moreau's paintings. In "Gretchen la pâle," Venus is "ce démon! / ... le Paros qui tue avec ses bras de marbre" (153). In "Le Vaisseau d'Or" semes of sexuality erupt as early as the third line in which a nude Venus is described as sprawled at the prow of the ship in a climate of excessive sun. It becomes evident in the second quatrain that the wreck of the ship results from the perverse attraction of female sexuality: "Mais il vint une nuit frapper le grand écueil / Dans l'Océan trompeur où chantait la Sirène" (312). The siren, said in classical mythology to attract sailors onto reefs, is also the symbol of the seductive woman. "La Cyprine d'amour" has caused the ship to plunge into the "profondeurs du Gouffre, immuable cerceuil" (312), that is, into the hell or nothingness this word had connoted in nineteenth-century French poetry since Hugo. The quest for the ideal has foundered on the reef of sexuality and ended in destruction. Clearly, Nelligan's understanding of female sexuality is not too far removed from that of Barbey d'Aurevilly and his decadent successors. Eros, in Nelligan as in decadent poetry, remains fraught with danger.

To what conclusions can these observations lead? Can we infer from his absorption of much decadent discourse that Nelligan is a decadent poet? Without doubt, the retreat from society, the turning away from nature, the preference for interiors, the vision of a world in decay, the obsessions with aging and death, the view of sexuality as threatening, all argue for a strong link between Nelligan and the decadent ethos. But there is something peculiarly striking about these convergences, for much of the discourse that Nelligan seems to share with the decadents was already part and parcel of Quebec culture and of its religious beliefs in particular.

As the discussion in chapter 2 demonstrates, ab der Halden, Camille Roy, and others who insisted that Nelligan avoids religious themes were simply mistaken. In the edition they would have used, namely Dantin's, religious themes play an important role in nearly one-fifth of the poems. The pervasive melancholy of this poetry is not unrelated to a religious thematics dating from the Fathers of the Church, which was appropriated by the popular spirituality of French Canada in order to stress that this life is hard, miserable, and necessarily sad. We live in a "valley of tears," as a popular prayer of the time put it. Consolation lay in the fact that this life is not the only life, that another lies beyond, if we merit it. "L'essentiel, c'est le ciel," the saying went. If this life is not the real one, should we be astonished that a sensitive adolescent might be obsessed by death? While we cannot discount Rollinat and Rodenbach as intertexts, we need to note as well that the liturgy of Ash Wednesday reminded the faithful that they were dust and to dust they would return.[4] A reading of the spiritual and moral discourse of the period reveals the extent to which many in this society had accepted Cardinal de Bérulle's affirmation that "ce Monde n'est qu'un Théâtre de Mort et cette vie n'est qu'une obligation de mourir, n'est qu'un engagement à la mort" (2:867).

Nor is the view of sexuality as threatening and destructive that Nelligan shares with the decadents surprising in a culture that viewed the body as evil. On numerous occasions, Nelligan yearns for purity, as in "Rêve d'artiste" where the desired woman is represented as pure, angelic, and completely disincarnated. Such desire coheres with the discourse of a society that taught that "les pensées et les désirs impurs" were capital sins. The nostalgia for childhood, so prominent in Nelligan, betrays a desire to return to a time prior to the awakening of his sexuality. His fear of losing his purity is clearly expressed in "Le Talisman," and his struggle against the flesh quite evident in "Châteaux en Espagne" where he despairs at his inability to withstand "le combat des vieux Anges impurs" (156). The latter image, absent from Nelligan's European sources, is, of course, common in the discourse of nineteenth-century Catholic moral theology where "les vieux Anges impurs" are the fallen angels who tempt us towards the sins of impurity.

But sexual urges are no less strong for being perceived as snares of the devil. If the poems on shepherdesses and most of those on Gretchen are fairly anodyne, "Gretchen la pâle" and "Le Vaisseau d'Or" reveal Nelligan as obsessed with the erotic and fascinated with the female body. The first two lines of the second quatrain of "Gretchen la pâle" depict a naked, wet woman unfurling her abundant hair. In answer to his own question as to whether this woman is from Eden or from hell, he is compelled to respond that she is "ce démon! / Ce Paros qui tue avec ses bras de marbre!" (153). Had not Jean-Jacques Olier reminded the faithful that "le démon a grand pouvoir sur la chair" (87)? Threatened by the sexual desire Gretchen represents, Nelligan falls back on a moral discourse that saw desire as evil. The eroticism associated with the wreck of the ship and its subsequent fall into the "profondeurs du Gouffre" in "Le Vaisseau d'Or" portrays sexuality as leading to the abyss of hell, a depiction coherent with the moral discourse of the period.

Since all descendants of Adam and Eve are inheritors of a primeval transgression, sin, for Nelligan and his co-religionists, is one of the realities of the human condition, for we are all, as the catechism affirmed, "participants [du] péché et de [la] punition de nos premiers parents" (*Catéchisme* 9). The preponderance of guilt in Nelligan's poetry, which distinguishes him from the decadents, most of whom experienced no sense of moral conflict, reveals a sense of culpability experienced at a level of anxiety rarely found elsewhere in poetry written in French. Guilt in Nelligan comes from the pleasures of the flesh that Olier had called "que des excréments, et une corruption de notre nature" (93), pleasures from which the talisman given to him by his mother was to protect him. The struggles of puberty, accompanied by an increasingly bohemian lifestyle, put him into conflict with the mother he so much adored. Whether or not Émilie Nelligan was a "mère dévorante" who wanted to be her son's sole object of love, as Doris-Louise Haineault has suggested (113), poems dealing with his childhood show him to have a strong fixation on his mother as the bearer of unconditional love. His childhood love for his mother and hers for him coincide with his moral purity. With adolescence came moral failures and hence the disappointment and disapproval of the mother.

Moral failures included writing verse that his mother considered scandalous. Nelligan seems to have been greatly anguished at the conflict between his poetic expression and his love for his mother. Anne-Marie Gleason, a journalist who wrote under the pseudonym Madeleine, reported in a fictional reconstruction of the only post-internment meeting between Nelligan and his mother, in November 1902,[5] that Nelligan said to his mother: "– Maman, tu sais, ces vers qui t'ont fait pleurer? Je les regrette, je les répudie, dis leur bien à tous que je les ai reniés. Demande à ces amis qui les ont lus, de les oublier, à ceux qui en gardent la copie, de la brûler. Émile Nelligan ne veut pas les avoir écrits. C'est mon testament à Dieu, et ma réparation à toi."[6] This repudiation of his poetry, or at least some part of it, because it caused pain to his mother is an indication of the anguish that his mother's disapproval caused him. While Nelligan's depressive condition may have been in part the result of psychosocial factors that included family dysfunction, a non-specific risk factor identified by recent research,[7] the deep melancholy of his adolescence may be linked to the loss of his mother's unconditional love. Freud's "Mourning and Melancholia" (1917) established that loss of a loved object is at the root of melancholia, an etiology to which mainstream psychiatry still subscribes. Melancholy is a mechanism by which the person experiencing the loss avoids the necessity of openly expressing his hostility towards the loved one. Donald Capps, in his study of melancholia in James, Otto, Jung, and Erikson, has argued that for them the lost love object was the unqualified love of the mother. In Nelligan's case, it is clear that the loss of the mother's unconditional love is intimately linked with his religious heritage. Bessette noted Nelligan's identification of his mother with religion (48), a trait discernible in Nelligan's *imaginaire*: "A l'autel de ses pieds, je l'honore en pleurant" ("Ma Mère" 110). In disapproving of her son's lifestyle, Mrs Nelligan became the articulator of the prevailing religious discourse. The mother, psychologists tell us, is frequently the source of moral feelings about one's sense of self (Douglas and Atwell 106). Nelligan's inability to measure up to her religious ideals and standards of behaviour, his sense that he has betrayed her, are clearly factors to be considered in accounting for his dysphoria.

Nelligan, then, adopts that decadent discourse which coheres with aspects of his own culture and upbringing. While Jacques Blais has successfully argued that a poem such as "Je veux m'éluder" incorporates features of decadent writing (dissonant phonology, rare or startling vocabulary, unexpected switches in register) "à son insu" (1999, 272), it is significant that Nelligan does not replicate aspects of decadent discourse that were incongruent with prevailing cultural norms within Quebec. There is no proud proclamation of incredulity in Nelligan, for whom faith was a given of his culture. There is no flirtation with the occult, an unnecessary move in a society that firmly believed in Satan's presence among us. He does not share the decadents' fascination for deviant sexual behaviour, an interest that would have been strongly reproved in his culture. No expressions of philosophical idealism are to be found in his poetry, for his society was already permeated with religious idealism. And no revolt against positivism and materialism appears here because these were hardly threats in nineteenth-century Quebec. Nelligan accepts and adapts those aspects of decadent discourse that are compatible with his own culture. His decadence therefore is an inculturated decadence. Nelligan owes much to the formulas and perceptions of European decadence; he owes perhaps more to the quasi-Jansenist discourse within his own society. Nelligan had internalized the teachings of Bérullian spirituality to the extent that his conscious adoption of the vocabulary and thematics of the legitimizing culture of France – the Parnassian to express nostalgia for the prepubertal life of innocence; the decadent to highlight the evil, decay, and death that marks postpubertal life – cannot mask that at a deeper level his intertexts are those of his own culture. In Nelligan, the prevailing language of European francophone poetic discourse operates in a different ethical space from that of its texts of origin, barely concealing how much he, who yearned for recognition from the centre, was entrenched in the mindset of the periphery.

Michel Butor once reminded us that "Nous écrivons toujours *dans* la littérature" (18). In reading Nelligan, we recognize that he participates in the community of nineteenth-century French poetic discourse, that he cannot be abstracted from the discursive space of nineteenth-century French culture. Yet that space, which provides the conditions for Nelligan's readability, cannot determine our reading. Nelligan is not a colonial echo of a Parisian ethos. What the French *collectivité discursive* provides must be "read through" to fully comprehend the contribution of Nelligan's personal drama as well as that of his French-Canadian discursive community. We need not subscribe to Harold Bloom's affirmation that a "poem's true subject is its repression of the precursor poem" (25) to accept his contention that "any reading of a poem is an inter-reading" (3), that a poetic text does not have "an ascertainable meaning or meanings without reference to other poetic texts" (2). Reading Nelligan is necessarily an inter-reading. The relationship of his texts to French texts is part of the production of meaning, even though that production of meaning requires that we ultimately put aside these same French texts.

Notes

INTRODUCTION

1 On this subject, see Michon 1988.
2 For a brief history of Nelligan criticism, see Wyczynski 1977.
3 For a listing of these, see Marquis 1995, 284–7; for a discussion of the poetic, theatrical, and fictional representations of Nelligan, see Marquis 1993.
4 See Giroux for a discussion of Nelligan's verse as set to music as well as music about Nelligan.
5 See Brissette's *Nelligan dans tous ses états: Un mythe national* for a thorough discussion of this evolution and its cultural significance.
6 See especially Wyczynski's *Emile Nelligan: Sources et originalité de son œuvre*.
7 Pierre Nepveu has provided a sophisticated analysis of the question of *américanité* (by which he refers to a sense of belonging to the Americas) in selected Québécois, Canadian, American, and Latin American writers (Nelligan is not included). See his *Intérieurs du nouveau monde*. For a briefer treatment from another perspective, see Morency.
8 For a succinct formulation of the relationship between intertextual and intratextual coherences, see Plett 5. A brief, probing discussion of interdiscursivity can be found in Angenot 1983.

CHAPTER ONE

1 For a detailed, season-by-season account of English theatre in nineteenth-century Montreal, see Franklin Graham, *Histrionic Montreal.*

2 For a discussion of this pre-avant-garde, see the substantial essay by Pierssens and Benardi.

3 Some interesting comparisons (and contrasts) between Lampman and Nelligan have, however, been drawn by Mezei 1979.

4 The multi-volume anthology *Les Textes poétiques du Canada français*, published from 1987, covers the entire corpus up to 1867. For a good example of the prevailing poetic tastes during Nelligan's childhood, see Louis-Hippolyte Taché's anthology, *La Poésie française au Canada* (1881), as well as its preface by Benjamin Sulte.

5 For a discussion of the status of the writer and the understanding of poetry in Quebec at mid-century, see Lemire 1993, 133–57, 161–7.

6 For a discussion of this aspect of Delahaye's thinking, see Filteau 133–60.

7 Verlaine's poem appeared in Montreal in *Le Samedi* where Nelligan published some of his own poems. All of Verlaine's works were available in Montreal in the 1880s, and there is ample evidence that Nelligan knew them well. See Wyczynski 1987, 124–8. Moreover, he seems to have identified Verlaine with "Clair de lune," since in an unpublished poem written during his internment we find the line "Verlaine clair de lune odorant des jardins" (ibid., 307).

8 On this subject, see Cohen.

9 In the copy of his poetry which Nelligan's mother gave to Guillaume Lahaise, Nelligan had inscribed "à Eva Nelligan" below the title (RW 530). Nelligan's sister, Eva, was two years younger than he.

10 "Telle durant la nuit la harpe éolienne, / Mêlant au bruit des eaux sa plainte aérienne, / Résonne d'elle-même au souffle des zéphyrs" (146).

11 The poem is followed in Lacourcière's edition by groups of poems titled "pièces retrouvées" and "pièces posthumes."

12 The text which apparently offended Nelligan is the following: "La poésie de M. Emile Nelligan n'avait pas toute l'originalité qu'annonçait le titre *Notre-Dame-Des-Neiges*. Son *Perroquet* était franchement mauvais, comme tous les perroquets qui ont une trop grande variété de couleurs dans leur plumage. *La Négresse* s'harmonisait cependant bien dans le tableau avec cet oiseau fastidieux. Je voudrais bien avoir l'avantage de lire d'autres œuvres de M. Nelligan, une petite thèse en simple prose, par exemple, afin d'émettre un jugement plus net sur son

mérite littéraire. Si tel est son désir, il pourrait l'adresser au *Monde illustré*, où nous la publierons avec commentaires s'il y a lieu, car nous encourageons les jeunes écrivains" (*Le Monde illustré*, 11 mars 1899). Bernard Courteau's assertion that de Marchy did not exist and was a pseudonym used by one of Nelligan's enemies (60, 62) must be rejected as contrary to historical evidence.

13 Nelligan maintained this perspective into his internment, if we are to judge from the poems of others he consigned to his notebooks, such as Fernand Gregh's on Baudelaire, in which he speaks of "le martyrologue de l'art" (M 118).

14 Verses 15 and 16 pose a grammatical problem. The verb *gémir*, normally intransitive, is in this case rendered transitive, unless *qui* is a faulty transcription on Dantin's part. Since the manuscript no longer exists, it is not possible for us to know if Nelligan might have written *que*, but it seems likely that the intransitivity was deliberate. The verses he dreams of writing, in Verlainian fashion, imitate the funereal sounds of autumn winds.

15 The reader is sure to note the irony of the title since *romance* normally designates a sweet and touching song. "La Romance du vin" is simply "the song of wine." Wine, whose god is Bacchus, is, we know, the drink of cheerfulness.

16 As Paul Wyczynski has noted, these lines recall Rollinat's poem "Le Rire," where we find the following lines: "Je ris toujours, je ris encore / Avec le cœur plein de sanglots!" (Rollinat 2:355). See Wyczynski 1960, 96.

17 This is the reading of Luc Lacourcière (1952, 15) and of Paul Wyczynski who has reiterated it a number of times (1960, 96; 1967, 25–6; 1986, 417–18).

18 The signifier *rose* has poetic and imaginary connotations in Nelligan. The expression "comme un rose poème" is found in "Devant deux portraits de ma mère," and "nos roses rêveries" in "Le vent, le vent triste d'automne."

19 Only once in his poetry does Nelligan adopt an ironic view of himself as a poet. In "Le Christ en croix," he refers to himself as "Récitant Éloa, les cheveux dans le vent, / Comme il sied à l'Éphèbe esthétique et bellâtre" (189).

20 See Sabatier 395.

21 The story of Martha the Negress was related in a short story appearing in *Le Petit Messager du Très-Saint-Sacrement* in 1898 and was probably written by Dantin. On this subject, see Wyczynski 1960, 219.

22 Mallarmé, reversing its connotations, speaks of a "poison tutélaire" in his "Tombeau de Charles Baudelaire."
23 The allusion is to George Sand.
24 This is an allusion to a detail of Chopin's life, specifically that in leaving Poland in 1829 he brought with him a bit of his native soil. See Wyczynski 1960, 218.
25 According to Paul Wyczynski, Denys Lanctôt gave Nelligan a copy of *La Jeunesse blanche* which he had brought back from Belgium. See Wyczynski 1987, 233.
26 The only other poem by Nelligan whose first word is "Maître" is "Pour Ignace Paderewski": "Maître, quand j'entendis ..."
27 The contrast with Rollinat's poem "Chopin" could not be more striking, for Rollinat's piece is most explicit: "C'est fini!" he announces in the second stanza. "Hélas! toi mort," he concludes in the last stanza. Rollinat 2:71, 73.
28 William Bonaparte-Wyse's contribution is exceptional in its bluntness: "So, Death at last hath ta'en thy hand, black Death." *Le Tombeau de Théophile Gautier*, 34.

CHAPTER TWO

1 This detail is based on the testimony of Nelligan's cousin, Béatrice Hudon-Campbell (see RW 460).
2 Faillon's book *Sentiments de M. Olier sur la dévotion à Saint-Joseph* sold 40,000 copies in Canada between 1854 and 1858.
3 It should be noted, however, that the taboos were not as strict as is sometimes believed. Consider, for example, the frank poems about prostitution penned by Nelligan's friend Charles Gill. See Gill 37–48.
4 This is one of several reasons why I do not follow Wyczynski, who reads this poem as an attack on Decadent poets (1960, 74).
5 Lest we lose a sense of perspective, it is useful to recall that the Victorianism that reigned during this period in Anglo-Saxon cultures, though not imbued with the same discourse of guilt, had its own strictures regarding sexual morality, at least in its public expression. On this subject, see Douglas and Atwell 19–20, 25, 111.
6 On this subject, see Jean Le Moyne's essay, "La femme dans la civilisation canadienne française" (1953), reprinted in his *Convergences* 69–100.
7 Only one of Nelligan's acquaintances alluded to his having had a girlfriend, a young woman named Marie Beaupré, but this recollection

was made more than a half century later by Louis-Joseph Doucet, some of whose other recollections have been proven to be false (see Lacourcière 1969, 50).

CHAPTER THREE

1 Fréchette likewise appropriated the term in *La Légende d'un peuple* (see Beaudoin 170–1, 176–7, for a brief discussion of Fréchette's usage).
2 The word "hospodar" is not used in its historical meaning (princes who were vassals of Turkish sultans), but as evocative, by a phonetic/exotic association, of "conquistador." As Jacques Michon has pointed out, exotic words in Nelligan "ne sont pas mobilisés pour leurs dénotations, leur contenu encyclopédique, ou pour produire un effet de réel" (1983, 52). In fact, it is frequently their secondary semes which are actualized.
3 Charles Dahlberg's translation is as follows: "Then you will remember her in incomparable manner and appearance. And I will tell you of a great wonder: there will be a time when you are holding her, with shining face, quite naked in your arms, just as if she had become wholly your sweetheart and your companion. Then you will build castles in Spain" (64).
4 Dahlberg's translation: "And [you] will take joy in nothing as much as in going around deluding yourself with the delectable thought that contains only lies and fables" (64).
5 In all editions of Nelligan's poetry prior to Robidoux and Wyczynski's, this poem began with "Ce fut ... ," following the language of its original publication by Dantin. In the extant transcriptions of the poem by Nelligan himself (all post-1900), however, the first line of the poem is always in the imperfect: "Cétait un grand Vaisseau taillé dans l'or massif." Wyczynski has concluded that Nelligan wished thereby to signify a continuity and duration in the past and suggests that the *passé simple* may have been an editorial decision by Dantin. Hence, in his and Robidoux's critical edition, the line is transcribed in the imperfect.
6 See, for example, Viatte, 144; Wyczynski 1965, 85, 101; 1987, 320–1. Réjean Robidoux discusses Nelligan's relationship to Rimbaldian *voyance* (Ethier-Blais 123–53).
7 Rimbaud's productive period extended from 1870 to 1875, that is from the age of fifteen to twenty; Nelligan's productive period lasted from 1896 to 1899, from the age of sixteen to nineteen. It had been

believed that Nelligan abandoned writing after his internment, but we now know that he continued to write some form of poetry almost to the end of his life. Most of those "hospital texts" that still exist have been published as the second volume of the *Œuvres complètes*, edited by Jacques Michon. Nelligan clearly maintained an interest in poetry throughout his internment, in sharp contrast to Rimbaud who, when Delahaye tried to discuss poetry with him in 1879, answered only, "Je ne pense plus à ça" (Bernard lxiv).

8 Wyczynski plausibly dates its composition as occurring between 26 May and 9 August 1899, that is, in the weeks prior to Nelligan's internment at La Retraite Saint-Benoît-Joseph-Labre. See Wyczynski 1971, 119–20, and his updated discussions in Wyczynski 1981, 77; 1987, 318; RW 77.

9 As Marie-Andrée Beaudet and Denis Saint-Jacques point out (16), the fact that Napoléon Legendre could in 1890 quote, though disapprovingly, Rimbaud's "Voyelles" in its entirety is an indication that his poetry was circulating, at least in some quarters, in Montreal.

10 In his *Les Influences françaises au Canada*, Jean Charbonneau also listed Rimbaud as one of the poets who had attracted Nelligan (93). Charbonneau appears to have been the only one of Nelligan's contemporaries to have included Rimbaud on the list of Nelligan's preferred poets, however. Wyczynski, who did extensive research on Nelligan's literary sources, was able to identify only one of Rimbaud's poems, "Le Buffet," as a source (for "La vieille armoire"). See Wyczynski 1960, 182.

11 Nor, for that matter, is *vaisseau* unfamiliar in nineteenth-century French poetry generally, Rimbaud excepted. Wyczynski correctly points out its presence in Baudelaire, Rodenbach, and Rollinat, among others (1960, 237–9). Etiemble also stressed that *Le Parnasse contemporain* contained numerous poems featuring sea crafts (2:77).

12 I see no reason to identify *Dégoût*, *Haine*, and *Névrose* with Rodenbach, Baudelaire, and Rollinat respectively, as Wyczynski once proposed (1960, 243).

13 Rimbaud's nautical text might be interpreted as signaling the end of his poetic project since "la flache / Noire et froide" (lines 93–4) to which he wished to return does not augur well for the continuation of poetic creation. Yet this would be misleading, since "Le Bateau ivre" is an early text followed by at least three years of poetic activity. Neither is the madness which Nelligan accepts an indication of the end of his poetic project since he continued writing even when interned.

14 For an analysis of its decadent components, see Blais 1999. Some pertinent remarks on the poem's language can be found in Robidoux 22.

15 Madness as a constituent of the poet's personality was occasionally evoked in Quebec, as in Albert Ferland's *La Consolatrice* (1898) in which the muse repeats three times, "Le poète est un fou" (9). Ferland's muse is not speaking, however, of clinical insanity but rather of the folly that the vocation of the poet represents.

CHAPTER FOUR

1 For a full discussion of Aubin, see J.-P. Tremblay.

2 *Le Samedi* 10, no. 11 (13 août 1898): 4.

3 *Le Samedi* 10, no. 12 (20 août 1898): 4.

4 *Le Monde illustré* 15, no. 735 (4 juin 1898): 68.

5 See, for example, J. Fleury, "Pensées misanthropiques," *Le Monde illustré* 12, no. 610 (11 janvier 1896): 558; L.-J. Béliveau, "Consolation," *Le Monde illustré* 14, no. 697 (11 septembre 1897): 310.

6 See A.L., "Un Soir sur la grève," *Le Monde illustré* 13, no. 645 (12 septembre 1896): 304.

7 See Aristide Trudeau, "Soir d'été ou méditation," *Le Monde illustré* 14, no. 702 (16 octobre 1897): 390.

8 See Marcotte, 90–7; Lemaire; and especially Pierre Nepveu's edition of Lozeau's poetry, *Intimité et autres poèmes.*

9 Nelligan used this pseudonym for the first nine poems he published.

10 The resemblance of these stanzas to Victor Hugo's "La Prière pour tous" has been noted by Laurence Bisson 129–30.

11 Rémi Tremblay, "Le Jour des Morts," *Le Monde illustré* 12, no. 600 (2 novembre 1895): 396.

12 Jacques Soulary, "Élégie," *Le Monde illustré* 14, no. 720 (19 février 1898): 676.

13 Fleury Desjardins, "Mortua," *Le Monde illustré* 14, no. 719 (12 février 1898): 662.

14 Such poetry was not uncommon in Montreal newspapers and magazines at the end of the nineteenth century. For examples, see "A une jeune fille au jour de sa première communion," *Le Monde illustré* 10, no. 474 (3 juillet 1893): 56; Louvigny, "A ma bonne petite sœur, Marie-Thérèse," *Le Monde illustré* 11, no. 524 (19 mai 1894): 28; Eugène Soubeyre, "Les Communiantes," *Le Monde illustré* 14, no. 681 (22 mai 1897): 53. See, in addition, Albert Ferland's "A ma sœur, le jour de sa première communion" in *Franges d'Autel*, 68.

15 As examples, see Jules Lanos, "'Santa Claus' des enfants," *Le Monde illustré* 11, no. 557 (5 janvier 1895): 428; J. Beaulieu, "Chant de Noël," *Le Monde illustré* 13, no. 660 (26 décembre 1896): 547; J. Beaulieu, "Hymne de Noël," *Le Monde illustré* 14, no. 712 (25 décembre 1897): 547.

16 Nelligan's need to exclude the father seems to have been long-lasting. In 1938, when he copied Rodenbach's poem "La Maison paternelle" into his own notebook, he altered the title to read "La Maison maternelle" (M 285, 510).

17 For a discussion of the treatment of mental illness in late nineteenth-century Quebec, see Viau.

18 It should be noted that Judge William's "answer" to the young man is not Kierkegaard's definitive response. The fictitious editor specifies in his preface that "these papers come to no conclusion" (1:14). In fact, in later works Kierkegaard offered a critique of the ethical state as well. For an excellent discussion of Kierkegaard's understanding of the spheres or stages of human life, see Ferguson 81–115.

19 Charles Vellay, "Petit poème en prose. Feuilles Mortes," *Le Monde illustré* 12, no. 598 (19 octobre 1895): 370.

20 Arthur de Bussières, "Soirée allemande," *Le Monde illustré* 14, no. 691 (31 juillet 1897): 211.

21 In an 1841 entry in his *Journals*, Kierkegaard wrote: "I ... have an intimate, confidential friend – my melancholy, and in the midst of my pleasure, in the midst of my work, she beckons me, calls me aside, ... she is the most faithful mistress I have known, what wonder then that I must be ready to follow her at any moment of the day" (90).

22 As examples, see Louvigny, "L'Hiver," *Le Monde illustré* 11, no. 556 (29 décembre 1894): 412; J.H. Legault, "L'Hiver," *Le Monde illustré* 14, no. 718 (5 février 1898): 622.

23 Maurice Champanile, "La Neige," *Le Monde illustré* 11, no. 559 (30 mars 1895): 573.

24 Augustin Lellis, "L'Hiver," *Le Monde illustré* 13, no. 657 (5 décembre 1896): 500.

CONCLUSION

1 For a history of decadence in France, see Marquèze-Pouey. Its thematics are discussed by Pierrot and Palacio, and wider ramifications are treated in Décaudin and Birkett. Spackman includes an important

discussion of Italian decadence. On decadence as a broader social and political term, see Angenot 1989, 369–407.

2 There appears to have been in French Canada only one contemporary discussion of the decadents as a group, namely Napoléon Legendre's entirely negative essay, "Réalistes et Décadents" (1890), which conflates these two divergent movements into a single threat to literary decency. Occasional warnings in cultural magazines of the period against literary "décadentisme" indicate a burgeoning interest in its aesthetics that few, however, such as E.-Z. Massicotte, seemed willing to embrace openly. On Nelligan's familiarity with contemporary French poetry, see Wyczynski 1960.

3 There may be a non-decadent influence here: François Coppée. On Nelligan's readings of Coppée, see Wyczynski 1960.

4 According to D. Hayne, aging and death were common topoi in nineteenth-century French-Canadian verse. See his "La Poésie romantique au Canada" 65.

5 Gleason, a friend of Mrs Nelligan, accompanied her to the asylum, but remained in the waiting room while mother and son met. Her fictionalized account, published two weeks later, is considered by scholars as a plausible representation on what actually transpired (although some doubts have been voiced by Larose 116).

6 "Testament d'Ame. Aux amis d'Émile Nelligan." *La Patrie* (15 novembre 1902): 22.

7 On this subject, see Puig-Antich et al.

Works Cited

ab der Halden, Charles. 1907. *Nouvelles Études de littérature canadienne-française*. Paris: Rudeval

Angenot, Marc. 1983. "Intertextualité, interdiscursivité, discours social." *Texte* 2: 101–11

– 1989. *1889. Un état du discours social*. Longueuil

Arnould, Louis. 1919. "La Tristesse de Nelligan." *France-Amérique* 10, no. 93: 343–6

Autran, Joseph. 1875. *Œuvres complètes*. 8 vols. Paris: Lévy

Bachelard, Gaston. 1943. *L'Air et les Songes: Essai sur l'imagination du mouvement*. Paris: José Corti

– 1949. *La Psychanalyse du feu*. Paris: Gallimard

Baillargeon, Noël. 1972. *Le Séminaire de Québec sous l'épiscopat de Mgr de Laval*. Québec: Presses de l'Université Laval

Baudelaire, Charles. 1964. *Les Fleurs du mal et autres poèmes*, ed. Henri Lemaître. Paris: Garnier-Flammarion

Beaudet, André. 1981. "Nelligan's Fake (le nom de Nelligan)." *La Nouvelle Barre du Jour* no. 104: 91–104

Beaudet, Marie-Andrée and Denis Saint-Jacques. 1996. "Lectures et critiques de la littérature française contemporaine au Québec à la fin du XIXe siècle." *Études françaises* 32, no. 3: 7–20

Beaudoin, Réjean. 1989. *Naissance d'une littérature. Essai sur le messianisme et les débuts de la littérature canadienne-française (1850–1890)*. Montréal: Boréal

Beausoleil, Claude. 1993. "L'Ange de la poésie." In *Émile Nelligan. Cinquante ans après sa mort*, ed. Yolande Grisé, Réjean Robidoux, and Paul Wyczynski. 215–21. Montreal: Fides

Bénichou, Paul. 1973. *Le Sacre de l'écrivain, 1750–1830*. Paris: Corti

Bernard, Suzanne. 1960. "Introduction," Rimbaud. *Œuvres*. Paris: Garnier

Berrichon, Paterne. 1910. *Poèmes décadents, 1883–1895*. Paris: Vanier

Bérulle, Cardinal de. 1960. *Œuvres complètes*. 2 vols. Montsoult: Maison d'Institution de l'Oratoire

Bessette, Gérard. 1968. *Une littérature en ébullition*. Montréal: Éditions du Jour

Birkett, Jennifer. 1986. *The Sins of the Fathers: Decadence in France 1870–1914*. London and New York: Quartet Books

Biron, Michel. 1992. "Nelligan: la fête urbaine." *Études françaises* 27, no. 3: 51–63

Bisson, Laurence A. 1932. *Le Romantisme littéraire au Canada français*. Paris: Droz

Bissonnette, Pierrette and Jean-Pierre Bouchard. 1970. "Analyse de 'Clavier d'antan.'" *Revue de l'Université d'Ottawa* 40: 597–604

Blais, Jacques. 1993. "L'Entourage libéral de Nelligan." In *Émile Nelligan. Cinquante ans après sa mort*, ed. Yolande Grisé, Réjean Robidoux, and Paul Wyczynski. 63–71. Montréal: Fides

– 1999. "Décadence chez Nelligan: le cas du poème 'Je veux m'éluder.'" *Voix et Images* 24: 264–76

Bloom, Harold. 1976. *Poetry and Repression*. New Haven: Yale University Press

Boileau-Despréaux, Nicolas. 1961. *Œuvres*, ed. Georges Mongrédien. Paris: Garnier

Bourget, Paul. 1899. *Essais de psychologie contemporaine*. Paris: Plon

Bouthillette, Jean. 1972. *Le Canadien-français et son double*. Montreal: L'Hexagone

Brissette, Pascal. 1998. *Nelligan dans tous ses états: Un mythe national*. Montréal: Fides

Brown, E.K. 1930. "The Claims of French-Canadian Poetry." *Queen's Quarterly* 37: 724–31

Butor, Michel. 1968. *Répertoire III*. Paris: Les Éditions de Minuit

Capps, Donald. 1997. *Men, Religion, and Melancholia: James, Otto, Jung, Erikson*. New Haven: Yale University Press

Catéchisme des provinces ecclésiastiques de Québec, Montréal et Ottawa. [1888] 1944. Quebec

Catta, René-Salvador. 1974. "Richesse de la langue nelliganienne." In *Émile Nelligan*, ed. Jean-Noël Samson and Roland-M. Charland. (Dossiers de documentation sur la littérature canadienne-française, 3) 75–82. Montréal: Fides

Champigny, Robert. 1954. *Portrait of a Symbolist Hero*. Bloomington: Indiana University Press

Charbonneau, Jean. 1912. *Les Blessures*. Paris: Alphonse Lemerre

– 1916. *Les Influences françaises au Canada*. Montréal: Beauchemin

– 1935. *L'École littéraire de Montréal*. Montréal: Éditions Albert Lévesque

Cloutier-Wajciehjowska, Cécile and Réjean Robidoux, eds. 1986. *La Solitude rompue*. Ottawa: Éditions de l'Université d'Ottawa

Cogswell, Fred, trans. 1983. *The Complete Works of Emile Nelligan*. Montreal: Harvest House

Cohen, Henry. 1989. "Le rondel dans la poésie d'Émile Nelligan." *Studies in Canadian Literature* 14: 105–27

Condemine, Odette. 1972. "Arthur de Bussières, cet inconnu." *L'École littéraire de Montréal*, ed. Paul Wyczynski et al. (Archives des Lettres Canadiennes, 2) 10–30. Montréal: Fides

Courteau, Bernard. 1986. *Nelligan n'était pas fou!* Montréal: Louise Courteau

Crémazie, Octave. 1976. *Œuvres*, ed. Odette Condemine. 2 vols. Ottawa: Éditions de l'Université d'Ottawa

Dandurand, Albert. 1933. *La Poésie canadienne-française*. Montréal: Lévesque

Dantin, Louis. 1932. *Le Coffret de Crusoé*. Montreal: Albert Lévesque

– 1997. *Emile Nelligan et son œuvre*, ed. Réjean Robidoux. (Bibliothèque du Nouveau Monde.) Montréal: Les Presses de l'Université de Montréal

Davies, Garner. 1950. *Les "Tombeaux" de Mallarmé: Essai d'exégèse raisonnée*. Paris: Corti

Décaudin, Michel et al. 1980. *L'Esprit de décadence*. 2 vols. Paris: Minard

Delille, Jacques. 1811. *L'Imagination*. 2 vols. Paris: Michaud

Delumeau, Jean. 1983. *Le Péché et la peur: La culpabilisation en Occident (XIII*^{e}*-XVIII*^{e} *siècles)*. Paris: Fayard

Desportes, Philippe. 1960. *Les Amours d'Hippolyte*, ed. Victor E. Graham. Geneva: Droz

DesRochers, Alfred. 1951. "Nelligan a-t-il subi une influence anglaise?" *Les Cahiers viatoriens* 3: 187–98, 300–7

Douglas, Jack D. and Freda Case Atwell. 1988. *Love, Intimacy, and Sex*. Newbury Park: Sage

Dudek, Louis. 1943. "Three Translations from Emile Nelligan." *First Statement* 2, no. 3: 18–20

Dugas, Marcel. 1929. *La Littérature canadienne. Aperçus.* Paris: Firmin-Didot

Emmanuel, Pierre. 1982. *Baudelaire, la femme et Dieu.* Paris: Éditions du Seuil

Éthier-Blais, Jean, ed. 1969. *Emile Nelligan: Poésie rêvée et poésie vécue.* Montréal: Cercle du Livre de France

Etiemble. 1952. *Le Mythe de Rimbaud.* Paris: Gallimard

Feder, Lilian. 1980. *Madness in Literature.* Princeton: Princeton University Press

Ferguson, Harvie. 1995. *Melancholy and the Critique of Modernity: Soren Kierkegaard's Religious Psychology.* London and New York: Routledge

Ferland, Albert. 1898. *La Consolatrice.* Montréal: Poirier, Bessette et Cie

– 1899. *Femmes Rêvées.* Montréal: Chez l'auteur

Ferron, Jacques. 1969. "Rimbaud, Nelligan et Jean Drapeau." *Le Petit Journal* 343, no. 52 (19 octobre): 87

– 1970. "La littérature utilitaire et l'écrivain engagé." *Le Magazine Maclean* 10, no. 7 (July): 46

Filteau, Claude. 1994. *Politiques de la modernité.* Montréal: L'Hexagone

Floupette, Adoré. 1984. *Les Déliquescences d'Adoré Floupette*, ed. N. Richard. Paris: Nizet

Franges d'Autel. 1997. ed. Réjean Robidoux. (Cahiers du Québec.) Montréal: HMH

Fréchette, Louis. 1863. *Mes Loisirs.* Québec: Brousseau

– 1899. Preface to *Femmes Rêvées* by Albert Ferland. Montréal: Chez l'auteur

Freud, Sigmund. 1963. *General Psychological Theory: Papers on Metapsychology*, ed. Philip Rieff. New York: Colher

Garneau, Hector de Saint-Denys. 1971. *Œuvres*, ed. Jacques Brault and Benoît Lacroix. Montréal: Presses de l'Université de Montréal

Gervais, André. 1987. "'Le Vaisseau d'Or': texte et après-textes. Codicilles." *Protée* 15, no. 1: 31–43

Gill, Charles. 1997. *Poésies complètes*, ed. Réginald Hamel. (Cahiers du Québec.) Montreal: HMH

Giroux, Robert. 1993. "Nelligan: si l'envie n'y est pas de le lire, chantez-le!" In *Émile Nelligan. Cinquante ans après sa mort*, ed. Yolande Grisé, Réjean Robidoux, and Paul Wyczynski. 15–25. Montréal: Fides

Graham, Franklin. 1902. *Histrionic Montreal: Plays and Players of a Century*. Montreal: John Lovell & Son

Gray, Thomas. 1993. *The Complete English Poems*, ed. James Reeves. New York: Barnes and Noble

Gregh, Fernand. 1897. *La Maison de l'enfance*. Paris: Calmann-Lévy

Grisé, Yolande, Réjean Robidoux, and Paul Wyczynski, eds. 1993. *Émile Nelligan. Cinquante ans après sa mort*. Montréal: Fides

Grisé, Yolande, Jeanne d'Arc Lortie et al., eds. 1987–2001. *Les Textes poétiques du Canada français, 1606–1867*. 12 vols. Montréal: Fides

Haineault, Doris-Louise. 1981. "Problématique de la création chez Nelligan." In *Crémazie et Nelligan*, ed. Réjean Robidoux and Paul Wyczynski. 106–16. Montréal: Fides

Hayne, David M. 1969. "La poésie romantique au Canada français." In *La Poésie canadienne-française*, ed. Paul Wyczynski et al. (Archives des Lettres Canadiennes, 4.) 51–73. Montréal: Fides

Hayward, Annette. 1994. "La littérature de la modernité et le libéralisme nationaliste au Québec entre 1899 et 1916." In *Combats Libéraux au tournant du XXe siècle*, ed. Yvan Lamonde. 159–84. Montréal: Fides

Heredia, José Maria de. 1981. *Les Trophées*, ed. Anny Detalle. Paris: Gallimard

Hesbois, Laure. 1981. "Le signe poétique chez Émile Nelligan." In *Crémazie et Nelligan*, ed. Réjean Robidoux and Paul Wyczynski. 96–105. Montréal: Fides

Hugo, Victor. 1968. *Odes et Ballades. Les Orientales*, ed. Jean Gaudon. Paris: Garnier-Flammarion

– 1969. *Œuvres complètes*, ed. Jean Massin. 18 vols. Paris: Le Club français du livre. 18 vols.

– 1970. *Les Feuilles d'automne. Les Chants du crépuscule*, ed. Marius-François Guyard. Paris: Garnier-Flammarion

Huston, James. 1982. *Répertoire national*, ed. Robert Mélançon. 4 vols. Reprint, Montreal: VLB

Jackson, Stanley W. 1986. *Melancholia and Depression: From Hippocratic Times to Modern Times*. New Haven: Yale University Press

Jankélévitch, Vladimir. 1974. *L'Irréversible et la nostalgie*. Paris: Flammarion

Karp, David A. 1996. *Speaking of Sadness: Depression, Disconnection, and the Meaning of Illness*. New York and Oxford: Oxford University Press

Kierkegaard, Søren. 1938. *The Journals of Søren Kierkegaard*, ed. and trans., Alexander Dru. London: Oxford University Press

– 1941. *Repetition: An Essay in Experiential Psychology*, ed. and trans., Walter Lowrie. Princeton: Princeton University Press

– 1987. *Either/Or*, ed. and trans., Howard V. Hong and Edna H. Hong. 2 vols. Princeton: Princeton University Press

Lacourcière, Luc, ed. 1952. *Poésies complètes, 1896–1899* by Émile Nelligan. Montréal: Fides

– 1969. "À la recherche de Nelligan." In *Émile Nelligan: Poésie rêvée et poésie vécue*, ed. Jean Éthier-Blais. 23–54. Montréal: Cercle du Livre de France

Lamarche, Thomas-M. 1932. "Notes pour la troisième édition." *Émile Nelligan et son œuvre*. Montréal: Excelsior

Lamartine, Alphonse de. 1963. *Œuvres poétiques complètes*. (Bibliothèque de la Pléïade.) Paris: Gallimard

Larose, Jean. 1981. *Le Mythe de Nelligan*. Montréal: Quinze

Lefaivre, A. 1877. *Conférence sur la littérature canadienne*. Paris: Bernard

Légaré, Romain. 1972. "Lucien Rainier, poète de l'art pur et de l'âme chrétienne." In *L'École littéraire de Montréal*, ed. Paul Wyczynski et al. 85–109. (Archives des Lettres Canadiennes, 2) Montréal: Fides

Legendre, Napoléon. 1892. "Réalistes et Décadents." In *À la mémoire de Alphonse Lusignan*. 229–56. Montréal: Desaulniers et Leblanc

Lemaire, Michel. 1997. "Le rythme dans la poésie d'Albert Lozeau. Contribution à l'étude du vers régulier symboliste." *Voix et Images* 22: 355–73

Lemay, Pamphile. 1879. *Une gerbe*. Québec: Darveau

Lemieux, Pierre H. 1991. *Nelligan amoureux*. Montréal: Fides

Lemire, Maurice. 1993. *La Littérature québécoise en projet au milieu du XIXe siècle*. Montréal: Fides

Lemire, Maurice et al. 1991. *La Vie littéraire au Québec I: 1764–1805*. Ste-Foy: Presses de l'Université Laval

Le Moyne, Jean. 1969. *Convergences*. Montréal: HMH

Leopardi, Giacomo. 1984. *Conti*, ed. Domenico de Robertis. 2 vols. Milano: Edizioni il Polifilo

Lewis, Paula Gilbert. 1980. "Emile Nelligan, *Poète maudit* of Québec: The Pervasion of Black and White Coldness." In *Pre-Text, Text, Context: Essays on Nineteenth-Century French Literature*, ed. Robert M. Mitchell. 229–36. Columbus: Ohio State University Press

Linteau, Paul-André. 1992. *Histoire de Montréal depuis la Confederation*. Montréal: Boréal

Lombroso, Cesare. 1889. *L'Homme de génie*, trans. F. Callona d'Istria. Paris: Alcan

Lorris, Guillaume de, et Jean de Meun. 1971. *The Romance of the Rose*, trans. Charles Dahlberg. Princeton: Princeton University Press

– 1974. *Le Roman de la Rose*, ed. Daniel Poirion. Paris: Garnier-Flammarion

Lozeau, Albert. 1908. *L'Âme solitaire*, 2e ed. Paris: Rudeval

– 1997. *Intimité et autres poèmes*, ed. Pierre Nepveu. Montréal: Les Herbes rouges

MacMechan, Archibald. 1924. *Headwaters of Canadian Literature*. Toronto: McClelland & Stewart

Mallarmé, Stéphane. 1984. *Poésies*. Paris: Gallimard

Marcotte, Gilles. 1962. *Une littérature qui se fait*. Montréal: HMH

Marmade, R. de. 1906. "La littérature française au pays de Jacques Cartier." *Mercure de France* 64: 21–33

Marquèze-Pouey, Louis. 1986. *Le mouvement décadent en France*. Paris: Presses Universitaires de France

Marquis, André. 1993. "L'Image intertextuelle de Nelligan." In *Émile Nelligan. Cinquante ans après sa mort*, ed. Yolande Grisé, Réjean Robidoux, and Paul Wyczynski. 151–67. Montréal: Fides

– 1995. "Tombeau de Nelligan." In *Émile Nelligan, Poésies en version originale*, ed. André Marquis. 275–88. Montréal: Triptyque

Masson, Alain. 1973. "Discordia concors. Analyse d'un poème de Nelligan." *La Revue de l'Université de Moncton* 6: 95–117

Mezei, Kathy. 1979. "Lampman and Nelligan: Dream Landscapes." *Canadian Review of Comparative Literature* 6: 151–65

– 1980. "Emile Nelligan: A Dreamer Passing By." *Canadian Literature* 87 (1980): 81–99

Mianney, Régis. 1980. "Esprit de décadence et poésie: la première vague." In *L'Esprit de décadence*, ed. Michel Décaudin et al. 1: 13–26. Paris: Minard

Michon, Jacques. 1979. "La Poétique d'Émile Nelligan." *Revue des Sciences Humaines* 173: 25–35

– 1981. "Nelligan faux-monnayeur?" *Lettres québécoises* 23: 58–9

– 1983. *Émile Nelligan: Les Racines du rêve*. Montréal: Les Presses de l'Université de Montréal

– 1988. "La Réception de l'œuvre de Nelligan." In *Problems of Literary Reception/Problèmes de réception littéraire*, ed. E.D. Blodgett and A.G. Purdy. 77–92. Edmonton: University of Alberta Research Institute for Comparative Literature

Miron, Gaston. 1993. *L'Homme rapaillé*. Montréal: Typo

Montigny, Louvigny de. 1907. "L'Âme solitaire." *Revue Canadienne* 43, no. 9 (septembre): 305–20

Morency, Jean. 1995. "Les modalités du décrochage européen des littératures américaines." In *Québécois et Américains: La culture québécoise au XIXe et XXe siècle*, ed. Gérard Bouchard and Yvan Lamonde. 159–73. Montréal: Fides

Nantais, Aude and Jean-Joseph Tremblay. 1992. *Le portrait déchiré de Nelligan*. Montréal: L'Hexagone

Nelligan, Émile. 1952. *Poésies complètes 1896–1899*, ed. Luc Lacourcière. Montréal: Fides

– 1991. *Poésies complètes 1896–1941*, ed. Réjean Robidoux and Paul Wyczynski. Vol 1 of *Œuvres complètes*. Montréal: Fides

– 1991. *Poèmes et textes d'asile 1900–1941*, ed. Jacques Michon. Vol 2 of *Œuvres complètes*. Montréal: Fides

Nepveu, Pierre. 1998. *Intérieurs du nouveau monde*. Montréal: Boréal

Nerval, Gérard de. 1965. *Les Filles du feu. Les Chimères*. Paris: Garnier-Flammarion

Nodier, Charles. 1961. *Contes*, ed. Pierre-Georges Castex. Paris: Garnier

Olier, Jean-Jacques. 1954. *Introduction à la vie et aux vertus chrétiennes*, ed. François Amiot. Paris: Le Rameau

Palacio, Jean de. 1994. *Figures et formes de la décadence*. Paris: Séguier

Paul-Crouzet, Jeanne. 1946. *Poésie au Canada*. Paris: Didier

Pierrot, Jean. 1977. *L'Imaginaire décadent (1880–1900)*. Paris: Presses Universitaires de France

Pierssens, Michel and Roberto Benardi. 1996. "*L'Écho des jeunes*: Une avant-garde inachevée." *Études françaises* 32, no. 3: 21–50

Plett, Heinrich F. 1991. *Intertextuality*. Berlin & New York: Walter de Gruyter

Poisson, Adolphe. 1895. *Heures perdues*. Québec: A. Côté et Cie

Proust, Marcel. 1964. *À la recherche du temps perdu*, ed. Pierre Clarac and André Ferré. 3 vols. Paris: Gallimard

Puig-Antich, Joaquim et al. 1993. "The Psychosocial Functioning and Family Environment of Depressed Adolescents." *Journal of the American Academy of Child and Adolescent Psychiatry* 32: 244–53

Rainier, Lucien [Joseph Melançon]. 1931. *Avec ma vie*. Montréal: Édition du Devoir

Renaud. André. 1972. "Silvio, poète prosateur." In *L'École littéraire de Montréal*, ed. Paul Wyczynski et al. 335–51. (Archives des Lettres Canadiennes, 2) Montréal: Fides

Rimbaud, Arthur. 1964. *Œuvres poétiques*, ed. Michel Décaudin. Paris: Garnier-Flammarion

Robidoux, Réjean. 1992. *Connaissance de Nelligan*. Montréal: Fides

– 1997. Introduction to *Emile Nelligan et son œuvre* by Louis Dantin. Montréal: Les Presses de l'Université de Montréal

Robidoux, Réjean and Paul Wyczynski, eds. 1981. *Crémazie et Nelligan.* Montreal: Fides

Rodenbach, Georges. 1933. *Œuvres*. Paris: Mercure de France

Rollinat, Maurice. 1972. *Œuvres*, ed. Régis Miannay. 2 vols. Paris: Minard/Lettres Modernes

Roy, Camille. 1907. *Tableau de l'histoire de la littérature canadienne-française*. Québec: L'Action sociale

Roy, Gabrielle. 1993. *Bonheur d'occasion*. Montréal: Boréal

Sabatier, Robert. 1967. *Dictionnaire de la Mort*. Paris: Albin Michel

Saint-Bernard-de-Clairvaux, Sœur. 1972. "Henry-Marie Desjardins." In *L'École littéraire de Montréal*, ed. Paul Wyczynski et al. 37–65. (Archives les Lettres Canadiennes, 2) Montreal: Fides

Smith, Donald. 1973. "Nelligan et le feu." *Voix et images du pays* 7: 113–19

Les Soirées du Chateau de Ramezay. 1900. Montréal: Senécal

Sollers, Philippe. 1968. "Écriture et révolution: Entretien de Jacques Henric avec Philippe Sollers." In *Théorie d'ensemble*. 67–79. Paris: Seuil

Spackman, Barbara. 1989. *Decadent Genealogies: The Rhetoric of Sickness from Baudelaire to D'Annunzio*. Ithaca: Cornell University Press

Taché, Louis-H. 1881. *La Poésie française au Canada*. Preface by Benjamin Sulte. St.-Hyacinthe: Imprimerie du Courrier de St.-Hyacinthe

Le Tombeau de Théophile Gautier. 1873. Paris: Lemerre

Tougas, Gérard. 1960. *Histoire de la littérature canadienne-française*. Paris: Presses Universitaires de France. Republished 1974 as *La Littérature canadienne-française*.

Tremblay, J.-P. 1969. *À la recherche de Napoléon Aubin*. Québec: Les Presses de l'Université Laval

Tremblay, Michel. 1990. *Nelligan, livret d'opéra*. Montréal: Leméac

Vachon, Georges-André. 1969. "Émile Nelligan et la mélancolie." In *Poésie rêvée et poésie vécue*, ed. Jean Éthier-Blais. 103–13. Montréal: Cercle du Livre de France

van der Leeuw, Gerardus. 1963. *Sacred and Profane Beauty: The Holy in Art*, trans. David E. Green. New York: Holt, Rinehard and Wilson

Vecchio, Sisto. 1989. "I luoghi della nostalgia." In *Nostalgia: Scritti psicoanalitici*, ed. Sisto Vecchio. 95–118. Bergamo: Pierluigi Lubrina

Verlaine, Paul. 1976. *Fêtes galantes*. Paris: Garnier-Flammarion

– 1977. *Poèmes saturniens*. Paris: Garnier-Flammarion

Vermeil, Abraham de. 1976. *Poésies*, ed. Henri Lafay. Paris-Genève: Droz

Viatte, Auguste. 1954. *Histoire littéraire de l'Amérique française.* Paris: Presses Universitaires de France

Viau, Robert. 1993. "'Quand les anges m'auront sorti de l'hôpital': grandeur et misère de l'institution asilaire québécoise à l'époque d'Émile Nelligan." In *Émile Nelligan. Cinquante ans après sa mort*, ed. Yolande Grisé, Réjean Robidoux, and Paul Wyczynski. 73–92. Montréal: Fides

Vigny, Alfred de. 1950. *Œuvres complètes*, ed. F. Baldensperger. 2 vols. Paris: Bibliothèque de la Pléïade

Wilson, Edmund. 1964. *O Canada: An American's Notes on Canadian Culture.* New York: Farrar, Strauss, and Giroux

Wyczynski, Paul. 1960. *Emile Nelligan: Sources et originalité de son œuvre.* Ottawa: Éditions de l'Université d'Ottawa

– 1965. *Poésie et symbole.* Montréal: Déom

– 1967. *Emile Nelligan.* Montréal: Fides

– 1969. "L'Influence de Verlaine sur Nelligan." *Revue d'Histoire Littéraire de la France* 69: 776–94

– 1971. *Nelligan et la musique.* Ottawa: Éditions de l'Université d'Ottawa

– 1977. "Nelligan devant la critique." *Québec français* (mars): 24–8

– 1981. "'Le Vaisseau d'Or' d'Émile Nelligan: Genèse, structure, signification." In *Crémazie et Nelligan*, ed. Réjean Robidoux and Paul Wyczynski. 75–94. Montréal: Fides

– 1986. "Le monde poétique d'Émile Nelligan." In *La Solitude rompue*, ed. Cécile Cloutier-Wajciehowska and Réjean Robidoux. 415–29. Ottawa: Éditions de l'Université d'Ottawa

– 1987. *Nelligan 1879–1941: Biographie.* Montréal: Fides

Wyczynski, Paul et al., eds. 1972. *L'École littéraire de Montréal.* (Archives des Lettres Canadiennes, 2) Montréal: Fides

Index